CREATIVE
NEWSPAPER
DESIGN

Heinemann Media Series

Series editor: F. W. Hodgson

CREATIVE
NEWSPAPER
DESIGN

VIC GILES
and
F. W. HODGSON

HEINEMANN PROFESSIONAL PUBLISHING

Heinemann Professional Publishing Ltd
Halley Court, Jordan Hill, Oxford OX2 8EJ

OXFORD LONDON MELBOURNE AUCKLAND
SINGAPORE IBADAN NAIROBI GABORONE KINGSTON

First published 1990

British Library Cataloguing in Publication Data

Giles, Vic
 Creative newspaper design.
 1. Newspapers. Layout.
 I. Title II. Hodgson, F. W.
 686.2'252
ISBN 0 434 90703 0

Photoset by Deltatype Limited, Ellesmere Port
Printed and Bound in Great Britain
by Butler & Tanner Ltd, Frome and London

Contents

Acknowledgements

We are grateful to the many publishers and editors in Britain and in other parts of the world whose newspaper pages form a vital part of this book. In particular, we are indebted to the editors of *The Sun* and *Today* for allowing us to reproduce layout sequences showing the development of pages from rough sketch to the finished product; to the editor of *The Independent* for allowing us to use some of the pre-launch designs for the paper's masthead, and to Autologic, of California, for the use of illustrations on the technology of type from their *Digital Type Collection*.

Our chapter on newspaper graphics owes much to the examples of work we were permitted to print from *The Times, Sunday Times, The Observer, Daily Express, Daily Star, Northern Echo* and *USA Today*. Other material is reproduced by permission of the editors of the *Daily Mail, Daily Mirror, The Guardian, Birmingham Post, The Scotsman, Glasgow Herald, Manchester Evening News, Liverpool Echo, Irish Independent, Irish Press, Sunday Sun* and *Kent Messenger*. Mr Dennis Morris and Mrs Helena Hind helped us by lending material from their collections of historic newspapers, while at the other end of the time scale News International plc allowed us to take pictures of modern production sequences. Our thanks are due to *News of the World* staff photographer Brian Thomas for setting up special pictures, and to Mirror Group Newspapers for permission to use the picture of Harry Guy Bartholomew.

Rolf F. Rehe's *Typography and Design For Newspapers* (IFRA, Darmstadt, 1985) was a valuable book to have by us and we are glad to be allowed to reproduce two of his designs from it. We are indebted in retrospect ot our predecessors in this field, Alan Hutt (*Newspaper Design*, Oxford University Press, 1960), Edmund C. Arnold (*Modern Newspaper Design*, Harper and Row, New York, 1969), and Harold Evans (*Newspaper Design*, Heinemann, 1973).

We hope that any other acknowledgements due for the help we have had in researching and writing this book are adequately recorded in the text and captions of the following pages.

Illustrations

Colour plates

Plate 1(a) The quill work is from Einhard's *Life of Charlemagne*, written in the early ninth century and demonstrates the style of illuminated letters known as the Caroline, upon which modern Black letter and Old English typefaces are based
(b) This example of early sixteenth-century printing shows how closely the formation of the letters follow the quill work of the monks
Plate 2(a) The *Daily Mirror* in this front page makes a virtue of the clashing disposition of headlines on a day when there was no prospect of a good colour picture
(b) The Athens newspaper *To Fos* (The Light), is almost surrealist in its approach with a very European saturation blurb technique. *Nice-Matin* uses a more reserved typography to project similar ideas
Plate 3(a) A superb *Today* page one in its three stages of production
(b) *France-Soir* page ones are noted for the strategic positioning of colour. *Abēndpost* suffers with 'portmanteau' words which demand plenty of Extra condensed type. However, this page one cries out to be read
Plate 4(a) The combination of a striking blue masthead, a dominant approach to full colour pictures and spot colour create a unique blend of tabloid and broadsheet techniques in *USA Today*. The newspaper's USA Snapshots feature is a good example of a down-page eye-catcher using colours drawn from the halftones in the page
(b) Colour shots of the Mississippi have been montaged for a holiday feature

The ever-expanding field of newspaper technology is a source both of challenge and heart-searching for journalists. Will newspapers as we know them continue to be possible in a systems-dominated environment? Or will the computer produce a great leap forward into a new visual world?

'Visual' is the key word, for what ever has changed, or is changing, we must not elevate the power of the machine over the words and content. They are what make a newspaper worth buying. We seek in page design simply to make the words and content more attractive and accessible to the reader in whatever market a newspaper exists.

It is the view of the authors that in doing this we can have it both ways. We can make the machine serve the purpose of good design, while at the same time grasping the challenge that new methods offer to improve standards and make more things possible.

Vic Giles and F.W. Hodgson
London, March 1990

1
Theory
of
design

Newspapers are such familiar things that it would probably surprise the average reader to learn that there are complex design factors at work behind the pages. It might be supposed that the news of the day and the features that support it – and the advertisements for that matter – are installed in the paper as they arrive, and that the resulting pages are the arbitrary result of this process, with perhaps a little soling and heeling to get things to fit.

And yet the very familiarity of the pages of a favourite newspaper bears witness to the success of its design. The choice and use of types – were the ordinary reader to examine them more closely – stamp the newspaper unmistakably with a visual character that sets it apart from any other. The size of the headline and position of a certain story denoting it to be the most important item on the page, the readability and easily found page slot of the television programmes, the location of the Parliamentary coverage . . . all these are the clearest evidence of design.

Design thus gives a newspaper its 'feel', attracting the eye while at the same time subtly guiding the reader through the contents of the pages; blending eye comfort and familiarity with a reasonable amount of surprise. In fact, for a newspaper design to be successful, the reader should be unaware of any tricks as such, aware only that the finished product is acceptable and readable and therefore worth buying.

It can be argued that design principles must be hard to identify since there is a great deal of difference between one newspaper and another, not only in the contents but in the appearance. This is true, but it does not alter the basic concept that lies behind newspaper design. Our opening remarks can be used to summarize this concept in the form of three precise functions:

1   To attract and hold the reader's attention.

2   To indicate the relative importance and location of the contents of the pages.
3   To give a newspaper a recognizable visual character.

These functions hold good for any newspaper, national or local; morning, evening or weekly; general or special interest. The differences in appearance that arise, which can be seen from the array of titles on a newsstand, are the result of the way in which the functions of design are used to commend the ingredients of the pages to the particular market of each newspaper. These ingredients, which are the raw material out of which the page design is created, are:

- Advertisements.
- Text.
- Headlines.
- Pictures.

Principles of design   Before we examine the principles of design as expressed in the three functions we have listed, it has to be said that however significant, or entertaining, or motivated a newspaper's contents are it owes its existence to being bought and read on a regular basis. Some newspapers, even some specialist ones, rely on a percentage of casual sales – which is why page one is so important in attracting the eye on the newsstands – but it would be a hand-to-mouth existence for editors were they not able to rely on loyalty and regularity of buying habits among their readers, expressed preferably in copies ordered and delivered. This need to target a newspaper on its readers and potential readers takes us into the first function of design:

To attract and hold the reader's attention

The design, or visual pattern, of the newspaper is intended not only to grab the passing reader, but to persuade existing readers to keep coming back for more. It has been made attractive and desirable in the sort of market the editor is aiming for.

It could be argued against this that some newspapers sell on their content and that design in their case is irrevelant. This is a facile view since it presupposes that other newspapers sell on their design rather than on their content, and there is no evidence – certainly not in readership surveys – that this is so. While ideas used in page design might vary from newspaper to newspaper depending (as will be explained shortly) on the type of readership market, there is the strongest evidence that certain types of content appeal to certain readers, that there is a good deal of consistency in the pattern of newspaper buying, and that it is rooted in content. The detailed breakdown of readership of the principal national and provincial newspapers, based on sex, age, education, spending habits and television viewing habits, as checked annually in the *National*

Readership Survey, published by the Joint Industry Committee for National Readership Surveys (JICNARS), points to this, and the survey is used to give each newspaper a readership profile which is greatly valued by the advertisers.

If people tend to buy the sort of newspapers whose views and content they like, where, therefore, do design techniques come in? The answer to this is that in order to attract readers in the first place a newspaper needs to advertise its existence and to establish a public knowledge of what sort of paper it is. Editors are aware that readers are being born, growing up, growing old and dying and that no readership can be taken for granted in the competitive market in which newspapers exist. The number of newspapers that have folded in recent years is evidence of readerships that have faded away or have failed to reach viable levels after launch. An editor must be constantly looking to attract new readers as well as seeking to hold on to existing readers, seeing that content is right and the standard is being maintained, and that the content is being properly drawn to the readers' attention so that they are not persuaded that their interests are better served by changing to a rival newspaper.

There is no doubt that if newspapers were the only medium of mass communication and if there were only one newspaper for a given body of potential readers, the need to project an image would not rate highly. Editors would simply be faced with the need to maximize sales in a closed readership area. They would not have to try more than a moderate amount of persuasion, and there would be no yardstick to measure how worthwhile or successful the product was. It would be like selling water to consumers to whom water is water is water.

But running a newspaper is very different from running a public utility. Since the extension of readership to all classes as a result of the 1870 Education Act and the growth of mass circulations of national daily and Sunday newspapers that followed, competition has been as much a part of newspaper publishing as it has of any other sector of the economy. If some provincial newspapers have been cocooned from this in recent decades by the collapse or absorption of rival titles, then the burgeoning of free newspapers in most readership conurbations has come as a sharp reminder that the community does not owe a newspaper a living. There are no solus sites any more. Add to this the competition that comes from television, radio, teletext and news magazines and it can be seen that editors – who are appointed to succeed – have no room for complacency.

In short, behind modern newspaper production, whatever the content, is the urge to create the sort of visual image a newspaper needs in order to become known and to succeed. It is thus that cynics have likened newspaper design to the packaging of products as part of a brand image. Yet, whatever its social, political or cultural influence, a newspaper is a product in that it has to be able to sell in order to survive. It is produced commercially by a management that is answerable to shareholders (in Western countries at least); it has no subsidy. At whatever level it operates it has to depend on its readers, and its design is part of the means by which its contents are commended to these readers. Upon this rests its circulation.

To indicate the relative importance and location of the contents of the pages

Here the page design, by its use of headline type of varying sizes, maps out the items on the pages. The reader's attention is drawn to the main story on the page, then to the second most important story, and thence through intermediate stories to the smallest items.

In the case of stories or features meriting a big visual display, especially where there is a long text or a wealth of pictures, the choice and size of type is combined with pictures to project the material so that it is comfortable to the eye and inviting to read.

Regular items such as the editorial, or opinion column, the television programmes, or even the horoscopes, are located in a familiar part of the paper, and in a recognizable visual form with perhaps a specially designed 'logo', that helps the reader to spot them. This familiarity is an important aspect of newspaper design to which we will be returning.

To give a newspaper a recognizable visual character

No two pages of a newspaper (unless it is formularized to an extraordinary degree) ever look alike. The number of ways in which type and pictures can be used to offset each other is so varied as to be almost infinite. Indeed, not to vary page design in response to its contents would destroy the attempt to catch the reader's eye which remains the first function of design.

Yet a reader buying, say, *The Daily Telegraph* and the *Daily Mail* would recognize the papers at a glance and would be in no danger of confusing the two. Since one of them is a broadsheet (or full-size) and the other a tabloid (or half-size) it could be argued that there is little chance of confusion. Yet the visual point being made holds good if the reader were choosing, say, between *The Times* and *The Guardian*, both broadsheet papers; or between two tabloid papers such as the *Daily Express* and *The Sun*, or, in fact, between the *New York Post* and the *New York Daily News*. This is because a newspaper chooses a particular range of types and type sizes in which to present its headlines and text and broadly sticks to them. It has a recognizable type 'dress'.

All newspaper publishing houses, whatever their typesetting systems, carry a varied range of types, both serif and sanserif (see Chapter 2), some decorative, some plain, some kept for special occasions, some used on contract work for other titles. These are listed in a house type book. It might seem tempting for the person drawing the page to go through the book and try everything, or to vary types at mood or whim, yet – and there are newspapers who seem to try this occasionally – the result would be a hotchpotch, with balance almost impossible to achieve and any hope of visual character destroyed. One of the accepted and universal rules of newspaper typography is that you go for a deliberate type style, using a limited range of types for headlines – probably one main typeface and a couple of subsidiary ones for contrast – and achieve variety and emphasis by using differing sizes of a type, and perhaps light or bold versions, or by a combination of capital letters and lower case letters of the same type range. This avoids visual clashes that readers would find harsh and unattractive.

The body text, or reading matter, is likewise standardized to a chosen typeface and size, varied perhaps with the occasional use of a bold version of the letters and with a bigger size of setting for the first or second paragraphs of important stories.

It is the selection and consistent use of chosen types and typesizes, whatever varieties of shape the page patterns might have and whatever the size of the pictures, that give a newspaper a distinctive visual appearance. To some extent the average length of items in a newspaper – *The Times* as against the *Daily Mirror*, for example – contributes to this visual appearance, yet the image is still being created by the way in which headline type is used to break up the varying mass of reading type.

Ingredients of design The shape or pattern that is imposed on a newspaper page is created, as we have said, from four ingredients: advertisements, text, headlines and pictures. It is useful, in examining these ingredients, to take advertisements first since, of the four, it is the one over which the designer has least control, and it constricts by the space it occupies on the page (which space is paid for) what can be done to project the editorial contents.

Advertisements

These are designed to please the client and not to fit into any particular editorial pattern. The job of the designer or creator of the advertisement ends once the space has been bought in the page. Advertisements in daily or weekly papers, local or national, can, in fact, be sold up to a month before the paper appears. In the case of some advertising campaigns the space might be booked several months before. Some companies plan a year's advertising in specific papers in advance as part of their budget spending. The content, typography and illustration used in an advertisement are chosen by the client or, on the client's behalf, by an advertising agency. The size of an advertisement is paid for at a set card rate and cannot be varied by the editor. Nor, in many cases, can its position on a particular page for which a premium might have been charged.

In what is termed the free press of the non-Communist countries the income from advertising is the means by which newspapers reduce their unit costs sufficiently to have a low cover charge. The high circulations and ingrained newspaper-reading habits in the Western democracies are the product of cheap papers. Effective design techniques which make the editorial content attractive and readable are the means by which editors have learned to live with advertising in exchange for being able to keep down the cost of their product.

The space occupied by advertisements can be a considerable part of the whole. All newspapers have a percentage target of advertising which ranges, depending on the paper and its type of circulation, from about 30 per cent to 47 per cent. Within each newspaper there is an agreed pattern of placement by which certain pages – page one and sometimes the back page for instance – are kept clear. Other pages, such as the page containing the editorial opinion, are kept 'light' to allow space for regular content, while a portion of the advertising sold consists of whole pages, either a display item or collections of small classified items such as jobs, holidays and postal bargains. The remaining individual advertisements, or sometimes small blocks of like advertisements, are spread around the rest of the paper, including some pages on which specific spaces and positions have been bought. Some of these are solus positions which means that, for an extra payment, no other advertisement will be allowed on that page. The effect of this is to concentrate the non-solus advertising in greater volume on other pages.

It will be seen from this that advertising has already given the paper a certain shape before the editor begins to think what to do with the editorial contents. More worrying for the editor is that to ensure sufficient advertising revenue per copy, the number of pages (pagination) of each edition is determined normally not by editorial requirements but by the total volume of advertising sold. A rush of late space-selling can thus increase the number of pages, while a shortfall of expected advertising can diminish the number. Except on occasions of exceptional importance the editor is expected to accommodate to this.

In fact the pattern of selling by which certain pages are kept light, heavy or clear of advertising does allow the editor to stick to a general plan for the paper so that a consistent contents formula can be followed. Even so, on most of the pages advertising shapes and volume (as well as their content) can vary a great deal. 'Trading' of space and positions can be carried out on some papers (when fixed positions have not been sold) to enable editorial matter on certain pages to be given adequate space and display, especially on those that are front half of paper or right hand, where reader traffic is known (from readership surveys) to be highest. The advertising department is urged to concentrate its material on left-hand pages or at least to keep premium top right-hand positions clear. Some advertisers, aware of this tendency, stipulate (and pay for) forward right-hand positions.

It is selling practice on some papers that pages of classified advertising such as postal bargains or holidays go to the back of the paper, though not usually on sports pages, which are not popular with general advertisers. Sports pages, in fact, are usually light on advertising.

In advert-conscious US papers page shapes can be chaotic. A few years ago a campaign to sell 'flexi-ads' left whole pages at the mercy of whatever bizarre shapes an agency could sell to its clients, so that adverts might appear in the form of a huge letter 'H' or a monstrous Christmas tree, with the editorial items fitted in the remaining space as best as possible. In British practice advert 'rate cards' stipulate available shapes and sizes and there is a general policy of selling and placing adverts to a pattern that broadly suits editorial requirements.

Another point the designer must keep in mind with pre-sold space is to see there is no clash between the type and illustrations of editorial material and that used in the adjoining adverts. A cut-out picture of a woman's head in a story about an actress would lose its effect against a cut-out woman's head advertising face cream. A heavy sans headline on a page lead would be robbed of its dominance if a nearby advert had type of the same sort and size. A story in black panel rules would be pointless against an advert panelled in with the same rules.

The way to avoid these troubles is for designers to see early proofs or copies of any display adverts on the page rather than have to alter the page at a late stage. Since advertising space is sold first this should not normally be a problem.

Text

Having taken account of the shape and contents of the adverts, the page designer's task is to locate the text of the stories on the page in accordance with the editor's estimate of its importance. On a news page the biggest story is called the *lead*, and the second biggest the *half lead*. Other stories of importance are referred to as *tops*, which derives from the practice in early newspapers of starting all the main stories at the top of the page and running them alongside each other. It is common practice today to give 'strength below the fold' by running some tops across in 'legs' down page. At the ends of columns come the one or two paragraph items referred to as *fillers*, though even the smallest filler is schemed in advance in a well-planned news page.

The text of all these stories is set in a standard size of reading type (usually 7-point or 8-point size), with a bigger size of type to indicate the start of more important stories. Newspapers depart from standard reading text only where special emphasis is called for, in which case bigger or perhaps bolder reading type is used.

12 ■ FOREIGN NEWS ■   Daily Post, Wednesday

Tibet rioters go on the rampage

New satellites go into orbit

12 killed in new China crackdown

by Daily Post Reporter

HUNDREDS of Tibetan rioters rampaged through Lhasa hours before the imposition of martial law, looting shops, starting fires, and attacking police and bystanders, the New China News Agency said.

"Despite police attempts to cool down the situation, hundreds of rioters continued to storm through the streets and lanes of the Tibetan capital," the agency said in a report monitored by the BBC.

It also gave a detailed account of rioting on Sunday and Monday and said armed Tibetans shot dead one policeman.

It said Lhasa was quiet when martial law took effect at midnight on Tuesday.

China ordered the clampdown after three days of nationalist riots that Peking authorities say killed at least 12 people and injured more than 100. Tibetans say they believe the death toll is more than 60.

The riots have posed the biggest challenge to Peking rule since the anti-Chinese revolt of 1959 which killed thousands of people. A Reuter correspondent in Lhasa quoted Tibetans as saying they planned to press on with their drive to gain independence.

In a report from Lhasa a few hours before martial law went into effect, China's official news agency said:"Soon after 11 a.m. hundreds of rioters regrouped in front of the Bargor Street police station shouting slogans and threatening to storm the police post."

It said they later marched into another part of the street "smashing and burning goods that had survived the violence of earlier rioting. The street was shrouded in dense smoke.

"Masked rioters in eastern Beijing Road intercepted and attacked passers-by and piled up stolen bicycles and burned them," the agency added.

It said one of its correspondents saw a businessman chased and beaten by rioters.

"At 2 p.m. an estimated 200 rioters gathered at a market in Bargor Street. One rioter standing on top of a stall was shouting at the top of his voice 'Tibet is independent."

The agency said the trouble began shortly after midday on Sunday when priests, nuns and youths shouted "independence for Tibet" outside the Johkang Temple.

European launcher Ariane 4 lifts off from its base at Kourou, French Guiana

29th Euro-rocket

THE European Space Agency has launched the 29th Ariane rocket, putting Japanese and European satellites into orbit 22,000 miles up.

It was the second flight this year.

Ariane put into orbit JCSAT-1, Japan's first commercial communication satellite, and MOP-1, a European meteorological satellite which will send weather pictures every half an hour to stations on earth.

The first Ariane rocket was launched a decade ago. There have been four failed flights, the last in 1986.

A geomagnetic storm warning

A MASSIVE flare, the most intense since 1984, has erupted on the eastern edge of the sun, sending a burst of radiation that interfered with a navigation system and other communications, federal officials in the United States said.

In Boulder, Colorado, forecasters at the National Oceanic and Atmospheric Administration's Space Environment Services Centre said the flare was detected at 9:05 am (1405 GMT) by satellite instruments.

A flare occurs when energy stored by the sun's magnetic fields suddenly becomes unstable and is converted to heat and radiation within a few minutes, said Gary Heckman, director of the centre.

He said solar telescopes recorded a flare of particles rising some 70,000 miles from the surface of the sun.

He said such a burst could black out shortwave and high frequency communications that travel through the high latitudes on Earth. He said the burst could interfere with communications between aircraft flying in the far north and south, and that some television signals from satellites could be affected.

Another effect, called a geomagnetic storm, may arrive at Earth about 1400 GMT today, said Heckman.

A geomagnetic storm is a wave of magnetically charged particles smashing into the Earth's magnetic field, disrupting natural currents and triggering the aurora borealis, or northern lights.

DIGEST

N-snub

FOUR Russian ports have refused entry to one of their own ships because of fears over nuclear power. The huge nuclear-powered container ship has been turned away after public protests from Vladivostok, Nakhodka and Magadan in the Soviet Far East, and a workers' protest in Vostochny made officials ban the vessel.

Suite music

FURNITURE which belonged to Beethoven until the composer's death in 1827 was sold for £4,800 at a Paris auction yesterday.

Reminder

THE West German city of Nuremberg plans to turn the vast coliseum in which Hitler held his Nazi rallies into a museum which will chronicle aspects of the era.

Two die

A 'PLANE carrying civilian passengers was destroyed on the runway by a rebel missile in the Afghanistan city of Jalalabad yesterday. Two women passengers were killed.

Gun crazy

A GUNMAN burst into a house in a black suburb of the city of Pietermaritzburg and killed four people, one of them a 12-year-old girl, police said yesterday.

Russian-U.S. talks open in good mood

THE new U.S. administration and the Kremlin made their first high-level contact yesterday and declared it a good beginning.

Soviet Foreign Minister Mr Eduard Shevardnadze and U.S. Secretary of State Mr James Baker spent two hours together in talks in Vienna that highlighted differences on human rights, arms control, the Middle East and Nicaragua.

But Mr Shevardnadze told reporters before leaving for Moscow: "I have the impression that Mr Baker and I can work together successfully."

And Mr Baker said before leaving Vienna: "Mr Shevardnadze said he thought this was a good beginning and I agreed with that."

Eduard Shevardnadze

Differences

They met during the launch of new disarmament talks between the 23 Nato and Warsaw Pact states, and their wide-ranging discussions pointed up some major policy differences.

Mr Shevardnadze said Moscow refused to accept that aircraft and troop cuts should be relegated to second place at the Conventional Forces in Europe talks.

The U.S. and its 15 Atlantic allies want to give priority to discussing cuts in tanks, artillery and armoured troop carriers, which they say could be part of a surprise attack.

The two men agreed to meet again in Moscow in May to discuss prospects for a first summit between Presidents Bush and Gorbachev.

Mr Shevardnadze said he expected their Moscow talks could also produce a date for resuming the U.S.-Soviet START talks in Geneva to halve strategic nuclear stockpiles.

The two men looked solemn as they emerged from their talks but they smiled and chatted together as they posed in brilliant sunshine for photographers.

Mr Baker criticised Moscow's failure to condemn publicly Ayatollah Khomeini's call for British author Salman Rushdie to be killed for his novel The Satanic Verses.

French jail Briton

AN ENGLISHMAN was jailed for 12 years by a French court yesterday after being found guilty of attempting to murder a young French woman in 1986.

Stephen Coates, 25, from Hemel Hempstead, Herts, tried to strangle Nadine Dauber after meeting her on a train between Paris and Marseille.

First he tried to steal her handbag. When she screamed, he strangled her until she stopped moving.

"I panicked," Coates told the French jury during his trial in the town of Carpentras.

"Thinking that she was dead I opened the window of the compartment and threw her out."

Mrs Dauber survived, suffering only cuts and bruises.

15 hurt at clinic

ISRAELI soldiers stormed a UN medical clinic in the occupied Gaza Strip yesterday.

Palestinians were demonstrating in the building. Staff said 15 Arabs were wounded.

Reuter joournalist Paul Taylor saw three women taken away on stretchers and said that the soldiers' commander told his men: "Good job, I congratulate you all."

Staff at the clinic said that an eight-year-old girl was among the injured, also two ambulance drivers and a local journalist.

PROPERTY POST
Homemaker

EVERY SATURDAY!
... starting this week

DAILY POST

Three survive desert ordeal

A PREGNANT woman, her husband and their two-year-old son survived a 13-day ordeal lost in the searing heat of the Kalahari Desert, partly by sucking moisture off plants during the night, the Botswana Press Association said yesterday.

Jonathan Hayman, his wife Laura and their young son were driving across the Central Kalahari Game Reserve when their truck broke down.

After six days they ran out of food and water. They had not seen any other people, so they decided to begin walking the 120 miles back the town of Serowe.

The mother and child were too weak to continue after three days, but Mr Hayman carried on. After four more days farm workers found him on Saturday and took him to Serowe.

A Botswana army helicopter found his wife and son, the news agency said.

"I had given up hope," said 23-year-old Mrs Hayman. "I thought we were both dead."

She and the child survived by drawing water from plants during the night.

Daytime temperatures in the Kalahari Desert often reach 104 degrees Fahrenheit at this time of year.

1   How a newspaper page strikes the reader – the visual highlights in type and pictures, shown here, aim to attract the eye and guide it round the page

Headlines

The importance on the page of the stories comprising the text is indicated, as we have seen, by the size of type chosen for the headline. Headlines, in fact, serve two functions: they draw attention to the contents of the stories, and they form part of the visual pattern of the page by creating highlights **(1)**. More specifically, they break up and separate the mass of reading matter to make for greater eye comfort. Varying the size also spares the reader the confusion that would occur if all headlines were to shout equally for attention.

Pictures

The remaining ingredient of the page design is the pictures (or any other form of illustration). These, like headlines, have two functions, in that they may form part of a particular story which they have been chosen to illustrate, while at the same time they create visual highlights in the page pattern **(1)**. The placing and size chosen for the main picture can be the key element in the page design and the contents of the pages are usually allocated so that no page is left without pictures. Thus the design element as well as their illustrative role in a news story or feature can be a factor in the choice of pictures.

Influences on design

The job of the journalist designer is to display the editorial contents of the pages to the best possible advantage within the design formula adopted by the paper, and in the space allocated for this purpose. There are a number of influences to take into account here and the success of a page design can be measured by how far it copes with and responds to them. Advertising, as can be seen from the above discussion, is one of them. Yet it must not be overstated. By far the most important factor is the nature of the actual editorial material – the text and pictures – from which the page is to be composed.

Contents

The planning of the paper and the main decisions about the stories and pictures to be used are taken at the editor's daily conference. Decisions on specific stories might be taken by the editor or the editor's delegated executive – who may or may not be the person designing the page. Thus not only must the subject or nature of the contents and length of stories be taken into account, but also any decisions about the space or prominence to be given to particular items and the accommodating of any headlines that have been put up at the planning stage. The aim of these decisions, and of the ideas that go into the page design – called the *layout* or *scheme* – is to root the design in the materials of which the page is composed. A good picture, as we have seen, can be the key to a bold layout, while the wording of a headline can sell a page. Any design which ignores these points or subserves them to some abstract whim of a shape, or to a rigid formula, is failing in its purpose.

The length and number of stories to be carried will decide whether it is to be a 'busy' page or one in which the design is going to have to cope with presenting a wordy text in a readable way. The purpose of later chapters in this book is to show how design copes with the different kinds of content.

Style

In drawing the pages the journalist designer will need to take into account the type 'dress' of the paper – the types and typesizes normally used – and the attitudes to picture size and presentation and story length so that the pages are not visually out of character or clash one with the other. Thus, different papers and different sorts of papers become known in terms of their design style.

Principal optical area

In placing the elements on to the page the designer is influenced by the known psychology of reading habits – the fact, based on readership research, that the top right-hand part of the page, and especially the right-hand page, is where the reader's first attention will go. This has been defined by Edmund Arnold, the American writer on newspaper design, as the principal optical area (POA).

Production methods

The sophistication of the editing and typesetting system and the availability of colour and high-speed printing and advanced camera room facilities can affect design techniques by limiting or expanding what is possible in the time available. The number of columns in the column format used is an important governing factor, although the modern tendency is more and more to standardize tabloids into a seven-column format and broadsheet papers into eight-column.

Editor/proprietor influence

Lastly, and of importance on some papers, is the influence that can be brought to bear by editors or proprietors to present certain stories and certain pages in a particular way as a result of some personal interest or involvement. It is as difficult for the journalist designer to resist an editor's whim as it is for an editor to resist a proprietor's whim, even though there might be some reasoned grounds for doing so. Some of the oddities of picture choice and story presentation that go against normal style and practice in a newspaper can be traced back to such pressures.

2
Typography

Typography is the basic stuff of newspaper design. The transformation brought about by the computer has not altered the importance of understanding and knowing how to use type in creating newspaper pages. In fact, it has made these qualities more necessary now that machines are carrying out work at one time the preserve of craftsman printers trained in the history and uses of 'movable letters'.

The 1200 or so typefaces commonly available in phototypesetters today have their roots in developments that go back to the invention of printing in Europe in the fifteenth century and earlier. The word text, which is commonly used for the body type of newspapers and books, is derived from textur, which was the name given in Germany to the script letter form imposed on his empire by Charlemagne in the ninth century. The tiny condensed lower case letters, referred to as the Caroline **(Plate 1)**, were a breakthrough from the then flowery style used in the scriptoriums and enabled monastic scribes to produce manuscripts at great speed. So tight did this script become that it appeared at a distance like woven material with a texture of stitches – hence *textus*. Decoration and relief for the eye was achieved by drawing illuminated capital letters at the start of sections, which practice survives today in the initial drop or stand-up capital letter round which the first few lines of a paragraph are set, especially in features display and in magazines.

As used at speed in the many Vatican and religious texts of the Middle Ages, the characteristic letters of the Caroline acquired a slope, to which was given the name *italic*.

In reaction against the plain but readable Caroline, scribes in various regions of Europe moved gradually from the rounded lowercase letters into condensed sharper versions. Out of this grew the black letter with its spikes and serifs formed by calligraphic diamond shapes as the quill reached the head and feet of the letters. This was referred to in England as the Old English, while in Germany it took on the name *Fractur* because of its broken look. Fractur, as later mechanically founded and refined by designers, remained the national type of Germany until 1940.

Serif types

The invention of printing from movable type by Gutenberg in Germany in 1450, which spread rapidly to France, England and the Low Countries, produced the first great age of type design, from which the early Bembo (1495) and the designs of Christopher Plantin (1570) still turn up in type books. Claude Garamond (1499–1561), Europe's first commercial typefounder, produced under the patronage of Francis I of France the first mathematically designed type in the 1540s, naming it Grecs du Rois. His Roman was to become the standard, or upright, letter for all printing. Garamond went on to produce a family of roman types based on the letters of the old Latin

abcdefghijklmnopqrstuvwxyz
ABCDEFGHIJKLMNOPQRSTUVWXYZ

abcdefghijklmnopqrstuvwxyz
ABCDEFGHIJKLMNOPQRSTUVWXYZ

abcdefghijklmnopqrstuvwxyz
ABCDEFGHIJKLMNOPQRSTUVWXYZ

abcdefghijklmnopqrstuvwxyz
ABCDEFGHIJKLMNOPQRSTUVWXYZ

ABCDEFGHIJKLMNOPQ RSTUVWXYZ
abcdefghijklmnopqrstuvwxyz

abcdefghijklmnopqrstuvwxyz
ABCDEFGHIJKLMNOPQRSTUVWXYZ

abcdefghijklmnopqrstuvwxyz
ABCDEFGHIJKLMNOPQRSTUVWXYZ

2   Serif faces that typify 400 years of type design: Garamond, Caslon Regular, Baskerville Old Face, Bodoni Bold, Ultra Bodoni Italic, Century Schoolbook, Times Bold

inscriptions, characterized by flat serifs, or tails, on the end of the letter strokes that were to influence generations of type design. Derivatives of Garamond's early faces are still in use.

Sir William Caslon, the first great English typefounder, issued his type specimen sheet in 1734. Caslon, a refinement of Garamond (2), was more comfortable to read, with the serifs cleanly bracketed, and it remains popular in British and many American newspapers. Official copies of the United States Declaration of Independence were printed in Caslon, the face being introduced into the American colonies by Benjamin Franklin. Computer digitizing has further cleaned up the well-cut characters and given them a new lease of life.

A more graceful serif type, though less favoured in newspapers, was Baskerville, introduced by John Baskerville, a teacher of calligraphy, twenty-five years after Caslon's first sheets. His faces, too, remain available in modern computer systems, though usually under changed names. It was an eighteenth-century Italian designer, Giambattista Bodoni (1740–1813), however, who was to produce type designs that would be taken up by every country using the European alphabet, Bodoni bold and italic, with their fine serifs and elegant lowercase letters being still today the most used stock headline type in newspapers. Bodoni, a meticulous artist, was reputed to have spent three years designing the letter 'a' for the alphabet of his revolutionary Ultra Bodoni in which he refined his faces down to the finest of thin lines in the up strokes to a point where they almost disappeared, with the down strokes exaggerated to an enormous thickness (2).

Among much used modern seriffed faces are those of Stanley Morison, with his Times New Roman, designed in 1931 for the relaunch of *The Times*, a classic series used in different variations by many broadsheet newspapers; and the widely used Century bold, produced by the prolific L. B. Benton for American Typefounders Inc., and first cut in 1890 for Century magazine, which wanted a heavier seriffed face with the hairlines given greater thickness than those then available.

abcdefghijklmnopqrstuvwxyz
ABCDEFGHIJKLMNOPQRSTUVWXYZ

abcdefghijklmnopqrstuvwxyz
ABCDEFGHIJKLMNOPQRSTUVWXYZ

ABCDEFGHIJKLMN rstuvwxyz
OPQRSTUVWXYZ abcdefghijklmnopqrstu

3 Slab serif types. Note the heavy squared serifs: Egyptian Bold Condensed, Rockwell Bold, Playbill

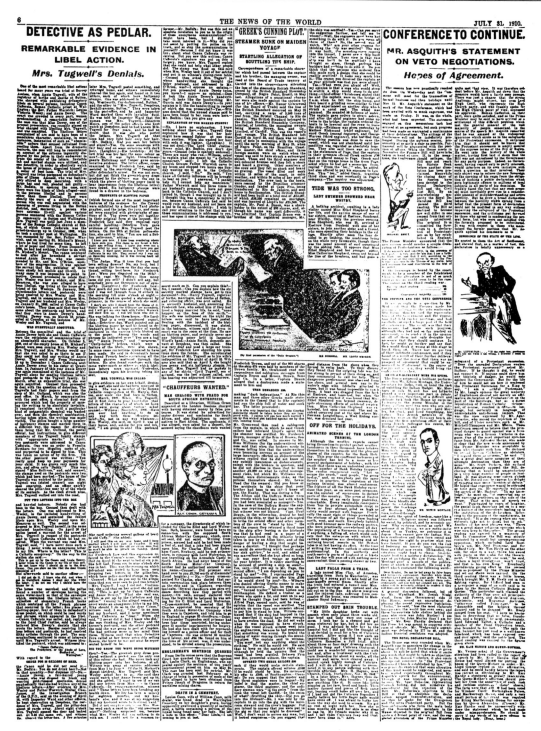

4 This 1910 page from the *News of the World* shows the shift into a primitive form of sans type for page lead headlines alongside the paper's ancient Cheltenham Condensed

Sans serif types By the late nineteenth century American newspapers on the new frontiers were inventing different type formats nearly every day, one of the favourite faces being the Egyptian family of slab-seriffed types **(3)**. Yet it was the British entrepreneur and newspaper owner Lord Northcliffe who started the move into Sans serif for tabloid papers with the *New York World*, which he launched in America four years after founding the *Daily Mail* in 1896. Alfred Harmsworth, as he then was, favoured the new Grotesques then coming into use which, in fact, derived from the primitive sans serif faces that had first appeared in the type specimen books of Figgins and Thorowgood in 1832, who called the faces Sans Serif, the first coining of this term. As used in the *New York World*, and soon to be copied in British papers **(4)**, these early crude sans faces have heavy solid strokes of equal width and are not attractive.

The Grotesques, or Grots as they became known, were to be the basis of all sans serif designs since, culminating in the elegant faces of typography and sculpter Eric Gill (1882–1940) with his Gill Sans, Perpetua, Joanna and Pilgrim **(5)**, and the German designs of the Bauhaus period of the 1920s, leading to Futura, sometimes called Future in computer systems, cut by Paul Renner in 1927. The Germans, in fact, despite their dalliance with the mediaeval look, had a major impact on modern sans serif, reforming, expanding and condensing to achieve a wide range of designs to which the digital computer designers of the late twentieth century have added their refinements.

abcdefghijklmnopqrstuvwxyz
ABCDEFGHIJKLMNOPQQRSTUVWXYZ

abcdefghijklmnopqrstuvwxyz
ABCDEFGHIJKLMNOPQRSTUVWXYZ

**abcdefghijklmnopqrstuvwxyz
ABCDEFGHIJKLMNOPQRSTUVWXYZ**

abcdefghijklmnopqrstuvwxyz
ABCDEFGHIJKLMNOPQRSTUVWXYZ

5 Some sans faces that typify the best of modern type design: Futura Medium, Gill Sans Bold Condensed, Franklin Gothic Bold, Univers

A popular American sans development in the 1890s was Medium Condensed Gothic – at one time referred to as News Gothic because of its versatility – along with its companion Extra Condensed Gothic.

EXCELSIOR

These are examples of body types used in newspapers in Britain. Some are serif face, some are sans. Roman is the standard reading type but italic and bold variants are also used.

EXCELSIOR ITALIC

These are examples of body types used in newspapers in Britain. Some are serif face, some are sans. Roman is the standard reading type but italic and bold variants are also used.

DORIC

These are examples of body types used in newspapers in Britain. Some are serif face, some are sans. Roman is the standard reading type but italic and bold variants are also used.

HELVETICA BOLD

These are examples of body types used in newspapers in Britain. Some are serif face, some are sans. Roman is the standard reading type but italic and bold variants are also used.

HELVETICA LIGHT

These are examples of body types used in newspapers in Britain. Some are serif face, some are sans. Roman is the standard reading type but italic and bold variants are also used.

BELL GOTHIC

These are examples of body types used in newspapers in Britain. Some are serif face, some are sans. Roman is the standard reading type but italic and bold variants are also used.

TIMES ROMAN

These are examples of body types used in newspapers in Britain. Some are serif face, some are sans. Roman is the standard reading type but italic and bold variants are also used.

TIMES BOLD

These are examples of body types used in newspapers in Britain. Some are serif face, some are sans. Roman is the standard reading type but italic and bold variants are also used.

METRO BOLD

These are examples of body types used in newspapers in Britain. Some are serif face, some are sans. Roman is the standard reading type but italic and bold variants are also used.

METRO MEDIUM

These are examples of body types used in newspapers in Britain. Some are serif face, some are sans. Roman is the standard reading type but italic and bold variants are also used.

6   Some examples of 8-point newspaper body type set across 8½ picas

Both these types, and later the adaptable Tempo bold and heavy range, were used in the *Daily Mirror*'s development of the tabloid style under Harry Guy Bartholomew in the 1930s and 1940s, and later under Hugh Cudlipp, the *Daily Mirror* being responsible for the successful exploitation of condensed sans faces by the British popular tabloids.

Univers, however, could be described as the modern typographer's most favoured face. Adrian Frutiger put this elegant and wide-ranging font together for Deberny and Peignot in 1957 and it appears in nearly all systems, a body type version of it being Helvetica, available in bold and roman (6). The beauty of this sans face is its clinical presentation and legibility in all sizes and weights.

Body types

Many of the body types in today's computerized systems (6) have an old pedigree, being derived in some cases from faces that appeared in early nineteenth-century type sheets. Ideal and Ionic, the latter still used, were shown in a Stephenson Blake specimen sheet as early as

1830, the long popularity of Ionic being due to its legibility under the stressful conditions of high-speed printing. The shortness of descenders and ascenders also allowed for economy of space. The modern version generally used was cut by Linotype for the *New York Herald Tribune* in 1926, with Intertype providing a version for the *New York Times* a few years later.

William Addison Dwiggins, a student of the designer Goudy, designed all the versions of the sans body face Metro in 1929–1930. Linotype produced this font with the names Metrolight, Metroblack. Metromedium and Metrothin. The square characters of the black became popular throughout Britain for wide intros for splash stories, and for captions and panels, being favoured over the older stock bold face, Doric, a Figgins and Thorowgood type dating back to 1854. The Metros sometimes appear in computer systems as Chelsea.

Another bold face, noted for its economy in depth, had a curious history. In 1938 the Bell Telephone Company of America needed a more economic type for the huge and ever-growing New York State telephone directory. A Bell typographer, who never merited a byline, joined forces with the Linotype Corporation to invent Bell Gothic, a clean and readable sans serif of uniform weight of line which offered them the visual boldness of types one or two sizes larger.

Imperial, cut by Edwin W. Shaar for Intertype, was another popular body type in hot metal cases, the bold version being noted for its blackness when used in captions or panels.

Faces and families

Every alphabet is in some sense unique. Some are dramatically different, others are adaptations of a previous face created to suit a particular purpose. Each is called a *typeface* and is given a name often, as can be seen, that of the designer. In the days of metal matrices, each letter was mathematically created on paper, transferred to metal, cut and countersunk. Outstanding type cutters such as Nicholas Jenson and John Baskerville would have been amazed and delighted at today's computer digitation of their type characters in which refinement and authenticity are produced by the computer breaking down the shape of the letters and re-creating them by bit-map editing to produce a result better than the original artist could possibly have hoped for. Every size is created in its own right with nothing being scaled down for fear of losing a characteristic.

Each typeface has its *family* which is made up of *fonts* of characters which are differentiated from other fonts by *weight* and *interpretation*.

The word font derives from the hot metal tradition and was the name given to a cabinet full of all the characters and sizes of a given type including punctuation, ligatures, cyphers, figures, fractions and asterisks, and which could range from 81 up to 160 characters depending on usage. The weight of a piece of type is determined by the visual heaviness or lightness of the strokes that make up the characters, giving bold or light letters. By interpretation the face

Helvetica
Helvetica
Helvetica
Helvetica
Helvetica
Helvetica
Helvetica

Helvetica
Helvetica
Helvetica
Helvetica
Helvetica
Helvetica
Helvetica

7   Weight and interpretation in type design – 18-point Helvetica lowercase in its various presentations

designer meant the condensing or expanding of the characters to produce narrower and wider variants for particular purposes. The weight and interpretation are signalled in the compounded names of types – Metroblack, Metrolight, Helvetica Bold, Helvetica Medium Italic, Extra Condensed Gothic and so on **(7)**.

Categories of type

To make the type map intelligible to the user it has become a convention to list typefaces, a selection of which we have now introduced to the reader, in five main categories:

Old English

Old English **(8)** is referred to as Fraktur in Europe. These are the alphabets derived from the hand-produced quill pen letters of the scriptoriums and sometimes referred to under their medaeval name of Black Letter. Fonts can be either in-lined or solid and vary in the degree of decoration applied to them. They survive mainly in newspaper mast-heads and in ornamental lettering.

Serif

This is an important range of typefaces, old and new **(2)** used in all manner of printing, which are characterized by letters that do not finish square on their strokes but carry a horizontal line or tail, sometimes at a slight angle (that is, the *serif*) which has the effect of adding dignity or authority to the letters. At the bottom of the letter the serif may be attached by a curve or bracket, to the main body of the character, or sometimes an angled attachment **(9)**. The serif, too, traces back to the flourishes given by the quill pen, as can be seen in

abcdefghijklmnopqrstuvwxyz
ABCDEFGHIJKLMNOPQRSTUVWXYZ

abcdefghijklmnopqrstuvwxyz
ABCDEFGHIJKLMNOPQRSTUVWXYZ

abcdefghijklmnopqrstuvwxyz
ABCDEFGHIJKLMNOPQRSTUVWXYZ

abcdefghhijklmmnnopqrstuvwxyz
AABCDEFGHIJKLMNOPQRSTUVWXYZ

8 Novelty and other little used faces, common in advertising display, sometimes find a place on features pages or in a special projection that looks to type to set the mood: Stencil Bold, Palace Script, Old English, Ringlet

the characteristic serifs in the range of *old style* faces such as Bembo and Garamond, which are not horizontal but sloping and rounded. By comparison the range known as *modern* (as in Bodoni) has thin unbracketed serifs, except in the capitals M and N, with a strong contrast between the thick and thin strokes, shown in its extreme form in Ultra Bodoni.

Transitional illustrates elements from the last two subgroups. Times Roman, for example, is a typical transitional face in which the serifs are slightly bracketed with just a little contrast between the thick and thin strokes. Finally, there is the square or *Slab Serif*, also known as Egyptian antique, in which the serifs are nearly as thick as the uprights of the characters **(3)**. These first appeared in the American type books of Vincent Figgins in 1815 as Antique. The name Egyptian was attached as a result of the antiquarian interest at the time in all things Egyptian. The theme was carried through in subsequent versions such as Karnak, Cairo, Pharon, Memphis and Scarab, although Rockwell and Beton are more recent versions in popular use.

Sans serif

Sans serif describes alphabets in which the letter strokes are without serifs **(5)**. The characters have generally a uniform thickness and weight throughout. The name Gothic has come to be attached to some of these designs – a misnomer since its origins go back to the Black Letter script of the monasteries. Helvetica, Univers, Grotesque, Franklin, Tempo, Futura and Metro are examples.

9 The terminology of type – this illustration from *Autologic's Digital Type Collection* shows the traditionally named parts of letters and the significance of the x-height

Scripts

Script and cursive – not for the news pages – are faces based on brush or pen strokes. Brush stroke letters can induce an air of urgency, while script type, much used on invitation and visiting cards, produces an effect of officialdom and authority. Occasionally, such typefaces will have some application on a features page but the subject needs to be exactly right **(8)**.

Novelty faces

These are the odd ones out. Modern designers encouraged by the transfer typographic sheets from Letraset and Mecanorma have produced alphabets constructed from sunbursts, brickwork and other elements. They can work on advertising posters and on television but have little application in newspapers **(8)**.

Measurement

Despite the onset of metrication in page design, typesizes even in the most modern of computerized systems are still measured in a 250-year-old system of points, of which there are, as a guide, approximately 72 to the inch and 28 to the centimetre. Strictly there are two points systems, the American, used throughout the English-speaking world, and the European, used in most of Europe, but the difference between the two is so small that in the ordinary run of typesizes it would pass unnoticed. Here we are concerned with the American system. We relate points to inches purely for convenience of learning since the two are different entities. If we are to be exact there are 72 points to 0.996264 of an inch.

BODONI   HELVETICA

10 How variations in x-height can create an optical illusion. These letters in Bodoni and Helvetica are the same size but have different x-heights

Type size is measured by its height in the page, but it should be remembered that sizes are derived from the metal base upon which the characters stood in the old hot metal system which had to allow space for ascenders and descenders in the lowercase letters f, g, h, j, k, l, p, q, t and y, and for the differences in height between capital and lower case letters. Thus, to say that a 36-point letter is half an inch deep is not strictly true, since without ascenders and descenders the actual size on the page is less than half an inch. The problem is complicated further by the fact that the proportion of space taken up by the ascender and descender varies in different type ranges so that the *x-height* – the mean height of a letter without the ascender or descender – can vary from one type to another **(10)**. Thus when a type is described as being 'big on its body' it means that its x-height is greater in relation to its descenders and ascenders than with other types. Such a type consequently looks bigger in any given size. An oddity occurs with certain types called *titling*, used for big headlines or posters, which exist only in capitals, since here the characters take up the full height available on their base. Consequently a headline in 72-point titling really is an inch deep.

Typesizes, originally for convenience of manufacture in hot metal days, are designated in a strict series of sizes. In body type they start at 4½ points, ranging through 5, 6, 7, 8, 9 to 10 points, then jumping in series to 12 and 14 points. Headline series run: 14, 18, 24, 30, 36, 42, 48, 60, 72, 84, 96, 108, 120 and 144 points **(11)**. Sizes can go beyond 144 points in computer software, and systems typographers, in response to American demand, have introduced 16, 20 and 22 point sizes to prevent distortion of existing sizes by having to reduce or enlarge type to get headlines to fit.

Computer systems are programmed at the outset with traditional series sizes for the very good reason that they enable page designers and production journalists to achieve a deliberate type balance at the visualizing stage which is essential if a newspaper's character is to be

Century bold   18 POINT

Century bold   24 POINT

Century bold   30 POINT

Century bold   36 POINT

Century bold   42 POINT

Century bold   48 POINT

Century bold   60 POINT

Century bold   72 POINT

11   Century bold lowercase showing stock sizes from 18 point to 72 point

preserved. While the sizing can be overridden by keyboard controls during design and editing, and types bastardized to within fractions of points of each other, the facility should be used sparingly if design is to be taken seriously.

Setting widths have always been in picas and points, a pica being a unit of 12 points (or one sixth of an inch) and this remains so with computerized systems. Standard column widths range from 8½ picas to 10 picas or more depending on the number of columns. The old English term for a pica, an em (or mutton), which was based on the width of the standard 12-point roman letter 'm', has now fallen largely out of use, and with it the en, or nut, based on the standard 12-point roman letter 'n'.

In subediting practice, except where setting format codes are used, setting is called up by keying in such terms as '12rom, 14p6', which means 12-point roman body type across 14 picas and 6 points, or, for example, '10MM, 8p4', which is the usual way of saying 10-point Metromedium across 8 picas and 4 points. Standard single or double column setting usually has a simpler one-stroke letter code to save keyboarding time. A system can be formatted with whatever sorts of standard width body setting are required to give maximum speed and simplicity in keyboarding.

Letter spacing

Letter spacing is a main area of faults in newly installed systems. If newspapers want to avoid interrupting the reading habits of their buyers, spacing is too important to be left to the systems manufacturers. This means that as far as possible it should imitate the hot metal system that went before. It must therefore be programmed in at the start, in body setting no less than in headline type. Body setting should tend towards being tight rather than slack, since open setting lacks impact, although justifying the lines in the typesetter will inevitably produce variations, especially in narrow measures. To achieve a good effect, the units of space should relate to the typesize rather than standard spacing being given across the board. A good test to detect faults in spacing is to prop a newspaper page upside down against a wall. The eye, untrammelled by having to sort out the sense of the words, can thus concentrate on the pattern of space between letters and between words and faults quickly become apparent.

Kerning

For ideal reading at all sizes, spacing between some letters needs to vary. While manufacturers might supply a system in which the letter spacing is satisfactory overall it is down to the user to modify this to improve readability by deleting or inserting units of space between certain letters, and also between words in which certain end letters occur. This is called kerning **(12)**.

Letters that will always require this visual balancing, especially in headlines, are the obviously badly shaped ones such as capital A, W, V and Y, where they fall together, and all rounded letters. Hot metal systems were clumsy in this respect in that the satisfactory lodging together of letters such as the Y and O and T relied on the eye of the operator of the casting machine. With hand-set headline type this often entailed permanently defacing metal characters by cutting with a saw into the waste or beard of a letter in order to draw it closer to its neighbour.

Computer setting allows for a much more precise attitude towards spacing since the system can produce units of space related to the widths of given characters and a judicious improvement can be carried out by keyboard commands. Using a one hundredth part of

AV Te Yo Y.

AV Te Yo Y.

AV Te Yo Y.

12 These letter combinations show the effect of kerning: from normal spacing in the top line, down to 4 units kerned in the bottom line

the width of a letter in larger sizes as a unit, an instruction can be given to the computer to remove space from between the letters by deleting the number of units required in proportion to allow a line a given density. Entire alphabets of every font in the house can be kerned in a uniform fashion in this way to the editor's taste. Thus not only is kerning easier than under hot metal, but it can be extended and made more uniform and standardized into setting formats across the setting so that greater readability is achieved.

The text

The act of reading is performed by the eye moving across lines of type in short jumps. These jumps take place at regular intervals with brief pauses for about a quarter of a second. The perception of the words covered takes place during the fixation period which is called the eye span and which, according to experts in these matters, covers in average newspaper reading text just 2 centimetres, or 5 picas. The eye then moves on to the next pause.

However, the eye also has to cope with the descent from line to line. To ease this function and to avoid lines becoming excessively long in characters, and the number of jumps required, it has been found helpful to set book texts in 10-, 11-, or even 12-point type. Newpapers, with their wider sheet and need to pack the space with content, have historically opted for columnar formats, which enable a

In a mass media system, the typographer is usually a member of the encoding team. He stands between the original source of the message and the channel (here: the printed page), which will carry the message to an audience. He has considerable control over the coding process by selecting type faces, type sizes, and by

9 point solid (no leading).

In a mass media system, the typographer is usually a member of the encoding team. He stands between the original source of the message and the channel (here: the printed page), which will carry the message to an audience. He has considerable control over the coding process by selecting type faces, type sizes, and by

9 point with ½ point leading.

In a mass media system, the typographer is usually a member of the encoding team. He stands between the original source of the message and the channel (here: the printed page), which will carry the message to an audience. He has considerable control over the coding process by selecting type faces, type sizes, and by

9 point with 1 point leading.

13   Lines of 9-point Crown set across 14 picas demonstrate the effect on body type of line spacing or leading (ledding)

smaller body face to be used, thus maintaining lines of acceptable length while easing the eye's descent through the text.

As a result of having narrower lines than books, newspapers find that they can set comfortably for the eye in a body face of 7 or 8 point, with even 6 point being used in tabulated information. Where prominence needs to be given to the beginnings of stories, however, especially important stories, a bigger typeface is used, often of wider measure. It follows, therefore, that subeditors must increase the body type size when setting to wider measure.

Where required for special setting, or to fill, line spacing equal to 1 point or 1½ points can be inserted by keyboard commands **(13)**.

Intros

A page lead introduction or *intro* across two or more columns might be established in importance for the reader by being in 12 point, or even 14 point, perhaps in a bold version of the standard face, and still be comfortable to read. A single column story might carry an intro in 10 point or even 8 point, on a body size of 7 point. A caution here: practice in intro setting varies from paper to paper, popular tabloids going for bigger and bolder intro sizes, while the qualities and more traditional papers settle for one or two sizes up in the stock body face. *The Times*, for example, does not deviate from a fixed one size up from its 8 on a 9-point body, relying on the effect of fine line spacing thus produced to help the eye through the longish texts.

Also a matter for house style is whether the first paragraph starts with the first word in capitals, or not (as in most of the qualities) or whether drop letters are used **(14)**. More universal is the practice of starting the first paragraph full out, while giving all the others a standard indent on the first line of 6 points or sometimes 12.

Drop letters

Drop letters are large size initial capital letters on the first word of the intro of a story set in a special house type style, from three up to six or seven times the size of the body, and round which the first few lines of the paragraph are set. The size indicates how many lines of shorter setting are needed – that is, a two-line, three-line drop, or in the case of the more magaziney layouts, up to a ten-line drop, a device much used on *The Times* features pages.

Drop letters, as we have seen, are descended from the illuminated capitals of monkish manuscripts and their job is unashamedly to decorate the text and attract the eye. For this reason they are used nowadays more on features pages where longer texts and deliberate projection give more call for them **(14)**, though two- and three-line drops still appear on the main stories on some newspapers. The drop letter also exists as a *stand-up drop*, in which it is aligned with the base of the first line and stands above the paragraph. Magazines and some up-market newspapers use these paragraph markers at up to 120 point as stand-ups giving a huge amount of display space above the first line of the paragraph. Body type can be set easily round the contours of drop letters by the use of keyed formats giving a snug fit and useful relief to the shape of the page.

To be effective, the size of a drop letter should be in proportion to the width of the setting, and thought must be given as to whether to use serif or sans serif letters. If a serif face is used then the body type of the paragraph should be larger than normal since the serifs on the letter will push the rest of the line further away from the initial. A sans letter will allow the rest of the word to be tightly set alongside it, thus increasing its readability. In either case the rest of the first word should be in caps of the body.

A more adventurous way in magazine or colour supplement layout is to draw a squared piece of artwork as a drop, more on the lines of the illuminated letter. A ploy here is to suspend it in the white of the gutter in front of the column. In this case it is best used squared up to

THE SCOTSMAN Wednesday, March 8, 1989

Lifestyle 16

Skirts for the flirts

When it comes to sheer sex appeal the Italians lead the world. In Milan this week some are going to great lengths with skirts which sweep the floor but others are taking hemlines up, up and almost away. **Ann Chubb** reports

LEFT: Gianni Versace is taking things to extremes with this short daytime suit. The chic jacket and skirt are designed to be worn without a blouse — in winter.

BELOW: Keep out the chill with a heavy sweater, leather culottes and a wide, soft coat from Byblos. Similar coats appear in many of the Italian collections this year.

A lesson on the catwalk

AT a time of recession, should fashion quietly evolve wearable good taste classics or titillate our appetites with clothes that are covetable and exciting? The Italian designers, first in the international fashion circuit to unveil their wares for autumn are doing both.

Georgio Armani, whose younger, sportier Emporio line kicked off the shows on Sunday morning, made a strong statement in favour of understatement with softly tailored sportswear that you could buy to wear for ever. Gianni Versace, on the other hand, stuck his neck out for the shorter (and even shorter) skirt in a show that revelled in pure, unadulterated sex — something the Italians are rather good at. And at a time when too many designers offer too many options, we have to admit admiration for such positive thinking.

Armani, whose main line collection will be unveiled tonight, is something of an international force these days. Not only with an awesome programme of international expansion — his Emporio superstore opened in London last month, ten more are planned for around the country soon and a new Armani shop opens in London this weekend.

The man whose tailoring is the most covetable in the world has softened his line considerably. Shoulders are now dropped and slightly rounded, jackets shorter and curvier, trousers often track-suit-style or else flattering jodhpurs of grey jersey. The cape, a strong Milanese theme, appeared in every shape from voluminous and flowering to bolero brief. And while the Milanese women happily saunter the streets in the currently sweltering spring weather wearing opulent minks and sables, Armani comes out strongly in favour of the frankly fake with Fifties-style stoles and shrugs.

Versace, on the other hand, came on strong with a collection that majored in sex. His skirts were universally cut short, and not only were they cut to mid thigh or higher but they were skin tight and often side slit to boot. Sometimes they were simply tiny fans of Fortuny-style diagonally pleated fabric. And the short skirt was worn with everything from swirling ankle length great coats to long tailored jackets, a mere one inch shorter than the skirt or with brief bejewelled bustier tops.

On less than perfect models (Versace imported three of the world's best at vast expense to show exclusively for him) it was the look that could have been tarty — in fact it looked terrific. These are the sort of clothes that men will positively urge women to buy.

ELSEWHERE in Milan, the longer hemline proliferates, often soft and voluminous and ankle length, with trousers the only other alternative. Dolce e Gabana actually manage to make the long skirt look sexy by cutting it tight and curvy in jersey and teaming it with corset-style tops or fresh white cotton shirts edged with lace or translating it into wispy black chiffon. The essential accessory to complete the outfit is a Corsican-style crocheted shawl with deep fringed edging. It helped, too, to have actress Charlotte Lewis as star model looking just like a young Claudia Cardinale. Byblos on the other hand offered pleated trousers so wide that they looked almost like ankle length skirts — very pretty for evening in black teamed with simple black waistcoat and crisp white shirt.

Colours are definitely brightening up here in Milan. Byblos showed Harris tweed jackets in delectable shades of yellow or mint green or apricot for colourful hacking jackets over tapered cord pants. And they gave tweeds a new twist with neat suits in cheerful checks of bright colour enlivened with Paisley print lapels and cuffs.

Huge Paisley patterns were also used for jolly sweaters in bright colours teamed with suede walking shorts and bright hooded coats. The newest winter coat, which appears in almost every Italian collection, is wide and swingy, with dropped shoulder lines, cape or shawl collar and is often made of unlined blanket-like wool.

There was a Scottish air about the Missoni collection which had wonderfully practical quilted cire coats lined with tartan or tapestry and bright tartan-inspired knits for knickerbockers partnered with striped multi-coloured sweaters and jaunty Tam O'Shanter hats. There were also big collared tartan-style knit coats mixing bright colours together, while those famous Missoni multi-coloured zigzag knits looked young and lively used for long lean cardigans teamed with short flirty skirts.

A Chinese influence brought kimono-style jackets in tree bark effect knit and trouser suits in quilted print teamed with coolie hats of black or brown velvet.

As always the Italians excel at throwaway luxury looks of sumptuous quality. Good examples this week have included Mario Valentino's sheepskin coats in delectable shades of pale blue, pink or mimosa yellow, their wide shawl collars delicately fretworked to imitate lace; Laura Biagotti's softest suede jogging suits of palest petal pink and her gently tiered cashmere smock dresses; Genny's bitter chocolate leathers, glossy and paper-fine, used for wonderful three-quarter length coats, beaver-collared, and widely belted over short ocelot print skirts.

Maybe we're all taking fashion too seriously though. Certainly designer Franco Moschino who doesn't, is currently a huge commercial success with his wild and wicked designs that frequently contain some sort of joke — he has no less than 23 licensees making everything he designs from jeans to lingerie, most of which are now available in Great Britain.

He thinks that clothes (including his own) are vastly over-priced so writes 'very expensive jacket' across the back of a plastic hacking jacket, or embellishes black shirts with their actual price in gold embroidery. And last night he closed the whole of chic Via Sant Andrea for one mammoth street party to launch what he calls "his first and last shop".

A SPARTAN split-level catwalk dominated by a curious human silhouette functioning as a surrealist clock created a suitably avant garde backdrop for this year's Glasgow School of Art Fashion Show. The audience might have anticipated the performance from the set: aggressive, up-tempo, and out for thrills, although there were regrettably less than usual of the latter.

Two girls skipping in soft, ballet-inspired costumes, and then suddenly adopting the stance of body builders supplied the sort of visual aid a disappointing collection required to give it impact. But, in the end, the medium was more pleasing than the message.

Ethnic influences were writ large, if belatedly: there were sarongs, saris, and an abundance of gold filigree as the young designers opted for the frankly opulent, led boldly (u where no man has gone before) by the exquisite printed gents' shawls designed by Alistair McCauley.

Glasgow has long been celebrated for its printed textiles, and *The Glasgow Print* was very positively tattooed on the forearm of this show. The two models who strode ferociously with their pink, turquoise and orange umbrellas spearheading their matching, animal print dresses epitomised the atmosphere of captive energy.

The triumph of colour confidence was probably Susan Telford's red, pink and green dress and jacket, delineated with sculptured flowers, which, unlike most of the evening's offerings owed no obvious acknowledgement to last season's couture collections.

GAULTIER'S recent venture into external boning was responded to at regular intervals, most notably in a curious black and green sculpted wedding dress. Jasper Conran and John Galliano both breathed their heady influences into the rich embroidery and chiffon of Donna Lewis's blouses, breeches and pants, but there was an occasional showstopper nonetheless. Pauline Collins should be a name to watch, as her grey marked blouson top, skirt and leggings stretched the limits of the fashion designer towards the three-dimensional vision of the sculptor.

Other intimations of (potential) immortality came from Gillian Orr, with an olive green silk gents' suit and Claire Hendry whose men's chiffon flares added avant-garde bite.

All in all, the Class of '89 had a lot to be proud of, though their deliberately moody and mannered show displayed a lot that could be improved on, too. If such obviously talented young designers would trust more to their own instincts, (as Geraldine Mitchell did with her glorious printed hats, swimwear and duffle bags), then the shows of the future could be more fun, more inspired and altogether more saleworthy.

Iain McCallum

Jane Torday examines how a fatal attraction has become a drag

Light at the end of the haze

Smouldering star: Marlene Dietrich set the trend

THE theatre is packed. On stage, faint ribbons of smoke coil like chiffon around Maria Aitken, as she paces restlessly about the steam drawing room set. The smoke drifts over the audience and it smells very pleasant; not any old vulgar Virginian, and yet not entirely French or Turkish but something rather herbal which will not offend the non-smokers in the audience.

Continuous smoking is required of the actors in the current production of Noel Coward's *The Vortex*, focusing as it does on a fading society beauty who is about to lose her 1920s toyboy and gain a much sadder young man, her own son of the same age who returns home from Paris as a cocaine addict.

In Coward's day, smoking was seen as an entirely civilised pleasure in sophisticated circles. At the other end of the scale, it was one of the few forms of pleasure available to workers on low incomes with little leisure, though some still insulated it was a decadent and disgusting habit.

Cigarette smoking really took off as a glamourous activity for the masses under the influence of Hollywood. Marlene Dietrich and other screen idols used cigarettes a to accentuate their smouldering looks — and the public followed suit.

Victorian country houses had smoking rooms where men were exclusively male preserves. Before that time, prejudice against smoking in polite society was often as pronounced as it has become again today. The Duke of Wellington made his guests smoke, if smoke they must, in the servants hall. The difference today is that smokers and non-smokers alike are united in agreement that smoking is an unhealthy habit.

Smoking has become unacceptable for valid reasons, and even a small child can tell you what those are, smoking can endanger your health and can cause lung cancer and heart disease. Cigarettes are seen as an implement of death and have become an unwelcome intrusion into the lives of non-smokers because of the threat of passive smoking.

But it has now got to the stage that when moderate smokers (who smoke a few cigarettes a day, or less than a packet a week) light up at a social function, they are increasingly regarded as murder suspects instead of mere suicidal simpletons. Non-smoking hosts often can't find ashtrays for their guests, having either burned them or given them away to jumble sales.

National No Smoking Day is thus a glorious opportunity for non-smokers and reformed smokers to point the finger at their fallen friends and relations who still indulge. Whether or not this year's No Smoking Day will provide a genuine opportunity for smoking sinners to renounce the evil of their ways and tread henceforth on the path of righteousness, remains to be seen.

Some interesting advice is offered in the leaflet for No Smoking Day compiled by the admirable "Europe against Cancer" group. 'Instead of smoking, breathe deeply, move around, do something else, think about the harm that cigarettes will do you, clean your teeth, take sips of water.'

Today, could prove to be almost as funny as Red Nose Day on March 10, if wherever we go we can be entertained by haunted figures with anxious expressions, breathing deeply and moving around aimlessly in between teeth-cleaning sessions and sips of water. Tea and coffee will not be a comfort because as the leaflet says: 'Tea and coffee can trigger off the smoking urge.' The leaflet also advises us 'Go easy on alcohol, it weakens resolve.'

National Days dedicated to the promotion of tree-planting, adult education or breast feeding are all providing a form of social service. So are days dedicated to the reduction of the use of aerosol sprays, lead petrol and cigarettes. But perhaps another National Day could be added to this list. National Tolerance Day, when for 24 hours, we could all unashamedly abandon our usual prejudices against beliefs, lifestyles and habits which do not correspond with our own. The experience could prove to be so beneficial, so relaxing, so liberating, that smokers like myself might not feel the need for a cigarette the whole day long.

14 Typographical variations in a feature page from *The Scotsman*. Drop letters and white space are used as eye-breakers in place of crossheads. The body setting is standard width, but with the main feature indented to show columnar white, and the column seven piece set ragged right, or unjustified. The 'standfirst' under the headline is bastard measure, also ragged right, to fill the space between the intro and the cut-out picture

the top of the first line of the body type it accompanies. Check that the gutter space available, however.

A warning: the drop or stand-up capital is for decorative use only and should not be peppered around the page indiscriminately. Avoid mixing it with cross-heads and other eye-catching ploys (see Chapter 12). Drop letters should be elegantly spaced out on a page projection so that they do not line up or cover each other. Rivers of white space can be caused by badly positioned drops or stand-ups.

Justified setting

The practice in newspapers, as with books, is to use justified setting – that is setting that is squared off to an even margin down both sides of the column. It helps the eye by providing lines of the same width for it to scan. The machine provides artificially a setting system that breaks and hyphenates words where necessary in order to fill the lines to meet the spacing parameters. This process is known as hyphenating and justifying, or to H and J. The only relief in solid setting is the normal indent on the left of the column at the start of each paragraph.

In the case of computerized systems a pattern of hyphenation is programmed in at the outset to ensure that words are correctly broken syllabically, avoiding breaks in one-syllable words or proper names as in the style practised under hot metal.

Unjustified setting

Justified setting has remained unchallenged from the days of the *Gutenberg Bible* – even from the period of quill pen manuscripts – to the present day. Now advertising and magazine design have brought unjustified setting into fashion in an attempt to appear different or give attractive variation **(14)**.

A cardinal rule here is never to unjustify at the front end. The eye requires a constant reference line on the left and is not equipped for the shock of having to look for the start of the next line. On the occasions when unjustified right was used under the hot-metal system the linotype operator would be told to set the text 'ragged right', allowing the machine to run to the extremes of a set width. Problems would occur by massively unregulated indents on one-word lines, dropping a full word to the next line. In this respect the electronic method is more accurate and better regulated. There can be commands even for 'soft unjustification' or 'hard unjustification' depending on how the designer wants the space to be used. Contrary to expectation, the text does not usually take up more space than with justified setting.

Unjustified setting is little called for on news pages, though it can give effective variation and a feeling of lightness on features, provided measures are not wide or text long. Used in parts of the paper on a regular basis it can key the reader into a specific feature such as the editorial comment – but beware of overkill! Blanket use of such setting can weary the eye and remind the reader of the familiar comfort of normal justified lines with their regular traverse for the eye. Beware also the temptation of using ragged right on too narrow a measure. At 8 ems and under this could result in one-word turns and be unreadable.

Setting variations

Variations in body setting are used for two reasons: to give emphasis to certain parts of a text, or to certain stories; and to ease the eye in its perusal of the pages.

Most body setting has italic and bold variants, or is used along with a bold intro setting of a compatible type. Special stress can be given to the odd paragraph by setting in bold or italic, while particular stories on a page can likewise be differentiated by being set in bold or (less commonly) in italic.

Paragraphs

While H. W. Fowler (of *Modern English Usage*) describes a paragraph as 'essentially a unit of thought, not of length' he also says: 'The purpose of a paragraph is to give the reader a rest.' In the case of newspapers the latter function takes precedence. With type in columns long paragraphs are tiring to the eye and make the text look solid and unattractive and so, depending on the pace of the writing, newspaper paragraphs tend towards shortness. This gives the eye the relief of extra white space resulting from the pica or 6-point paragraph indent. Some quality papers also relieve their longer texts by putting a 2-point space between paragraphs, as well as setting stock type on a larger body to give fine linear white.

Cross-heads

A much used method to provide eye breaks with runs of text of more than 4 or 5 inches is to drop in cross-heads, which are usually single lines of display type in a regular stock face of the house taking one key word from the part of the story that follows. Sometimes, for uniformity, the type chosen is a smaller version of the headline type of the story. (See development of this in Chapter 12.) Some newspapers use pieces of decorative rule in place of cross-heads. Features pages sometimes rely simply on drop letters with a pica of space above, or run the text with heavy leading (ledding) between paragraphs making crossheads unnecessary.

Indention

Another way to vary setting is to indent it either 6 points (nut) front or 6 points each side (n.e.s.), which gives vivid columnar spacing **(14)** to set a story off against its fellows. A variation of this is the *hanging* or *reverse indent*, which has the first line of a paragraph standing proud full out and the rest indented usually six points. It works best with bold setting and with single column type. It is also known as nothing and one, or 0 & 1, and has periods of vogue on various newspapers, often being rediscovered by new editors.

Bastard measure is any type setting of non-standard width and can occur against a non-standard width picture. Sometimes a story will start, for design purposes, in a bastard measure intro, and then turn into single column. Type is also set bastard measure to fit into panelled shapes to suit a page design, in which certain texts are enclosed in a frame of print rules or borders. As with other type and setting variants the designer should avoid using too many of the devices in the same page or design format.

Headlines

Headlines are a dominant element in any page design. At its simplest, headline typography consists in the use of a few chosen types and type sizes to produce page designs that conform generally to a house style and give the pages their particular visual character. There are factors in the constructing and placing of headlines that are common to all newspapers. For instance, as we have seen, all pages have a lead story with a dominant headline. This can either take the form of a *banner* across the page, or a number of lines stacked on top of each other. The use of a *strap-line*, in smaller type, above the main headline is also common. Likewise the descending order of importance of stories is indicated by items of double or single column in reducing order of type size as shown in the tabbed page **(15)**. And yet within these parameters there are plenty of variations of approach.

In many broadsheets and the more traditional of tabloid papers the practice is to design pages to a modular or formula style with headlines of predictable shape and size, and even position. With the exception, perhaps, of the lead story the headline shapes come first and the words are generally made by the subeditors to fit. Headlines are located in regular sizes and widths, sometimes centred and sometimes set left according to a paper's style, occasionally with a wordy single column kicker to give variety to the middle of the page.

Features pages in most newspapers tend towards free-thinking on headline display. It is important, with this approach, that the shape and size of the headline on the lead story should reflect the mood of the headline words and the projection decided upon, even if some of the supporting stories are of more conventional shape.

Here, the working relationship between subeditor and page designer (the same person on many provincial newspapers) is vitally important as the page begins to take shape on the layout pad or screen. This can entail perhaps a main headline consisting of one or two words, exaggeratedly big, with perhaps a wordy, discursive second deck. It can have a mood headline linked to a dominant picture. It can involve special type, or type used in an innovative way to match the mood or content of the text. A sense of fun or a feeling of tragedy can be induced by the choice of words or type. It can entail layout in which pictures rather than headlines become the dominant factor. It is an approach to design that offers a more challenging and imaginative world for the designer, though the context of a type style remains important. (See development of this in Chapters 9, 10 and 11.)

Type choice

Fashion can dictate type use and the prevailing fashion is for wholly lowercase headlines, especially in those newspapers using a serif type dress. Lowercase type, because of its varied contours, is considered to be generally more readable, yet the danger, in unsophisticated hands lies in producing pages of a lulling uniformity – a fault that occurs even in such a design-conscious paper as *The Guardian*. For those papers using a free-style approach or seeking impact, especially on features pages, an embargo on headlines in caps can be constricting, the page one splash headline being a particular victim of this fad. However, the careful juxtaposing of light and bold lowercase faces and a balanced variation in sizes can produce pages of great elegance, especially where there is good picture content, as with *The Times*, *The Independent* and the *Sunday Correspondent*.

The essential thing in type choice is not to introduce too many permitted variants but to utilize type weights and sizes of a given range so that the page has a sense of pattern. Of the main variations *italic* is one that has been discontinued on many papers. Its use now is often as a form of labelling, sometimes reversed as white on black, to indicate to the reader where a particular subject or section is regularly located.

In more traditional layout styles, special emphasis within a type range can be given by the occasional multiple line heading of smaller than usual size with extra line spacing, while a predominantly sans format can give emphasis to a soft feminine subject by using a fine sensitive serif face as an alternative.

The main difference between the broadly traditional styles and the free-style tabloid approach lies in the type sizes used. While 72 point is often the largest type on a traditional broadsheet page, it is customary, in the search for impact, to go up to 120 point or even 144 point and bigger, on a poster-style tabloid front page. *The Sun*, in the hot metal days, in order to achieve the most telling effect in the fastest time, evolved a kind of Lexicon game in which letters in 108-, 120- or 144- point sizes of its headline titling were proofed and stuck to stout cardboard. These would be 'set' by the art desk until the best possible headline in terms of letter count and space had been achieved by the headline writer – usually the editor – who could alter and polish at will before consigning the line to metal. The alphabets were then returned to their headline box, the copy sent to the case-hand and the line would make a perfect fit.

Arrangement

A strap-line can run either above the main headline, or be bunched together alongside it. It should be about four sizes down from the main head, in order to fulfil its explanatory role and not to appear too dominant, and should be lowercase on top of caps or vice versa. The length of the lines is a matter of fitting the page design. It is sometimes an advantage, depending on the design style of the paper, to reverse the strap as a white on black (WOB) or white on 50 per cent tint (WOT). Another variation is to run the strap in black type on a lighter (25 per cent) tint. It should be well separated by space from the main head. A reversed strap requiring more space. Underscored straplines can look effective, provided underscores (usually in 2 point or 4 point) are not overused on the page. Contrast can be enhanced with a very light typeface on top of a thicker black underscore even up to a pica in the case of bold tabloid pages. The thicker the underscore the more massive should be the space below it. A useful guide is that a 72-point headline and accompanying strap with, say, a 4-point underscore, needs to be separated from the intro below by 18 points of space, with 24 points of space if the main headline or underscore is bigger. (See examples in Chapters 10 and 11.)

Centred headlines, whether single column, double column or wider, are now in style, although no headline should be significantly narrower than the space allotted to it. *Set-left headlines* can look effective but only as a variation to a broadly centred style. To make all headlines set left, as some papers did at one time, has neither point or advantage to it, and often left splodges of white all over the page. Headlines on the right-hand edge of the page should not be set left, on account of the raggedness it leaves on the outside column. *Set-right headlines* baffle the reading eye and should not be used. *Staggered heads* with the first line set left and the last set right are an American fashion which has never caught on in British newspapers.

Two-deck headlines are commonly used and enable two angles of a story to be explored. The second deck (in fact, a separate headline) should be a smaller version of the main type. *Three-deck* or *multi-deck heads* are seldom found these days outside the pages of the *Wall Street Journal*.

Line spacing

Capital letter headlines are easier to line-space than lowercase, since there is not the problem of ascenders rising out of the line below against descenders hanging down from the top line. Whatever system has been formatted, it is still visual experience that counts here. To make the space acceptable, either the format should be overridden at the keyboard or, with cut-and-paste, the scalpel should be used to 'overlap' ascenders and descenders, tucking each neatly in to the white space. In this way regular space from x-line to x-line can be maintained. With small sizes this is not possible, but then the space inconsistencies are not so affronting.

The general rule is to maintain a consistent standard of line spacing using computer formats as far as possible. Excessive line space makes a headline look weak, and is also a waste. As far as possible a line should fill laterally the space it is given, unless indented white is used for effect. Space, remember, is there to aid the eye. (For general letter spacing in typesetting see above.)

Effect of the computer

The digital conversion of typefaces from original matrices for the purposes of photosetting has enhanced the work of the old type designers. Caslon, Garamond and Bodoni would have been excited by the new lease of life now being given to their fonts.

A leading method in this digitizing has been the Ikarus Concept, developed by the German firm URW, of Hamburg. One of the typesetter manufacturers using it is Autologic, who describe in their *Digital Type Collection Book* how the work is done: 'The production process begins with the drawing of each character based on the historical development of the face. Along with original drawings come preliminary space specifications. Since Ikarus deals with contours rather than with bit-mapped information, the necessary outline points are defined and fed into the system for processing. . . . After conversion from Ikarus to digital format, each character is studied carefully on a bit-mapped screen and edited as needed **(16)**. The kind of refinement accomplished in this way is exemplified by Autologic's rendition of Athena, originally the Linotype Corporation's Optima face.'

The change of name of familiar faces which is common in the new digitized type masters is a tacit acknowledgement that what is being offered to clients is an edited refinement, or improvement, of a known typeface in the same way that in the past, tried and popular faces were constantly being improved upon and brought out under variant names.

In the process of refinement subtle bows and cuppings are retained even down to the 10-point master through the patterning techniques now being used. There could have been no such advanced refining by even the most modern metal type-cutting experts. Master matrices would not have had the efficiency of reproduction that applies with computer outputs. Herein lies the breakthrough in modern computerized typesetting.

The notes in the Autologic manual are instructive to systems users in that they point up the subtlety of individual sizes and counsel caution in the use of compensatory kerning and other house methods to vary letter spacing. The manual continues: 'Proofs showing all

MASTHEAD, LOGO or SEAL

DATE LINE

WHITE ON BLACK (WOB)

ANATOMY OF A MIRROR FRONT

BOLD – SINGLE COLUMN

BY LINE

INDENTED COLOUR PICTURE

SOLID BLOBS

42 POINT SUB-HEAD

DAILY Mirror

Friday, April 28, 1989   National Sale: 4,025,418 Incorporating the Daily Record

Life for boy who wanted to wipe out the world

By FRANK CORLESS

A BRILLIANT science student experimented with deadly chemicals in a plot to destroy the human race.

He planned to invent a deadly plague and use mutant flies to spread it.

A judge, ordering evil Matthew Williams to be locked up for life yesterday, said he was clearly highly intelligent... and VERY dangerous.

Williams, 20, whose father once stood as a National Front candidate, conducted a terror campaign, leaving bombs in phone boxes and launching arson at-

PLAN: Williams

tacks. But it wasn't until he fired a crossbow at neighbours because their radio was too loud that police caught him.

They then discovered the secret laboratory in his quiet Merseyside home — and his diary.

The diaries told how in his lab, under a large picture of Hitler, he planned the destruction of the human race.

In his diaries, Williams — who had 10 O-Levels and 4 A-Levels — wrote: "I hate people. The majority of people I come into contact with are filthy, ignorant, agressive scum who should not exist.

them all by whatever means I can."

● Full story — Page 9

FIND EVIL PAI

By SYLVIA JONES and RAMSAY SMIT

AN evil couple are being hunted by police investigating the baby food blackmail plot.

The pair hatched their twisted scheme to spike tots' food FIVE YEARS ago, it was revealed last night.

They have alread £18,000 — and now ing £1 million.

At least 220 conte spiked with glass, ne les, razor blades and now been discovered.

They were bough breadth of the coun to Cornwall, in Uls Irish Re

But a have be tal to do not turers i and Ga draw th

A seni last nig and pe have be

"But beef, bu thing ne

The c man a lieved t

● Tur

● **£18,000 taken from joint account**

● **Now they ask for another £1m**

HILLSBOROUGH APPEAL ➤ **£302,850**

STRAP LINE

EAR-PIECE AREA

WHITE ON BLACK

UNDERSCORED ITALIC CAPS

SPLASH HEAD, 56mm DEEP

SIX POINT RULE BOX

FOUR COLOUR PICTURE

INTRO, SET AT 1½ COLUMN

SIDE HEAD AND CAPTION

CROSS REFERENCE

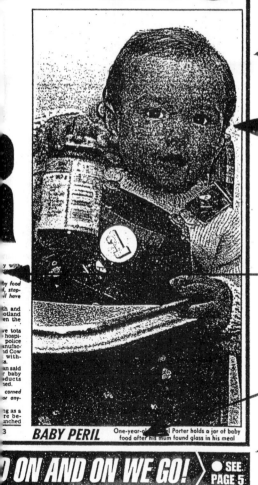

REVEALED: THE BLACKMAILERS' FIVE-YEAR PLOT

22p

THIS

BABY PERIL One-year-old ... Porter holds a jar of baby food after his mum found glass in his meal

ON AND ON WE GO! ● SEE PAGE 5

relevant character combinations are generated for each master size and put through a final spacing check. If necessary, adjustments are made and proofs submited to quality control for approval. For smaller masters, to retain the appearance of continuity with the large masters, it is often required to modify individual character structures. The ability to detail fonts in this manner is one of the advantages of a multimaster database arrangement. A 9-point typeset image does not and should not emanate from the same data as a 36-point image of the same character.'

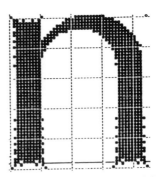

16   The Ikarus concept: this enlargement of a 10-point Athena 'n' is produced from the bit structure on the right which is based on a recreation by Ikarus of the original letter

An oddity of type design is that round letters, in addition to needing to be closer to each other than square characters, also need to be marginally deeper in body in order to convey visual balance. It is for this reason that the practice of the original type designers, who made round letters – o, e, c, etc. – in a given size fractionally deeper than their fellows, has been followed in the digitizing process. The justifiability of this difference in actual height between round letters and square did not stop some old-time printers from trimming off the tops and bottoms while tidying up a page!

The soft and hardware producers, thorough though they are, cannot be expected to cater for every newspaper's requirements, however. As the majority of these manufacturers are American-based their briefs in evolving font style are dictated by American usage. For instance, US newspapers go for generous letter, word and line spacing, particularly in headlines. It therefore follows that systems users, while respecting the integrity of the digitized designs, should take care to adapt such a basic feature as letter, word and line spacing to suit the individual newspaper. Spacing, as we have seen can be varied from letter to letter, according to the kerning points already discussed by the use of unit hundredths. However, Autologic, in particular, caution that kerning adjustments must be very fine and tested thoroughly from laser outputs (proofs).

Unless careful checks are made and formatting carried out on a house-style basis at the fitting-out stage in a computerized system, there will be dissatisfaction and messy changes to make later, and the type character of the newspaper may be damaged. A fully trained systems person and an editorial expert should combine to examine the countless permutations and possibilities offered and to see that sizes and spacing requirements are formatted exactly as wanted, while at the same time making discreet adjustments that might be overdue. A useful function, for example, is to have paragraph spacing on a command key. Even drop letters and big quotes (see Chapter 12) can be so programmed. But above all, in a system where types are being presented under new names, an editor or proprietor must be able to ensure that a successful newspaper is not landed with unwelcome changes in visual appearance. To cover negligence at the fitting-out stage by suggesting to the readers that a newspaper is undergoing a vibrant and exciting re-design can presage disaster.

A variation of the saw-happy old warrior who trimmed off metal letters is the philistine subeditor who instructs typesetters to 'squeeze it' to prevent a wanted headline from 'busting'. This is the way to destroy the careful original programming that was carried out to retain type balance in the pages. Such a headline will instantly look wrong. There are occasions when, as a deliberate plan, the versatility of the computer can be utilized – when a headline stands alone on a page of pictures, for example.

In the early days of newspaper design, one of the artists whose job it was to enliven the features pages would be asked to read the copy and come up with a drawn headline which reflected the mood of the piece. These exponents of incidental type design are redundant in the face of the achievements of systems and systems people whose creative key-stroking produces undreamed of typographical effects.

3
Historical influences

Newspaper design is an organic thing; it is not a few notions thought up on the spur of the moment aided by a quick glance through a type book, important though type is. The concepts behind page layout have been refined through more than 200 years of evolution in the use of typography and response to readership needs. An examination of early papers and their readers will disclose a world far removed from the sophisticated products we are familiar with, and yet embedded in them are the roots of today's practices.

Early newspapers   The first newspapers, carrying mainly foreign news because of the censor, began circulating in Britain in the 1620s though few copies have survived. With the outbreak of the Civil War, newspapers were harnessed by each side along with pamphlets in the propaganda war. *A Perfect Diurnall of the Proceedings* of Parliament, of 1645, of which copies can still be found **(17)** shows vividly how these partisan early journalists and editors set about wooing their readers on their front pages during the war of words.

Through the Commonwealth period and the restoration of the Stuart monarchy from 1660 the censor clamped down again and newspapers, hampered as they were in the coverage of national and political news (Parliament was not open to the press until the 1780s), concentrated on performing a service for the sort of people who could afford to buy them. The heavy *Stamp Duty* imposed in 1711, and which was to last, at sums that varied to suit government policy, until 1855, ensured this, though there were some short-lived political sheets that circulated illegally untaxed.

As a result of the cost, readers comprised mainly farmers, landowners, brewers, merchants, traders, the clergy, the aristocracy and academics. As newspaper publishing took off through the eighteenth century it was inevitable that editors (who were frequently the printers) went strongly for shipping news, grain and stock prices, the weather, royal news, law reports, social gossip and the advertising of goods and services appropriate to their patrons.

This modest content was presented usually in four of what we would call tabloid-sized pages, though the broadsheet size was becoming more common by the end of the century. Newspaper circulation was concentrated in London and the home counties, by far the biggest population centre, though the first provincial weekly paper, the *Norwich Post*, had appeared as early as 1701, in Britain's then second biggest city.

A four-column format was usual, with simple labels or even just place names above each item. *The Public Ledger* for September, 1760, for instance **(18)** carries on page one the very detailed running order for the Coronation of George III under the heading of PLAN OF THE PROCESSION AT THE CORONATION, a poem on the occasion entitled THE PATRIOT CORONATION, a letter TO THE PRINTER OF THE PUBLIC LEDGER, an item headed STATE LOTTERY 1761 and a collection of shipping movements datelined from various ports, under the heading of PORT NEWS, turning at the foot of column four without warning to the next page (turn lines had yet to be invented).

The first issue of *The Newcastle Chronicle* of March 24, three years later **(19)** is of the same size and format, with page one having a similar style of black letter masthead, with subtitle and ruled-off date

18   *The Public Ledger*, September 22, 1761

and number. The news is collected together under the headings THE INTRODUCTION, FOREIGN NEWS, LONDON and AMERICA. The individual items include cattle plague, the death of Viscount Townshend, the arrival of a wheat cargo, beef prices in Germany, regimental movements, murders in America, the shortage of grain in Naples, and various royal functions. Some are quoted from London papers. There is nothing on page one of interest to the seven northern counties the paper claims to serve. There is also not a whiff of political news or comment.

The aim of these two papers, neither of which carries advertisements on the front page, was simply to provide readers with public announcements, commercial news and summaries of events from various parts of the world. Most items are dated, the date showing how long the message has taken to reach the paper. The label headings are one size up from the body type and in capitals, and one item follows another wherever it happens to fall in the column, with items turning, if need be, on to the next page.

It is page design at its simplest. The content of the first item in each of the pages is obviously the most important on the page but thereafter there seems to be no particular order given to things and one visualizes the printer–editor assembling the pages from the galleys of type as they are set. The paper grows out of the contents of which the pages are composed, which are the sort of items the editor expects to be of interest to the readers.

And yet there is a basis of design and plan there. Already it is realized that to make the paper worth the high price, fairly small type (down to 4½ point in some items) has to be used to get a lot in, and that this is more easily readable if divided into narrower columns. Some sort of guidance is needed for the reader and so the items are broken up into sections under headings, sometimes each item having a run-on heading. So the headline, albeit primitively, has made its appearance. News from abroad usually appears with a date-line, a practice still used in some papers. The sections are ruled off and some of them are given emphasis by a drop letter on the first item; the *Newcastle Chronicle* having quite elaborate drops including one with a woodcut of Britannia with the scales of justice – or perhaps in this case impartiality.

The *Public Ledger* boldly departs from its four column format on page one to give a quite detailed numbered plan of the coronation procession across two columns. The eye is compulsively drawn down the numbers to check the identity of the celebrities listed alongside, a clear example of page design aimed at the reader's eye. One could visualize it as a subject for a graphic chart. There is, however, no illustration, and although woodcuts and copperplate engravings were already common in book production, and had appeared in newspaper advertisements as early as 1652 (in an advert for goldsmith's work in *The Faithfull Scout*), they were not thought necessary on editorial pages, which simply listed what

The Newcastle Chronicle.

Or, GENERAL WEEKLY ADVERTISER.

VOL. I. SATURDAY, MARCH 24, 1764. NUMB. I.

This Paper is circulated by the most speedy Conveyance thro' the Counties of *Northumberland*, *Durham*, *Cumberland*, *Westmorland*, and *Lancaster*, and the *West* and *North Ridings* of the County of *York*; also thro' *Annandale*, *Nithsdale*, *Galloway*, *Tiviotdale*, *Liddesdale*, *Tweedale*, and the *Mers*, or *Berwickshire*, in *Scotland*.

The INTRODUCTION.

THE Public generally expect something or other by way of prelude, or introduction, to publications of this sort; but as we have already given our friends their bill of fare in our proposals, which we hope they have perused, it only remains necessary to enlarge upon and explain the general heads thereof.—And,

1st, By way of apology, we may possibly be arraigned by several in points of prudence and policy, for an undertaking of this kind at this time; and by others, for introducing a new paper where they may imagine the country is already sufficiently supplied; but we hope by substituting ingenious and social entertainment in place of the horrid details of war and bloodshed, to recommend our paper to all the humane and generous part of mankind, and even to convince every one that our scheme is not chimerical, but founded on a plan full as extensive, and as well calculated for public utility, as that of any paper extant: For

"*As long as chequ'd variety shall please,*
"*And labour'd science wear the dress of ease;*
"*Whilst morals, bus'ness, novelty unite,*
"*Be ours the task to profit and delight.*"

We do not hereby mean to insinuate any better abilities towards conducting a paper than our neighbours, (tho' we will exert our utmost) or that the public should receive our attempts to serve them as a favour, when we candidly confess, that we were in the course of trade unwillingly necessitated to it; and tho' the term *necessitated* may seem to want explanation to the public in general, yet it must be very plainly understood and assented to by our senior news-writers here, who consequently must least of all disapprove our measures. Our friends, however, who please to favour us with their advertisements, may be assured that we have a double and indispensible interest in having this paper to succeed (and even to exceed) both as to numbers and extent of circulation, to which no pains or expence will be spared; and if thereby it answers our own purposes in point of advertising, &c. it must in consequence answer the same to the public in general.

We would willingly have obliged our friends in and about town with a WEDNESDAY'S paper, as was most generally wished for and expected, but the expence of circulation would have been intolerable, and not sufficiently expeditious on any but a market and post day.

2dly, We have proposed, that in this paper will be exhibited news foreign and domestic, the prices of grain, stocks, &c. and to render it a magazine of entertainment as well as a paper of intelligence, there will frequently be inserted characters of, and extracts from, new books, with other select and original literary articles in prose and verse:—As for the *select*, we have no great doubts about having fund enough to collect from; but for *originals*, should our literary correspondents which we have engaged, and rely on for that purpose, fail us, we are alas! unwarily bound by virtue of our proposals (like other ingenious publishers) to *write to ourselves*.

3dly, We have proposed the strictest impartiality in all points:—But as different people often tack different definitions to one and the same word, we beg leave to explain our own ideas in this point, *i.e.* What we would express by the word *impartiality*, is not to avoid all disputes whatsoever, offensive and defensive, since disputes will naturally arise among individuals, and often for the good and edification of the whole, such as criticisms, different opinions, &c. but to publish indiscriminately for all, so consequently to please and displease all parties by turns, which bids the fairest for impartiality in our sense of the word; for as few persons or parties are right in every particular, "that man who goes blindly into all "the measures of his party, and vindi- "cates all their proceedings, cannot justly "vindicate himself."

4thly, And consequently in matters of state, what we mean by not infringing the liberty of the press, or running into licentiousness, is, That after rendering to our superiours all deference and due respect, we shall not be biassed by, or particularly attach'd either to these who are Out, or those that are In, but occasionally insert interesting particulars for and against both: We shall always be particularly attached to our gracious sovereign, and to the interest of all his worthy, loyal subjects, who (tho' out of power) are ready upon all occasions to exert themselves in the support and defence of their king and country in their just rights and liberties, and who, as the sinews of state, better merit the freedom hitherto enjoy'd, than those greater personages (if any there are) who, from the pride and luxuriancy of private or public wealth, &c. and for sinister or ambitious motives, wantonly provoke and maintain party-spirited faction, to the prejudice and abuse of public tranquility, and constitutional welfare.

5thly, Despising the base, despicable spirit of calumny and detraction, we shall never officiously meddle with private characters, either by insinuation or otherwise, but when we can do it with justice, and to their advantage; and tho' we will not admit of scurrility on any occasion, or an aggressing affront or offence, to oblige any person or party, yet the injured and aggrieved shall never want an asylum in our paper, or even a weapon of defence to pelt down licentious insolence and tyrannic oppression, *i.e.* Our title of GENERAL ADVERTISER, shall continually remind us, that we will not, from sinister or selfish motives, refuse any fair and warrantable advertisements (the subject and language thereof being decent and delicate) to the diminution of his majesty's revenue, the prejudice of commerce, or to the disadvantage of any individual in his own legal property.

We thought it necessary to explain ourselves on the fore-mentioned heads, that we might not hereafter be mistakenly taxed with deviating from our own proposals; consistently with which, as above explained, the public shall be most zealously served, by

Their very humble servants,
The PUBLISHERS.

Saturday and Sunday's POSTS.

FOREIGN NEWS.

ROME, *Feb.* 18.

WE hear of nothing but clamours and insurrections on the confines of the kingdom of Naples, where the scarcity of grain is extraordinary and general. This has engaged our magistrates of the office of provision to send commissaries into divers parts to provide sufficiently for the ecclesiastical state, for fear a scarcity with us should be productive of the same tumults and disorders.

Paris, March 2. The author of *An Appeal to Reason*, (a work condemned to the flames by the chatelet) is condemned by a sentence of the same court to perpetual banishment, after being exposed to the carcan (an iron collar wherewith a malefactor is tied to a post); and his printer, the Sieur Grange, is banished the kingdom for five years. It is known, that this author is the Abbe de Caveirac, the same who some years ago had the wickedness and temerity to publish an apology for the massacre of St. Barthelemi.

By an arret of the 19th ult. four other pieces are ordered to be burnt.

LONDON, March 15.

They write from Brandenburgh, and other parts of Germany, that the distemper among the horned cattle was very much abated, which has been effected by hanging four or five onions about the beasts necks directly after they are taken ill, and will not eat. Those onions draw the infection out, and look the next day as if they had been boiled. This remedy is to be repeated several times, and the onions which have been used, are to be buried in a deep hole. And in a few days after the cattle are taken with a running at the nose, which carries off the distemper; it is also proper at that time to hang up some onions in the distempered cattles stables.

Yesterday was held a general court of the Russia company, at their court room over the Royal Exchange, on some affairs of importance; when, after debate, the question was put, whether an agent was necessary or not? which, on a division, passed in the affirmative by a majority of six. After which, an elegant entertainment was provided at the King's Arms tavern, in Cornhill, at which were present the earls of Sandwich, Egmont, and Halifax, with several other persons of distinction, as also M. De Grosse, ambassador extraordinary from the empress of Russia.

On Tuesday night an express arrived at the Rt Hon. Lady Townshend's in Whitehall, which brought an account of the death of her husband, the Lord Viscount Townshend, who died on the road coming from Bath on Monday evening. By his death 3000 l. per annum devolves to her ladyship. His lordship is succeeded in title and estate by his eldest son, the Right Hon. George, now Viscount Townshend, of Rainham, in the country of Norfolk, lieutenant-general of the ordnance, colonel of the 28th regiment of foot, as also of the western battalion of militia of the county of Norfolk, a major-general, and knight of the shire for the said county of Norfolk.

It is said orders are given for all the officers in Great-Britain and Ireland, upon absence of leave, who belong to the forces in the East-Indies, to hold themselves in readiness to embark on board the first ships that shall sail for those parts.

We hear his majesty will certainly visit his German dominions, soon after the rising of the parliament, and that he will be accompanied in his journey by his brother Prince Henry.

A grant of 650,000 l. is ordered immediately to pay off part of the navy debt.

Yesterday the money brought from Lisbon in the Hampden packet, Hill, on the merchants account, was lodged in the Bank.

On Tuesday Capt. Griffin, of the Lapwing, took leave of the directors of the East-India company, going express to Bengal.

Tuesday and yesterday several hundred men and boys, many of them disbanded soldiers and sailors, were sent down the river, in order to be shipped off for the East Indies, to complete the broken regiments there.

It is said that press-warrants will shortly be issued out, in order to man the fleets going to the East and West Indies.

On Tuesday 2200 quarters of wheat were shipped for the Straits; and a considerable quantity of gunpowder for Virginia.

The proceedings of the supreme Council at Martinico against the jesuits, dated in Dec. last, are just published at Paris. It appears that the jesuits there are to be treated exactly in the same manner as in the jurisdiction of the parliament of Paris.

By a letter received on Monday from Hamburgh we are informed, that beef, mutton, and pork, are sold there for sixteen-pence a pound; and the other necessaries of life equally as dear.

A shock of an earthquake was felt the 26th of last month at Mantua, but it did no damage.

They write from Dublin, that on a late calculation, the number of Roman Catholics in Ireland are found to exceed his Majesty's Protestant subjects in that kingdom by ninety-five thousand souls, which is thought to have greatly augmented the late opposition with regard to granting the former the proposed security on lands.

Monday and Tuesday's POSTS.

From the LONDON GAZETTE.

TURIN, *March* 3.

HIS Royal Highness the Duke of York is in perfect health, and greatly satisfied with the manner of his reception here. His Royal Highness has employed his time in visiting some of the strong places in the neighbourhood of Turin, and whatever else is worthy his attention; and has been often at court in his private character, where he is constantly received by the whole royal family with every possible mark of esteem and regard.

The Duke of Modena has sent hither the Count Belgiojoso, a person of the first distinction of that country, to compliment his Royal Highness the Duke of York, and to invite him to honour Milan with a visit; offering him an apartment in the Ducal palace; or, upon his refusal of that, a hotel in the town. His Royal Highness made a suitable answer to these civilities, and proposes spending the three last days of the carnival at that place. The Duke of Parma has also followed this example, and has sent the Marquis Calcagnini to compliment his Royal Highness, and to invite him to his capital, which invitation it seems to be his Royal Highness's intention to accept, upon his return from Rome and Naples.

Ratisbon, March 4. The college of princes, having received an imperial rescript, brought hither by Prince John of Lichtenstein, notifying to them the resolution taken the 20th past by the electoral ambassador at Frankfort to proceed to the election of a king of the Romans on the 3d day of this month, and having presented this evening the conclusum, notifying their assent therein, by Count Saurau the Saltzbourg minister, to the prince of Tour and Taxis, the chief imperial commissary to the diet, came immediately to an agreement to separate till the 1st of April.

Brussels, March 6. The scarcity of provisions is so great in the parts adjacent to Francfort, and near all the great rivers, occasioned by the late vast inundations, that a very large quantity of provisions is dispatched daily from hence for that city, where the consumption is immense, thro' the unusual concourse of people assembled there upon account of the approaching election and coronation of the king of the Romans. [Gaz.

FOREIGN NFWS.

Lisbon, Feb. 14. The court is at Salvatiera. Recruits continue to be raised; and being allowed to bear arms, they have committed great disorders in the city, and rob and assassinate with impunity. The inhabitants are afraid to leave their houses after dark. These excesses are the more inexcusable, as the troops are paid with the greatest exactness.

Naples, Feb. 18. Since the 11th inst. eleven ships are arrived here with corn, and more are impatiently expected. These, however, have had a happy effect in calming the populace, whom necessity had made outragious.

AMERICA.

Charles-Town, Jan. 11. Several expresses have arrived here from Augusta, &c. with accounts of the murders committed at Long Canes by the Indians. The news threw the people, in and about Augusta, into great consternation; all the settlers on Savannah river, above that place, fled thither with their families for shelter, even some of the inhabitants of Augusta have sent their families farther down the country for safety.

Jan. 18. The Indians who murdered the settlers at Long Canes, are now undeniably known to be Creeks, and it likewise appears that they are not of the Mortar's gang, so that the number of our enemies among them is greater than was imagined; and it is supposed they will soon commit other hostilities.

LONDON, March 17.

The Hereditary Princess of Brunswick has received a letter from the King of Prussia, written by himself, congratulating her on her safe arrival at Brunswick, accompanied with an invitation for their Serene Highnesses to pass some time this summer at Berlin; at which place (it is said) they will be met by his Royal Highness the Duke of York.

A ship lately arrived from Newfoundland, has brought over a few chaldrons of coals, the produce of that island; which for pitchiness and clear burning, are esteemed equal to the best Long Benton.

We hear that the fleet destined for the East-Indies will consist of three seventy-four, two sixty, and three new fifty-gun ships, with two frigates; each ship to be manned with their full complement of marines, as in time of war; which squadron will be under the command of commodore Arbuthnote.

Lord Robert Manners's regiment is ordered to march from Chatham barracks to Portsmouth, in order to embark for Jamaica.

19 *The Newcastle Chronicle*, March 24, 1764

editors thought the readers wanted to know.

With circulations remaining modest – only a few thousands an issue for the most successful – despite their growing numbers, and their readership still tied to the educated and better-off classes, newspapers did not have a great deal of incentive over the next few decades to improve their appearance. A more important influence on their development was the political freedom and extension of voting franchise that came with the nineteenth century. These brought a rapid growth in political news and comment as the press spearheaded the development of democracy. The result was a great expansion in words, political analysis and endless punditry which make Victorian newspapers such heavy fare when one turns back their tightly packed pages.

A peep at the first issue of the broadsheet *Sunday Times* in 1822 **(20)**, ten years before the first Reform Act, shows a modest four-page sheet of five 16-pica columns of mainly 6-point type, in which page one is divided between advertising and a lashing attack on the activities of the government. The two page one headings, ORIGINAL STRICTURES and ASPECT OF PUBLIC AFFAIRS are in capitals but still only a size up from the body setting. The title-piece is in the familiar black letter type, but ruled off below it, and significant of the new ethos of the press is a quotation in 9 point and running across the page: 'Let it be impressed upon your minds, let it be instilled into your children, that the LIBERTY OF THE PRESS is the PALLADIUM of all the Civil, political and RELIGIOUS RIGHTS of an ENGLISHMAN.'

The inside pages still have the news divided up into sections, but the content is broader and the items appear under the headings: POETRY, AGRICULTURE, SPORTS, MISCELLANEOUS, FOREIGN PAPERS, POLITICS OF THE TIMES, THE STAGE, IRELAND and LAW, with the headings set in an expanded seriffed face of about 10-point caps. Under each head are run-on headings in small capitals of the body face denoting the items: MARRIAGE PREVENTED, DESTRUCTIVE FIRE, MELANCHOLY CASUALTY, HORRIBLE OUTRAGE, HORRID MURDER, ANOTHER COACH ROBBERY, WEST INDIAN PIRACIES and the like. Though still labels, these now show more attempt at reader involvement. The main breakthrough is in content. Sport introduces readers to prize-fighting, a walking contest and trotting races. The Stage column reviews the opening of the new Drury Lane Theatre with *The School for Scandal*; with *The Jealous Wife* and *Venice Preserved* at Covent Garden. There is a letters column (despite being issue number one) and some animated court reports as well as the traditional market prices and a small column of stock prices.

The Times of November 4, 1854, **(21)** apart from a massive increase in classified advertising now, in common with other Victorian papers, occupying the whole of the front and back pages, and an even greater length of texts, shows little change in presentation from

32 years earlier. If anything it is set more solid with not a whisker of white space impinging on the words. It contains, in this issue, the superb war reports of William Russell from the Crimea; politics and government, with Britain midway between the two great Reform Acts, have become a staple ingredient. It has now moved into a six-column format and a wider page. The type, though still small, is a clearer, more legible face, well-printed by the standards of the day, as befits the advanced plant of Britain's top-selling daily, with its circulation of 40,000 an issue. Its news is still grouped under headings in capitals scarcely bigger than its body type. It has three and a half columns of editorial opinion without a headline, law reports, wide foreign coverage, court circular, city news, market prices, weather, shipping . . . but, unlike the *Sunday Times*, no sport for its daily readers.

Its price is still 5 pence, including *Stamp Duty*, and its readership, despite its campaigning record, remains the elite of the day.

The new readership

If, by 1850, newspapers showed only modest advances in presentation and circulation, the second half of the century was to change that. And the key to both was to be readership.

In 1855 stamp duty came off for good and for the first time a penny newspaper became a possibility. By now, the take-off of the Industrial Revolution had begun to alter the face of Britain's cities, bringing regular work, higher wages and, despite the social problems that went with it, an improving standard of living. More significantly it began to spread wealth down the social scale by producing, for the first time, a salaried middle class of managers and technocrats and a new upwardly mobile class of skilled workers. More people could afford more papers, and had more reasons for buying them. At the same time the new rail network had made national distribution on the day of publication a reality. Whether editors realized it or not the scene was set for expansion.

The vitality of *The Times* as the top-selling daily from 1820 under its great editors, Thomas Barnes (1785–1841) who built up the world's first network of news correspondents, and John Thaddeus Delane (1817–1879), ran out on the threshold of the new challenge, and it was *The Daily Telegraph* that took up the lead. Founded as the first penny national paper the year stamp duty ended, *The Telegraph* quickly moved from a radical standpoint to a broadly Right-wing stance that suited the new middle class readers who found its wider news content, heavy crime coverage and sport and theatre reviews preferable to the elitist content of *The Times* and the old Victorian dailies.

The *Telegraph* was also the first paper to use stunts and promotions to push its sales some three decades before that arch publicist, Lord Northcliffe. In 1873 it discovered the 'Loch Ness Monster', in 1877 it gave a Jubilee party for 30,000 children in Hyde Park which was reviewed by the Queen. It went for young readers, crusaded against

The Sunday Times.

Let it be impressed upon your minds, let it be instilled into your children, that the LIBERTY OF THE PRESS is the PALLADIUM of all the Civil, Political and Religious Rights, of an Englishman.

No. I.   LONDON: SUNDAY, OCTOBER 20, 1822.   **PRICE 7d.**

capital and corporal punishment, and claimed to be the first paper 'to treat prostitution boldly and plainly'. It passed *The Times* circulation of 60,000 in 1860, went to reach 200,000 before the end of the century and remained the top-selling daily for forty years until 1900.

Cheaper papers and the arrival of reading literacy with the Education Act of 1870 led to a rash of new weekly and evening papers appearing all over the provinces, including many of the titles still being published today. An inside page from an early copy of the *Daily Gazette* **(21)**, which went on sale in Middlesborough in 1869 at a halfpenny (and is still appearing) is typical of local papers of the period. It has a column of LATEST NEWS from London 'by telegraph' quoting items from *The Times*, the *Morning Post* and *Daily News*, and four well-filled columns of local news and readers' letters.

The prestigious London dailies could now aim at a national circulation, with the expanding rail network providing the means of reaching breakfast tables from Plymouth to John O'Groats. *The Daily Telegraph* was the first paper to cater in this way for the new readership produced by the Industrial Revolution, and yet it made disappointingly little attempt to change its presentation. Opening the edition of July 3, 1872 **(21)**, we find twelve pages of six-column format, seven of them, including the front and back, crammed with classified advertising. The news, varied though it is, is set tightly into the remaining pages, with headlines little bigger than fifty years earlier. There are five columns of editorial opinion without headlines, though on the main stories, such as the sensational:

DR LIVINGSTONE'S SAFETY

OUTLINE OF HIS DISCOVERIES

THE NILE SECRET SOLVED

the three-decker headline has arrived, even if still only in 14 point.

A look at the densely packed pages of small classified advertisements in these Victorian papers carries the clue to the conservativeness of their presentation. Until there was a truly mass market to be exploited in terms of spending power and expectations, the need to display a newspaper's contents visually, either editorial or advertising, did not arise. The competitive consumer environment of mass circulation newspapers and mass produced food and goods in which communicators exist today had simply not dawned in the 1870s and 1880s; and while such a market might be just round the corner, editors, who live notoriously day to day, were unlikely to be its prophets. In the conservative world of newspapers *The Telegraph* had already taken a giant leap ahead of its fellows in recognizing that newspaper readership was changing.

21   (a) *The Times*, November 14, 1854. (b) *The Daily Gazette*, November 22, 1869. (c) *The Daily Telegraph*, July 3, 1872. (d) *Daily Mail*, December 28, 1899

22   Lord Northcliffe (1865–1922), 'father' of the popular press

Lord Northcliffe   The catalyst of change was to be Lord Northcliffe **(22)**. Born Alfred Harmsworth, the son of an impoverished barrister in Dublin, and largely self-educated, he discovered as a young reporter from his contributions to the magazine *Titbits* (founded in 1881 by George Newnes) the new world of 'snippet' journalism. *Titbits* thrived on stories of adventure, gossip about the famous, readers' letters, advice columns, competitions and potted paragraphs giving unusual facts. It was aimed perceptively at a largely family and young working class market that had not yet developed a newspaper buying habit. By 1890 *Titbits* had reached the unheard circulation of 200,000 an issue.

Envious of its success, Harmsworth launched his own magazine *Answers* at the same market in 1888. After several successful magazine launches in the new popular field he bought the failing *London Evening News* in 1894, took it down market and made it profitable. In 1896 he realized his greatest ambition when he used his now considerable funds to launch his own daily, the *Daily Mail*, as the first national paper to reach, in its content, the working class reader who had hitherto been ignored.

Northcliffe's new daily (he was given his barony by Edward VII in 1905) was scorned as a 'newspaper for office boys' but its rising circulation soon proved that a paper strong on readers' letters, tales of battle, adventure and human interest was what the new readership wanted and its sales, in 1900, became the first to pass the million mark. The popular press of the twentieth century had been born.

Northcliffe sensed that there was spending power to be tapped in the new wage earners, and he cleverly married the new mass production of goods to the growing consumer market to create in the *Daily Mail* a truly national advertising medium. The income from this enabled him to price the paper at a halfpenny by offsetting its production costs against advertising revenue. Like all good ideas, Northcliffe's recipe for success was blindingly simple. The cheaper the paper the more people bought it; the more the circulation grew the more attractive it became to the advertiser; the greater the advertising revenue the more Northcliffe spent on improving the paper and its sales by hiring the best journalists, getting the best stories and financing stunts to get the paper talked about – and the richer became Britain's first newspaper tycoon. The press had become big business.

The effect of Northcliffe's ideas on the newspapers of the period was two-fold: it spawned a new growth of down-market dailies – the *Daily Express* (1900), the *Daily Mirror* (1903), and *Daily Herald* (1912). It drove the *Daily News* and *Daily Chronicle* to widen their market towards their eventual merger as the *News Chronicle,* and it spelt a decline in fortunes of the more conservative Victorian dailies – the *Morning Post* and *The Standard,* causing even *The Times* to totter and sell out to Northcliffe in order to survive. In the big conurbations of Manchester, Birmingham, Newcastle and Bristol the competition between titles likewise intensified in the race to capture the new markets. The battle for readers had begun, a battle in which some old and influential titles were to go to the wall.

It was inevitable that with a new and very different body of readers, and in an age in which spending power was expanding across the board, newspapers would have to change in image as well as content. What the critics of the press described as its commercialization had revealed newspapers to be a product with a capacity for making money as well as having influence. Yet influence on its own was not enough. There can be nothing less influential than a paper that is failing to attract readers in an expanding market.

23   New-style features – inside the *Daily Mail* of 1899

When it came to design, a vital part today in the image-making process, it has to be said that Northcliffe was no innovator. To him ideas and words were the market weapons. He left advertising to occupy the front and back pages of the *Daily Mail* **(22)** as in the old Victorian papers, although display adverts with line drawings on such big sellers as Yorkshire Relish sauce (with a cookery book offered for a shilling to those reading the advert), and the many soaps, cocoas and medicines began to adorn the paper. Looking inside **(23)**, we see that the type sizes in 1899 are little changed from 1855, though the busy eight-column format he instituted is easier to read, with shorter and more varied items, many with two-decker headlines, and with distinctive features pages (*Woman's Realm, Daily Magazine*) lightened by line drawings.

It fell to rival Sir Arthur Pearson's *Daily Express*, much influenced in content and market by the *Mail*, to be the first national daily, in 1901, to put news back on to the front page, though it was not until 1966 that *The Times* became the last British paper to give in to this trend.

Photographs

The breakthrough that made modern design techniques possible came with the perfecting of the means of reproducing photographs on newsprint by the halftone process. The first successful photograph had been taken by Henry Fox Talbot at Lacock, Wiltshire, as early as 1835. The need for a viable means of reproduction, however, delayed the use of photographs in newspapers until March, 1880, when the *New York Daily Graphic* became the first when it published a picture of the city's shanty town using the new halftone process. In this the tones which made up the details of the photograph were broken up into tiny dots on an engraved plate which, on picking up ink, reproduced by their varying density the tones of the actual picture. The method solved the problem of ink pick-up and only by looking extremely closely could the eye detect that the picture had been 'reconstructed' by means of a screen.

It was another decade before newspapers in general began installing process-engraving departments to produce halftone blocks, though even then the pictures used were mainly studio portraits, and it was not until 1904 that Northcliffe's new *Daily Mirror* became the first newspaper in the world to employ its own staff photographers to provide news photographs as a day-to-day ingredient. By this time page design was already on the move with newspapers beginning to utilize artists' line drawings of news events and personalities, as can be seen in the *Daily Mail* **(23)**.

It was an example of Northcliffe's indifference to visual presentation that, while accepting pictures as viable news content, he did not rate them in the same class as words, and the idea of photojournalism as an independent journalistic skill would have been anathema to him. His ideas were pervasive and news pictures up to 1914 were considered to be more appropriate in picture papers such as the *Daily*

24   Early picture newspapers exploit the new photo journalism: the *Daily Graphic* of July 26, 1909, and the *Daily Mirror* of November 12, 1918

Graphic and his own *Daily Mirror* **(24)** which he had founded in 1903 as a paper for women readers (about whom he did not entertain a very high opinion). Such papers existed side-by-side with the orthodox 'news' dailies, which continued to concentrate on the words.

The vintage years   Edwardian newspapers with their conservative up-and-down layout show the cautious onset of ideas – two and three decker headlines in spindly 14 to 30 point, with static photographs of seldom more than two columns still vying with artists' drawings. *The News of the World* for July 31, 1910 **(4** and **25)** was advanced in its time in using a crude sans typeface alongside its Cheltenham Condensed, and for its daring gimmick of printing an entire popular song sheet as a circulation booster.

It was the First World War, with all its visual horror and squalor, that brought home to editors the vital role of news pictures as an ingredient on a par with – and occasionally superior to – the words, and newspapers from the 1920s onwards show a lively awareness of this in their presentation. The page patterns of the *Daily Express* **(26)** demonstrate both increased picture use and more creative headline writing, though type quality is still fairly poor. The front and back pages of the *Daily Express* of October 6, 1930, with its famous coverage of the R101 airship disaster, is an example of what can be achieved by picture journalism. It also shows the advent of the new Century type, which was to be used by the *Express* and the *Mail* with such distinction during the next three decades.

But it was in the words and the headline writing, and ultimately in typography, that the newspapers of the 1930s made their greatest advances. Journalists look back on the period as the golden age of reporters when, untrammelled by rival media, newspapers combed the world for exclusive stories, fought to be the first on the street with them, regarding detailed coverage of their market as the entitlement of readers. Writers were backed up by technician editors such as Arthur Christiansen, of the *Express* and Harry Guy Bartholomew **(27)** of the *Mirror* (and co-inventor of the first picture wiring system), who knew their markets and who harnessed typography and powerful headlines to hit their readership targets and make their newspapers the best and most talked about on the newsstands.

It was the age of 'busy' papers with multideck headlines that covered stories from every angle, pictures scattered about like an optical joyride, and endless fillers rolling up the columns, ensuring that no newsworthy items were left unexploited. Prodded by the ebullient Lord Beaverbrook, Christiansen exploited traditional forms to their limit, reducing headline sizes with the importance of the story as the eye moved down the page, polishing every line of every filler so that each word earned its place on the page. It was the something-for-everybody approach in which the aim was to dazzle the eye with a cornucopia of goodies spread around the basket.

And yet design techniques were moving forward. The text size pages might carry a lot of headlines, but editors were becoming fussy about type style. Types were being used more consistently and in a set pattern of sizes so that the *Daily Express*, the *Daily Mail* and the *Daily Herald* and the other dailies were assuming a distinctive appearance of their own. Good pictures and series of pictures were being given special spreads. The circulation war of the 1930s resulted in a greater stress on exclusiveness, on appearance, on the use of blurbs and promotions and in an increase in type sizes and more imaginative type use as page one became a weapon on the news-stands.

The tabloid revolution

The sale of the *Daily Mirror* by Lord Rothermere in 1934 to a new company, Daily Mirror Newspapers, threw into prominence Harry Guy Bartholomew, its former picture editor under Northcliffe, who

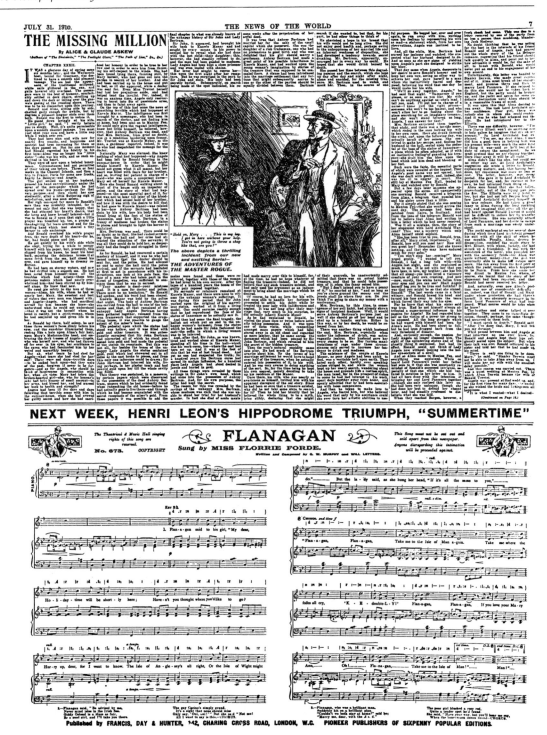

25   Circulation pullers of their day – a *News of the World* fiction series, *The Missing Million*, circa 1910, sharing a page with one of its famous half-page song sheets of popular tunes of the time

became the editorial director. It was the moment Bartholomew had been waiting for to put into effect a theory he had long held that none of the existing papers – and certainly not the *Daily Mail* since Rothermere had inherited it from his brother, Lord Northcliffe – truly served the working class market then just emerging from the depression of the 1930s.

Bartholomew was a rough diamond, a cantankerous man, rude and ruthless in his dealings with people, but with a genius for understanding the mind of the ordinary man in the street (he was not heard to mention the ordinary woman in the street) and with the technical skill to devise newspapers to reach him. He could see that a good deal of newspaper content was outside the interests of such readers. A new sort of product was needed. For him this meant a handy tabloid-sized paper, down to earth in its viewpoint, which entertained as well as informed, was easy to read, with competitions and lots of reader participation. It should get away from wordiness and hit the reader with big bold headlines and bold layout. Above all things it should be about people and the things that affected people – ordinary people.

It was thus that the *Daily Mirror* threw off its staid picture tabloid image and blossomed forth in the mid-1930s in bold new clothes which were to take it to Fleet Street's all-time peak circulation of 5,250,000 and make it the most powerful influence of the century on British newspaper design. It appeared on the newsstands distinctively **(28)** with thick black type headlines of a size not used before in dailies. The length of the news items shrank, foreign news almost disappeared, pictures became bigger, a page of comic strips appeared, and lots and lots of readers' letters. Human interest stories abounded, and where serious matters concerned the ordinary person they were spelt out in short words and paragraphs and charts with symbols and hurled at him (or her) in a way that could not miss. Into the paper came a vivid political cartoon and hard-hitting by-line columnists who berated the authorities on behalf of the readers and embodied the paper's us-and-them philosophy.

In design terms, the *Mirror*'s style was often referred to as poster journalism. In fact, on one or two celebrated occasions the front and back pages were upended to make one gigantic headline poster to smash a message home to readers on a page carrying the minimum of words.

The new journalism   The 1940s and 1950s were traumatic years for British newspapers. With wartime newsprint rationing reducing them to eight tabloid or four textsize pages the profligate use of space for headlines and text that had characterized the pre-war pages ended, never to return, and papers became leaner and more deliberately planned in order to put space to the best use possible. The *Daily Mirror* news page for May 8,

Daily Express

TO-DAY'S WEATHER: Rain at Times.

NO. 9,493.   MONDAY, OCTOBER 6, 1930.   ONE PENNY.

The R101 Crashes And Is Destroyed: Lord Thomson, Sir Sefton Brancker And 44 Others Burned To Death.

THE TRAGIC AFTERMATH.—Dead bodies shrouded in sheets near the wrecked airship.—Special "Daily Express" Picture.

THE KING'S "HORROR."

The King immediately on hearing of the disaster sent the following telegram to the Prime Minister:—

"I am horrified to hear of this national disaster which has befallen Airship R 101, and the consequent serious loss of life, including that of Lord Thomson, my Air Minister.

"The Queen and I sympathise deeply with the relatives and friends of those who have perished in the service of their country, and also with the injured survivors.

"GEORGE R.I."

LATE NEWS.

REVOLT AGAINST BRAZIL GOVERNMENT.

NEW YORK, Sunday, Oct. 5.

According to despatches received here to-night, Brazil is in the flames of revolution. Practically the entire State of Rio Grande do Sul has revolted against the Federal Government, while outbreaks are also reported in the States of Parana, Minas Geraes and Rio de Janeiro, owing to the strict censorship the extent of the uprising is not known.—Reuter.

Broadcasting Programmes on Page 13

NUNS' VIGIL OVER BODIES.

BEAUVAIS, Sunday, Oct. 5.

While the rain beat down on the smoke-blackened girders of the wreck of the R101, six Sisters of Mercy at the Beauvais convent gathered at the little children where most of the victims' bodies lie, to begin an all-night vigil.

They will spend the night in prayer. The wholeroom is too small to accommodate all the bodies, and eleven are to remain in a field outside, protected by tarpaulins.—B.U.P.

TRAPPED MAN'S ESCAPE.

Mr. A. Disey, wireless operator, told of his escape by tearing and being her way through the fabric. "I used both my arms and nails," he said. He became exhausted; then suddenly felt though a ragging inrush of fire, and found himself safe on wet grass.

GREAT AIRSHIP STRIKES A HILL AFTER BATTLE WITH A STORM.

SLEEPING PASSENGERS ENVELOPED BY SWIFTLY RUSHING FLAMES.

THE giant airship R101, which left Cardington at 7 p.m. on Saturday for India, crashed on a hill near Beauvais, France, at 2.5 a.m. yesterday, and 46 of those on board—including Lord Thomson, Minister for Air, and Air Vice-Marshal Sir Sefton Brancker—were burned to death.

A quarter of an hour before the crash those on board had no warning of danger, although the weather was stormy. At 1.50 a.m. they received a message from the French Air Ministry, telling them they were one kilometre from Beauvais. They replied "Thank you"—nothing more.

The next few minutes sufficed to produce the worst disaster in air history. Low-lying clouds had prevented the R101 rising, and the storm, which left masses of rain-water on the top of the envelope, forced her down until she struck a low hill by a wood near the village of Allonne.

A few moments and the vast airship was a mass of flame. Many of the victims were killed in their sleep, so swift was the rush of the fire when the hydrogen of the R 101 was ignited.

Some of the survivors owed their escape to the fact that the water tanks broke, and the flood washed them through the flames to safety. Rare heroism was displayed by three of the survivors who, though injured, returned to the burning wreck in the hope of finding some comrade to help.

One survivor's last glimpse of the wreck was Flight-Lieutenant Irwin standing at his post quietly giving orders. He was still there when the flames enveloped him.

Lord Thomson was considered by many to be the Government's nominee as next Viceroy of India. Flight-Lieutenant Irwin, the captain of the airship, was among the victims, who include a number of distinguished officers and air experts.

Biographies of victims are on Pages Two and Ten.

MAJOR SCOTT IN THE R 101.

M. LAURENT EYNAC, the French Air Minister, talking to Rigger W. G. Radcliffe, one of the survivors, in Beauvais Hospital.

LATEST NEWS.

An emergency meeting of the Air Council was held at the Air Ministry last night to hear Air Chief Marshal Sir John Salmond's report on the disaster in which five chiefs of the Ministry perished.

* * *

It is announced by the Air Ministry that a public inquiry will be held in this country, subject to co-ordination with the arrangements which are being made by the French Government.

* * *

The bodies of the victims will be brought to England for burial. They will be carried across the Channel in a warship.

* * *

Engineer H. J. Leech was in a cabin with two other engineers when the crash came. "We shook hands," he said, "and swore we would not be burned to death, but that somehow we would make our way out. We had no idea how." All three escaped.

* * *

When the disaster happened only twelve men were on duty, navigating the airship. Every one else was asleep.

"A DRUNKEN, REELING MONSTER."

By HAROLD PEMBERTON.
"Daily Express" Special Correspondent.

(who flew from London at dawn yesterday to the scene of the disaster.)

BEAUVAIS, Sunday, Oct. 5.

LET me tell the story of the most terrible disaster in the history of British flying as simply and as faithfully as possible. Let me reconstruct an accurate picture of how brave men of state high and low met their death in the fabulous palace of the air.

It needs no gloss. No mind could conceive a drama more pitiless than the one unfolded to me by eyewitnesses in this stricken and terrified town, a few short hours after the flaming sky had lighted terror in a thousand eyes.

From my airplane flight over the wrecked R 101, and stories told to me by survivors as having something of divine Providence about them, it is from these that I reconstruct for you a narrative of facts that must sear the heart.

Beauvais, a small French town some forty miles from Paris, was sleeping peacefully when, about 2 a.m., the great ship appeared above the housetops.

It was a fearful shadow, for

PAGE THREE, COL. FIVE.

Lord Thomson, his valet, and all the others of R 101 had taken out special accident policies for substantial amounts. It is understood that Air Sefton Brancker had not taken any special precaution against accident, and that the crew were not covered.

* * *

In common with all other Government property, the airship itself, which cost £500,000, was not insured.

* * *

There can be no question of a stowaway being on board the airship," said an Air Ministry official last night, referring to French reports that more than fifty bodies had been recovered.

* * *

An expert inquiry will be opened to-day on the scene of the crash, Major Cooper, Inspector of Accidents, Air Ministry, presiding.

Mr. H. J. Greenwood's full story of the disaster and rescue scenes is on Page Three. Survivors' narratives are on Page Eleven.

WHAT WAS THE CAUSE?

AIRSHIP IN PERIL THREE MONTHS AGO.

LEAKING GAS BAGS.

"Daily Express" Air Correspondent.

I am able to reveal the complete details of an alarming experience which overtook R 101 during her flight over Hendon during the Air Pageant last July which now casts a mysterious shadow across the wreckage and destruction of the airship yesterday morning.

There were elaborate precautions against the publication of the following facts and until now the secret has been kept successfully. The destruction of the great air liner with its toll of forty-six lives, however, makes it vital that the truth should be laid at once before the public.

PREVIOUS ESCAPE.

Officials have carefully concealed the fact that disaster almost ended the career of R101 on the day that she made her public appearance at the Royal Air Force display.

There were moments of her cruise on that day shortly before noon, and spent a considerable time hovering over the east coast before starting for London, so that she would arrive over the flying field at her appointed time. Directly on leaving Hendon, after being in the air for more than four hours, the officers in control of the vessel discovered that she continued to lose height.

Members of the crew who examined the gasbags found that the small balloons, which are made of goldbeaters' skin, were chafing against the metal framework. A report was immediately made to the senior officer, who set in force a series of precautions and ordered all available speed from his engineers.

R101 returned safely and moored. The airship, however, was saved solely by the swift action of Flight-Lieutenant Irwin, the captain, who dumped his entire water ballast and two tons of heavy oil fuel, and employed every other possible means of reducing weight.

HOLES WORN.

Shortly afterwards R101 was taken from the mast and put into her shed for repairs.

It was discovered on examination of the deflated balloons that more than sixty small holes had been worn through the gas containers.

The re-design of the airship's hull, which meant inserting another bay and increasing her length by forty-five feet, was subsequently undertaken, and it was understood in some quarters that a new method had been introduced for the arrangement of the gas balloons.

THE PRINCE INFORMED.

Air Ministry officials at Beauvais were in constant touch with the Prince of Wales throughout the day. It is possible that he may fly to Beauvais to-day.

THE theory of yesterday's disaster points, however, to a recurrence of the same trouble which the R 101 encountered on the day of the Air Pageant.

The Last Message: "Going To Bed."

The last of a series of wireless messages received at Le Bourget from the R101, states Reuter, was timed 7.40 a.m. Eleven minutes before the crash. It read as follows:—

"At the moment, the passengers, after an excellent meal and after enjoying a number of cigars, are getting ready to go to bed."

Five 'Pound Birthday Voucher

£5

Isn't Mr. Drage fine and his Furniture and Gift topping?

MRS. EVERYMAN

Mr. Everyman: Here's your £5 birthday voucher I cut from the paper. As my order comes to £105 I take off the £5 gift, leaving £100 to pay. Is that so, Mr. Drage?

Mr. Drage: Quite correct—the £5 is my birthday gift to you.

Mr. Everyman: Well, how do I pay the £100 on your 50 Pay Way terms?

Mr. Drage: Why, £2 now and £2 monthly for 49 months after.

Mr. Everyman: That's more than 4 years' credit—thank you, Mr. Drage, for your most liberal terms and most kindly present.

Coupon

Name

Address

D.E. 6.10

CUT OUT AND POST IN U.K. STAMPED 1d. ENVELOPE TO—

DRAGE'S

HIGH HOLBORN · LONDON

S181

26 Disaster coverage Fleet Street style – the front and back pages of the *Daily Express* for October 6, 1930

Daily Express

MONDAY, OCTOBER 6, 1930.

AERIAL VIEW OF GREATEST BRITISH AIR DISASTER.

A "DAILY EXPRESS" PHOTOGRAPH, taken from an airplane, of the wreckage of R 101 at Beauvais, France.

ONE OF THE ENGINE GONDOLAS.

FRENCH OFFICERS EXAMINING A WRECKED ENGINE.

THE AIRSHIP'S FLAG, WHICH BY SOME CHANCE ESCAPED THE FLAMES.

27   Harry Guy Bartholomew (1885–1962), creator of the modern *Daily Mirror* and architect of the 'tabloid revolution'

1945, shows the careful dovetailing and tight subbing by which fifteen items could be contained in a tabloid page **(29)**.

It was the age of radio, but fears that the spoken word would dampen the appetite for print proved groundless. The immediacy of broadcasting might force newspapers to follow up rather than lead in the more important spot news, but it did not stop people rushing out to buy newspapers to get 'all the facts'. Moreover, there were whole areas of news that had no chance of being among the handful of items which were all that could be included in a news bulletin; and so circulations leapt up in the 1950s as newsprint restrictions were eased. Even television, from the late 1950s onwards, did not have the effect on overall sales that the gloomiest prophets foretold, although it reminded editors of the importance of pictures, and forced them to take background and magazine features more seriously, and to take

28 The war in the pages of the *Daily Mirror* – the first day, September 4, 1939, and the day Japan surrendered, August 15, 1945, an edition that carried a famous Zec cartoon

more care over the visual side of page design now that there was such visual competition. The more perceptive editors could see, even when colour television arrived, that there was a permanence in a good newspaper picture that was denied to something of which you got a quick glimpse 'on the box'.

The wartime period was also the high watermark of hot metal and the craft of the skilled printer, soon to be approaching its swansong. At the height of the London blitz, when Lord Kemsley's Gray's Inn Road plant was hit by a bomb and the underground Fleet River surged into the basement, the composing room continued to set as water reached the lead pots of the Linotype machines and sent clouds of steam swirling. Imperial printer George Eggington shepherded his flock until all was complete and the Kemsley titles came out on time. After the war, on his visits to the vast Kemsley composing room at Withy Grove, Manchester, George would review his men and machines like a general, walking down the long ranks, greeting each operator as he rose from his seat and stood to attention.

The history of newspaper design has a number of watersheds. The launching of the first 'popular' daily by Lord Northcliffe and the ideas

29 A *Daily Mirror* page for May 8, 1945, shows the tight dovetailing needed to use every inch of news space in an eight-page wartime tabloid

that went into it, was one. The birth of press photography in the early 1900s was another; Bartholomew's tabloid revolution was a third, and the traumatic effects of two world wars on attitudes and practices could be said to constitute two more. Another such watershed occurred in the 1960s when, under the new Thomson ownership, the *Sunday Times* was revamped first by Robert Harling and later by Harold Evans, as a sectional newspaper on the American lines, but with a new type dress employing mainly lowercase light and bold serif faces **(30)** in a horizontal format with multicolumn single line headlines crossing the pages below the fold, and with the pages tabbed and segmented by horizontal thick and thin rules. The most

30 Revolution in Gray's Inn Road – the new-style *Sunday Times* of the 1960s as it blossomed under the Thomson ownership

potent effect of the new approach was that it gave genuine strength below the fold to text size pages, which was something they had previously lacked.

The style, taken up by *The Observer* and, later, *The Guardian*, was ideal for newspapers who wished to compartment their news and features and to make imaginative use of their text size untrammelled by traditional forms. The pages that resulted were characterized by a more daring and artistic cropping of pictures as design elements, the creative use of white space around headlines and pictures and the liberal placing of logos on regular items. The style also set off a shift into wholly lowercase type formats across the board in quality and many provincial titles, of which *The Times* and the *Financial Times* are notable examples today.

In its development, it instituted what might be termed the modern approach to type use and page patterns that was to herald – and to some extent challenge – the next great watershed in newspaper design, the availability of full page composition on the computer screen.

4
Technology and the designer

Printing technology determines what is possible in newspaper design since it provides the tools and the plant to give the editor the sort of paper that is wanted. At the same time the editor's ideas on presentation and printing – the end product of design – have to bear some relation to the means available. Editing and printing thus exist in a reciprocating relationship to each other.

In talking of printing technology we assume now the use of some sort of computerized system into which writing, editing, typesetting and printing capability have been built; an all-in main-frame computer system of the sort designed by Atex, Linotype-Paul, Ferranti and the other big printing systems manufacturers.

It is possible, with the advances made in computer design, to produce a newspaper very cheaply by what has come to be known as desktop publishing (DTP). This can be a basic one-person operation consisting of a word processor with disk drive, using programmes for copy origination, editing and make-up, connected to a laser printer which provides a useful though limited range of types and the facility to output made-up pages. These pages can be fed into a printing platemaker and simple sheet-fed offset press, or can be sent on to a printer who will do the platemaking and printing side of the work at a contract figure on more sophisticated equipment. The design element involved here has to be simple and within the typesetting and page composition capacity of the system. Such an operation can produce a satisfactory though modest in-house newspaper and is being used more and more in schools, press offices and organizations.

The purpose of this book, however, is to examine design from the point of view of general newspaper practice, and of this chapter to look at the relationship between design and technology within this context. (Chapter 14 looks at how design methods can be adapted to in-house newspapers and other special markets.)

**Hot-metal
technology**

Newspapers as they appear today, though every stage in their production has been computerized, are in essence the end product of old printing technology. The concepts of typography, design, page make-up and press work are rooted in methods based upon the use of hot metal at all stages, and the purpose in building computerized systems has not been to evolve a new printed product, or to bring about changes in newspapers, but to reproduce exactly by cheaper and more efficient means the sort of newspapers being produced by the old methods. The facilities built into the new systems are thus orientated to working parameters that already existed.

Pages were made up – and had been from the very earliest newspapers in the seventeenth century – by putting into a frame called a *chase* the lines or slugs of type that had been set by compositors and assembled ready for this purpose in long metal trays called *galleys*. The galleys of type represented the editorial input of news stories and feature articles written by reporters and feature writers for the edition and edited to fit the spaces on the pages. The checking and editing to length of this material was carried out by subeditors who had marked, on the original typed or handwritten

31   Page make-up hot-metal style

text (called copy), the type and setting instructions for the compositors to follow. Once typeset, this material was further checked for setting errors (called *literals*) by proofreaders working from proofs pulled from the galleys of type.

The pages were then put together by a page compositor, or *stonehand* (31) to an editorial plan, or layout, which indicated the positions of the text, headlines, pictures and adverts. The pictures and adverts, like the type, were of metal, being engraved on to *plates*, or 'blocks', and then mounted on metal mounts called *stereos* to give them the same height in the chase as the lines of type.

In the early days, as can be seen from examples in the previous chapter, design played little part in this. Often the printer was the editor and, apart from the first items on page one or two and a crude sequence or pattern for the different parts of the paper, the order of items was often that in which they had been received, with the headlines being simple labels scarcely bigger than the type of the reading matter. While design techniques developed rapidly from the late nineteenth century onwards, typesetting, page make-up and printing methods underwent little basic change other than the

32 A bank of rotary presses – still performing good service for many newspapers in a hi-tech environment

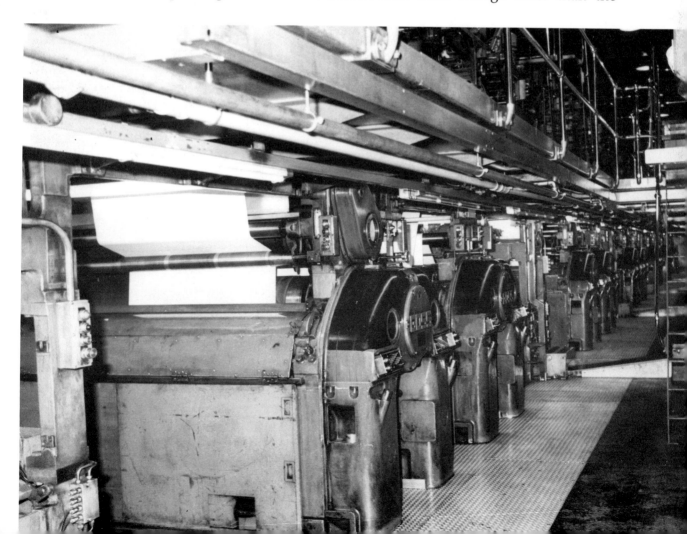

introduction of keyboard-operated *linecasters* for the setting of body type in the 1890s.

The pages under the hot metal method just described were made up on a stone-topped bench, later of metal but still referred to as 'the *stone*' (hence stone-hand, stone subeditor, etc.). A completed page was called a *forme*. From the forme, moulds were taken under high pressure using a composition material called *flong*, from which were cast the curved printing metal plates used to print the pages by the letterpress method on the rotary presses **(32)**. These presses, though greatly refined so that they could comfortably print up to nearly 70,000 copies an hour, remained in essence the sort of press first used by the *Philadelphia Ledger* in 1843, by which curved metal plates attached to a revolving drum picked up ink from a bath and printed the pages by direct impression on to a revolving web of paper as it passed over them, that is, by *letterpress*. The rotary had replaced the earlier flat-bed, or sheet-fed presses.

Modern design techniques grew up in this working environment, as indeed did the whole concept of a newspaper as a product. As markets and revenue expanded so editing and design became more sophisticated and the functions required for them more refined. New types with extended sizes were designed for special roles, in particular some of the versatile modern sans ranges, influenced by designer Eric Gill and, among seriffed types, Stanley Morison's Times New Roman. Type-composing machines had been designed and built since the 1840s, but Ottmar Mergenthaler's Linotype machine, patented in Baltimore in 1884, by which an operator on a keyboard **(33)** produced slugs of type from matrices, proved the first practical one. Instead of the laborious hand-selecting of tiny letters it could set lines mechanically at five a minute. Meanwhile, press speeds were being improved and also ink and paper quality, while automatic etching machines replaced the old hand engravers and speeded up the process of blockmaking.

Yet typesetting, picture reproduction, page make-up and printing remained a hot-metal, labour-intensive operation with the basic routines and attitudes little changed, and costing and work practices rooted in earlier days. Typesetting speeds increased hardly at all from the breakthrough with the Linotype machine in the 1890s until the 1950s, when experiments began with computer-fed tape which (against some opposition from print unions who were understandably worried about jobs) increased the setting speed from linecasters to fourteen lines a minute. Hot metal was not without its advantages: complex setting could be delivered by a good operator intelligently aware of a page's special requirements; the wide availability and easy replacement of headline types in standard sizes from 14 point to 96 point and beyond, which were visible for inspection in their cases, enabled good type balance to be achieved; a skilled page compositor could refine the spacing on a page by the use of standard 1-, 2- and 3-point leading and move type around to fit in with changes; attractive

33 The workhorse of old technology – Linotype machines

results could be achieved by the right cooperation between designer and page compositor. Indeed the cooperation was vital since the tools needed to turn a design into a finished page were in the hands of printers.

A disadvantage from the designer's point of view was that any special type effects, or the use of type reversed as white-on-black (WOB) or as black-on-tone (BOT), had to be prepared by photographing the type and creating a metal block or plate. This, together with the growing use of graphics for special display and generally greater demand for halftone and line blocks, including those for adverts, put ever-increasing pressure on the process-engraving department, and it was here that the most spectacular bottlenecks occurred in hot-metal production. The poor quality of labour relations, and the failure of print union agreements to take proper account of the growing sophistication of editorial requirements, plus the general problems of old machinery, outdated methods, demarcation disputes, noise, dirt and slowness inseparable from the hot

34 Electronic editing – a subeditor using an Atex keyboard and monitor, or VDU

metal operation, made it harder and harder for editors to get the sort of paper they wanted.

It has to be remembered, nevertheless, that in ideal conditions the hot metal system worked and produced great skills which made possible the advances in design techniques that established the British newspaper in the postwar years as a model to Western Countries. When faced with the demand for colour from the mid-1960s onwards, the pre-printing on newsprint of colour advertising gave a high quality result long before run-of-press colour became commonplace with the web-offset presses of the new systems.

Cold type

It was not the pursuit of quality that forced the computerization of the printing industry from the 1960s but rather the need to solve the chronic problems of costs, over-manning, poor labour relations and (by contemporary standards) spectacularly old-fashioned technology. Rotary presses had a forty-year life; Linotype machines and page moulding presses had been in use unchanged in some offices for more than seventy years; some Fleet Street composing rooms in the 1970s, with their mallets and space bars and iron trolleys and chain-driven proofing machines, looked like museums of industrial archaeology.

Early problems both with photo typesetting and with printing presses delayed the take-off of 'new technology' but by the mid-1960s most American papers, which were smaller and cost less to re-plant, and a growing number of British provincial papers had changed to the new methods. The development in the 1970s of hard polymer for printing plates and the introduction of faster web-offset presses with better paper control made the new systems suitable at last for the longer print runs of the national titles. By the end of the next decade most British papers had switched from hot metal to 'cold type' to secure advantages in cost-saving and efficiency, once it was clear that product quality could be maintained. The move was helped by the new generation of fast main-frame computers which greatly improved editing and typesetting capability. Through the move into 'new technology' it also became possible to secure improvements in picture reproduction by the use of a finer screen acceptable to the smooth web-offset printing plates.

The changeover broadly meant the electronic origination and editing of copy **(34)** through visual display terminals or units (VDUs) connected to the main computer, the use of the original keystroke to activate phototypesetters, and the making up of pages either by paste-up from type bromides delivered from the typesetters, or on screen. Thereafter the made-up pages were fed as page negatives into a platemaker which produced the smooth polymer printing plates used to print the paper on web-offset presses. The page image could be transferred to polymer relief plates where a company wanted to continue using its costly investment in rotary presses for printing by letterpress, although this sacrificed better picture reproduction, added to the cost and time of platemaking and deprived the company of access to the run-of-press colour capability of web-offset. As a result, most offices still using rotary presses planned towards changing, when the time for replanting came, to web-offset presses.

The success of the systems builders in designing and manufacturing custom-made text and picture origination systems to suit individual newspapers meant – provided there was editorial involvement in fitting out – that page design could achieve the same visual results for each paper as with hot metal. There was also the advantage of generally better quality reproduction and the option of colour.

At each stage of the operation there were other advantages. With electronic copy origination, or what came to be known as direct input, writers typing out their stories on the keyboard of their VDUs could revise and alter copy on screen by cursor without the need for retyping. Editing could likewise be carried out on screen instead of having to cover text with unsightly crossings out and editing marks for an operator to sort out and set. The text was called up by the subeditor and religned itself accurately on screen as editing proceeded. When complete it could be checked for length and instantly hyphenated and justified showing the lines as they would appear when set. The edited story was then called up by the revise subeditor for final 'reading' and checking before being sent to the photo typesetters, where the electronic signals were turned into type and printed out as bromides. With photosetters using cathode ray tubes (CRTs) setting at 1000 lines a minute, page-ready type bromides were being produced to enable pages to be created by paste-up in a fraction of the time taken under hot metal. And there was the alternative of page composition on screen in which the entire process of page make-up was carried out inside the computer by means of a make-up screen and special controls.

Influences on design

Page design, in its routine, is the part of newspaper production least affected by computerization. Layouts still have to be visualized and drawn whatever method is used for making up the pages. While art desk work is generally the same, the changes in editing, typesetting and make-up methods do, however, influence the ideas that can be used and also the time scale of the work. Vital to the whole concept of page design is whether pages are made up by paste and scalpel or on screen.

Paste-up

Under this method the text and headlines are outputted from the photosetters in galley form as sheet bromides looking exactly as they will look in the paper when printed, each story with its headline and captions. The bromides are cut up from their sheets, which might contain several stories for different pages each under its header and catchline. These are waxed on the back and then attached to the page card with the help of a scalpel. The page card is an exact replica of the layout sheet used to design the page and is graduated in centimetres marked in non-reproducing blue lines, with a pica space between each column to guide the compositor in placing the columns of matter accurately **(35)**. Where stories need to be separated, or ruled off, 'electronic' sticky tape of the appropriate points-width is attached. Headline and body setting is automatically spaced in the photosetter, but space can also be adjusted optically by cutting up lines and words with the scalpel until the production journalist in charge of the page is satisfied with the effect.

Pictures, having been scaled and prepared (see Chapter 5), are 'shot' to size and are delivered to the page as bromides, as are the adverts, and these also are waxed and attached by the make-up compositor. When the page is complete and every item is in position according to the layout plan and looking exactly as it will look when printed, it is photographed and the page negative fed into a platemaker.

The skill in the operation lies in the speed and accuracy of the make-up compositor and the facility to reproduce, with a combination of eye and scalpel, the design of the layout, however complex. Speed is helped by the fast setting and the ease with which cuts and reruns of text can be keyed into the photosetter, although at peak setting times it is useful (to avoid overload) if simple cuts can be done on the page with the scalpel. Likewise, pictures can be scalpelled to fit, and space adjusted infinitely to get a page optically right.

From the designer's point of view the advantage of paste-up is its flexibility in accepting any design style, being able to achieve complex and unusual effects with speed, and being able to change text or pictures quickly to suit editorial purposes.

Full page composition

The alternative – and what some people believe to be the ultimate – method of page make-up is to keep the various ingredients inside the computer and assemble them into a page on screen. This is done by a handheld control called a 'mouse' or bit-mover which can block out a layout shape on screen and call up pre-edited modules of material, and also stored digitized pictures and graphics, including adverts, move them about and fit them into the page. A special keyboard and screen is used, and the system needs to have built in a facility for inputting, storing and retrieving prepared pictures and graphics, as well as the computer graphics now supplied with most systems. This method has a lot of logic to commend it and it undoubtedly represents the ultimate utilization of the computer, with the original keystroked material being fed straight through the system and into a platemaker without the intervention of typesetter, paste-up room or

35 Preparing the edition – paste-up compositors making up pages

camera. Yet even with the most advanced mainframe computers it poses problems.

It is difficult at present to break out of rectangular-based modules in working to a design by means of computer controls, and this makes it impossible to use on-screen page make-up for certain layout styles. It is also a worry to editors of successful papers who feel its adoption might change or damage a layout style that is successful and familiar to the readers.

Moreover, the screen manipulation of pictures and adverts and other elements involving graphics generation has caused such difficulties, mainly owing to its slowness, that some papers which have adopted screen make-up have found it quicker to print out pages as bromides and attach the pictures and adverts by scalpel afterwards in order to obtain a complete page image to feed into the platemaker. The result of these problems is that at the time of writing only a very few British papers had adopted full page composition, and fewer than half of US papers, despite the tendency there towards modular styles, the view being that developments in computers may later make on-screen, or electronic, make-up more acceptable.

Page production

An important gain to the designer from computerized systems is the shortening of the time gap between page drawing and make-up, whether by paste-up or on screen. From subediting, type can be in the page within three or four minutes, provided the system is not overloaded by bunched setting. A scaled picture can be shot and delivered as a page bromide ready for paste-up in about the same time instead of half an hour, or often much longer, under the hot metal system.

The ability to 'see' the result of type-and-picture artwork at an early stage helps in complicated visualizing jobs, or where an editor is anxious to see a proposed effect while, with paste-up, the help of the scalpel to carry out instant amendment to text and picture bromides can make fine adjustment at the make-up stage free of bother.

The pervasive use of the camera in the computerized systems is a boon to the designer. Difficult enlargements and reductions of pictures can be tackled and inspected using a laser printer such as the Autokon. Type can be quickly reversed into white-on-black (WOB) or black-on-tint (BOT) for big or complicated jobs outside the range of the photosetter's reverse video facility, and delivered to the page without the delays that would have happened under the old system. Complicated art work can be shot and the bromide inspected in advance of page make-up. It is also possible to re-shoot difficult picture originals for quality improvement by lens adjustment to enhance work already done by the retoucher.

Page design also benefits from the general improvement in the printing quality of pictures as a result of the use of the finer screen acceptable for half-tone (fine dot) reproduction with web-offset printing plates.

Colour

The run-of-press colour capability (described fully in Chapter 16) of web-offset presses makes the use of colour for those papers that want it both easier and cheaper than the preprinted colour evolved for letterpress printing. To what extent colour is appropriate on news pages remains a matter for debate. It is an extra dimension and a challenge for the designer, with the right pictures and subject, and a worthwhile option to be able to offer the advertiser who might prefer a newspaper with run-of-press colour capability.

Technology and type   Early problems of poor match of types on changeover to photosetting have been overcome and now all main manufacturers carry a full range of standard and not-so-standard faces to suit the most fastidious users. There can be, as a result of the American provenance of most of the type masters, slight design variations in popular types such as Century, Ludlow Black and Tempo but this has not prevented papers converting to photoset from maintaining a striking continuity in presentation with even an added clarity of reproduction.

Matching existing body faces has offered more problems, though some papers, addicted to a battered and old-fashioned Ionic or Jubilee long overdue for the bin, have been delighted to find their photoset columns taking on a new sharpness and readability.

Traditional body and headline type sizes, to suit each customer's type format, from 5½ point right through the range to 144 point where applicable, are programmed into the computer for ease of command in editing, and to make type balance more calculable. Yet, in fact, with electronic typesetting you can have any size you like down to half a point variation, and the facility to override formatted commands and produce 'bastard sizes' exists in all systems. Used sparingly and sensibly, it is invaluable for getting into a measure a much wanted headline – especially one written by the editor – or avoiding excessive tightness of set or wasted or ugly white.

The command facility to italicize or 'lean' a typeface is also useful, if used sparingly, although not all faces italicize successfully. The best italic types are those that were designed that way, and it is useful to have some stock italic masters in the photosetter, if they are likely to be used (see Chapter 12).

Spacing, both linear and letter-spacing, should be programmed in at the outset to maintain style and give visual consistency although, as with type sizes, formula spacing needs to be overidden to give special effects or to solve difficult setting problems. With paste-up, of course, spacing can always be adjusted at the make-up stage by scalpel – a useful ploy with lowercase headlines when awkwardly placed ascenders or descenders, or the lack of them, require lines to be optically spaced. The systems give what they are asked to do and it is wrong to endure setting and spacing faults that can be put right by re-programming. It is not a good idea to vary spacing by command formulas when spacing consistency could be maintained simply by using more words or letters, or re-writing a headline.

5
Pictures

Newspapers are so dependent upon pictures performing a design function as well as an informative one that it is hard to imagine how editors coped in the days before the camera. In fact, as we have seen, design in early newspapers played such an insignificant part in the marketing of a product that consisted simply of sheets of information for a limited audience that the lack of illustration was not felt. It was when circulations and markets started to expand towards the end of the nineteenth century, accompanied by a broader content and deliberately targetted readership, that presentation began to matter.

Certain news stories, it was found, gained in actuality if the words could be accompanied by a picture. Certain features, even the most mundane how-to-do-it ones, were more intelligible if a point could be made visually. At the same time a picture on a page, it was realized, created a focal point for the eye of the reader and so how the picture was located began to matter.

Role in design

Whatever the design style or market (the two are connected) of a newspaper, pictures form, in modern page design, a fundamental ingredient of the mix along with text, headlines and adverts. In an ideal world every page would have a right size, right subject picture forming a main focal point along with the bigger headlines, around which the text and the other headlines and pictures would be arranged. Such a picture would sit neatly in the editorial space left by the placing of the adverts as if the space had been designed for it. Nothing is so simple. In fact, the choice and placing of pictures is the product of a mixture of planning, good luck, compromise and the sheer inspiration that produces the display idea to unite the ingredients.

Planning a paper's contents, including even some feature pages, is geared to a news coverage dependent on the events of the day and often has to be undertaken without some of the material being at hand. While many events (Parliament, courts, meetings, weddings, etc.) can be allowed for in advance, some of the best stories will happen without warning. As a result, the allocation of pictures to some pages might have to be made before they have been received or, alternatively, left to a fairly late stage if the page production slot allows this.

Compromise is of the essence. The most newsworthy text might be the least productive of pictures, and it is unlikely that every page will have a main story supported by a main picture, or that the most wanted picture turns out to be the right shape (that is, horizontal or vertical in composition). A superb picture, or the relative failure of a picture assignment (often a clear case of luck), can cause early plans to change. As a result, editorial material might have to be moved around so that every page gets its share of pictures, and so picture-worthiness as well as news value can become an element in the space and position stories are given. The picture possibility of a feature can likewise govern the space and position it is given.

While change and compromise can play a part in allocating the contents to a page, it does not mean that any old picture – any more than any old text for that matter – will do. The criteria for choosing and using the right picture is as important as the criteria for choosing and using the right story and much care and judgement goes into the process, and so in addition to the basic requirements that a picture should illustrate the text and be an element in the page design, we have to take into account other factors. There are, for instance:

- *Composition*. The grouping and position of the people and main objects in the picture must form a pleasing shape. It has to be the most eye-catching picture of its set or of those available.
- *Balance*. It must balance with the rest of the page and with the picture material of the adverts. It is no use if, for the position it is required to fill, the subject faces out of the page or out of the story it is illustrating.
- *Quality*. There must be sufficient contrast in tones between dark and light for the picture to reproduce properly. A lack of good tonal values can produce a grey effect on printing, although the versatile Autokon machine (see Chapter 7) can enhance poor original quality.

If the main picture is supporting the page lead or half lead then it must be integrated into the main text and headline area but in such a way that it plays a structural part in the page. If it is with a secondary story then picture, text and headline must be combined to serve a structural function in order to get the best visual effect from it. If the picture is being used for its own news value – say, the first release of a Royal portrait – then with its caption story, rather than just an identifying caption, it must be given its own prominence as a focal point in balance with the main headline area. If there are secondary pictures on the page, even if they are just single-column head shots, they must be balanced against the main picture so as to provide lesser focal points. The examples described below show how these considerations work in practice.

Picture workshop

The news page from the tabloid *Birmingham Post* **(36)** shows how to get the best out of a handful of pictures supporting a dramatic page lead. The decision to top the page with the most vivid one of a

One of the carriages derailed in Saturday's crash at Purley, Surrey, is hoisted above the houses before being taken away for examination. Five people were killed in the accident.

Warning to egg producers

By NIGEL HASTILOW

The Government last night promised tough legal action against food producers who continue to sell infected eggs.

After months of criticism of the Ministry of Agriculture's delays in responding to growing public concern over salmonella in eggs, a clear warning was issued to producers last night.

Mr Richard Ryder, the junior Agriculture Minister, told egg producers: "Clean up your act or face the full brunt of the law."

He was speaking during a Commons debate on the Government's £19 million package of assistance to the industry which came after the slump in sales caused by a remark by the former Junior Health Minister, Mrs Edwina Currie, that most egg production was infected with salmonella.

Mr Ryder rejected the claim by the all-party Commons agriculture select committee that his department had been sluggish.

He said the Ministry had put forward 17 new measures to control salmonella in eggs, the most comprehensive package in the world.

Though egg sales were still down by 20 to 25 per cent, the Govern-

ment's rescue package had restored stability.

He said: "Consumer sovereignty is the key to the market place.

"It can be threatened by monopoly and cartels, trade protectionism masquerading as protection, or neglect of public health standards."

Earlier, Mr John Biffen (Con Shropshire North), the former Cabinet Minister, condemned Mrs Currie (Con Derbyshire South), for her reluctance to give evidence to the select committee and described her as "a political health hazard."

Sir Hal Miller (Con Bromsgrove) said some caterers had still not reacted positively to the Government's measures to improve egg quality.

Some small farmers were still finding their supplies to caterers were down by 90 per cent.

Dr David Clark, the Labour agriculture spokesman, accused the Government of mishandling the whole affair by "incompetence, excessive secrecy and delaying tactics.

"By their failure to act speedily, they have allowed the problem to become exacerbated."

Driver 'failed to report Clapham signal change'

A British Rail driver could have prevented the Clapham disaster in which 35 people died by reporting signal irregularities he noticed only minutes before the crash, the inquiry was told yesterday.

But Mr George Christy did nothing, it was claimed.

The reason was that he should not have been driving the train, but had agreed to an "illegal" swop with another driver, said Mr Benjamin Browne, a lawyer.

Mr Christy rejected the allegations from Mr Browne, who was representing Mrs Sue Rolls, widow of the driver killed in the crash, and John Rolls.

In an emotional gesture yesterday, she handed back the union badge her husband was wearing when he died.

Mr Tony Staton, district secretary of the Associated Society of Locomotive Engineers and Firemen, told her to keep it, but she said between sobs: "I am sorry, you don't understand. They have let everyone down."

It is understood she was upset at the union decision not to cross-examine Mr Rolls's fel-

Mr George Christy: denied 'illegal' swop as driver.

Mrs Sue Rolls: handed back husband's union badge.

low drivers about the failure to report the signal irregularities.

The inquiry has heard that a wiring fault during signal modernisation caused the fault, which the driver of a Basingstoke train stopped to report. The signals then allowed a Bournemouth train — driven by Mr Rolls — to run into the back of it.

Mr Christy, aged 60, said he had driven a Bournemouth-Waterloo train past the spot just 10¼ minutes before the crash in December.

But he dismissed Mr Browne's claim that the swop he had agreed to — by taking over the train from another driver — was "illegal."

However, he admitted it

was unauthorised and a disciplinary offence but the management found out.

He did not report sudden changes in the lights shown by the signals because he thought they were no more than unusual. He thought the reason was that a Clapham signalman had rerouted a train in front.

Mr Browne said: "If you had realised the importance of what you had seen and reported it this tragedy would never have occurred, would it?"

Mr Christy said he did not know how to answer — there was a signal irregularity, but he was not aware of it at the time.

Mr Browne said: "May I

suggest that you are so anxious now to say that this wasn't an irregularity and didn't report it at the time because you were well aware that you should not have been driving that train and, had you reported it, you would have got yourself into trouble?"

Mr Christy: "That isn't the case. If there had been an irregularity I would have reported it."

Mr Christy, of Hammond Close, Basingstoke, Hampshire, said he had seen the three signals approaching the one at the centre of the crash, number 138, change to green as he approached the first of them.

Then signal 142, the one before 138, suddenly "flicked" from green to yellow, he said.

A BR official responsible for supervising signals modernisation said he had feared there could be more loose wires like the one that caused the crash.

Mr Alfred Court was being questioned by Mr Michael Spencer, counsel for the bereaved and injured, about why he had agreed to cut off part of the old loose wiring responsible for the disaster after signal engineers found it within hours of the crash.

Mr Court, aged 48, signals supervisor at Wimbledon, said he had obeyed orders from senior engineers to make the wire safe by cutting it and had left it in their hands.

Mr Spencer, asking why Mr Court had not left it in place to be photographed and examined later, said: "You appreciated the importance of this evidence, did you not?"

Mr Court said: "Yes, but I had just finished 16 commissions similar to this one and I was a bit worried about wires on my job hanging loose.

Mr Court said: "You were worried that some of the wires that you have been involved in could be in the same state?"

Mr Court said: "I was worried. But when we checked there were none."

He said the remaining wire, still connected at the other end to a fuse, was taped up with black tape with a marker to distinguish it.

The next day two senior engineers asked him to remove the wire completely, but he refused. He cut off a short length and gave it to one of the engineers.

The inquiry continues today.

Take another look at the 190 series. Mercedes-Benz have.

Take a look at the subtly refined lines. Take a look at the new more aerodynamically efficient front aprons and bumpers. Take a look at the new high-impact door and wing panels. Take a look at the totally new seats with softer top cushioning and wider side support. Take a look at the extra legroom for rear seat passengers.

Take your choice from six models.

Take a test drive by visiting our showroom or calling us on the phone.

SWINFORD MOTORS..

Swinford Motors (Continental) Ltd. Grange Lane, Lye, Stourbridge, West Midlands. Telephone: Lye (0384) 424471

ENGINEERED LIKE NO OTHER CAR IN THE WORLD.

Dangerous myths on cancer causes

Myths among children that cancer is caused by eating burnt toast, operating computers or falling off a chair backwards must be destroyed, the Cancer Research Campaign said yesterday.

Survey results published by the campaign showed that children had various misconceptions about the disease and were deeply confused about its causes and curability.

The campaign is worried that children will grow up with false ideas and fail to seek early treatment as adults for possible symptoms.

A hundred children around the country, aged between 12

and 16, were asked their views of the disease.

Dr Anne Charlton, of the campaign's Manchester-based education and child studies research group, found that a third of the children were correctly aware of the dangers of smoking. A fifth knew that excess sunlight could cause cancer, but many were wildly wrong in their view of the disease.

"Old wives' tales are developing all the time about cancer. Schools can help to project a more accurate message and expose some dangerous misconceptions," said Dr Charlton.

Tesco pays half costs

Tesco is to pay half the costs of the case in which two sisters were awarded £300 damages each last week after suing for unlawful arrest, false imprisonment, libel and slander.

The sisters, Mrs Frances Warby and Mrs Ann Chantrell, from Hertfordshire, faced a costs bill which some estimates put at £30,000, because they pursued their court action after refusing a settlement offer of £1,500 each.

Tesco will pay costs up to the time it paid its settlement offer into court. The firm is not paying the sisters' portion of the costs.

Jail for father who caused son's death

A drunken driver was jailed for four months at the Old Bailey yesterday, for causing the death of his two-year-old son in a car crash.

Paul Swaby, who was already banned for another drink-drive offence, was two-and-a-half times over the legal limit when he set off home with his son from a party.

Swaby (35) put the boy in the front passenger seat with an adult safety belt over him.

Mr Tobias Davey, prosecuting, said that as Swaby went through the Blackwall Tunnel he overtook on the inside at speed.

The car careered from side

to side before smashing through a crash barrier on to the opposite side of the road.

The toddler was killed almost instantly.

Swaby had denied causing death by reckless driving.

Mr Andrew Bright, defending, said the boy's death had had an appalling effect on Swaby.

The judge was told that Swaby, unemployed, of Sheridan Road, Manor Park, East London, is already serving 16-months for deception and handling. He ordered yesterday's sentence to be served concurrently.

36 Handling a news picture – the *Birmingham Post*

Irish Independent, Wednesday, March 8, 1989 7

US Yuppies to burn up the ould sod

• Exporting a well-packaged product.

By TIM HASTINGS

BORD NA MONA is to make its first major pitch for the American market later this month with the introduction of Irish Peat Bricks as an "upmarket lifestyle product".

The new Yuppie fuel — which is designed to be used for special occasions — will sell at nine dollars and 95 cents a half bale. That's almost 10 times the price of the half bale here — but the difference is largely accounted for by transport costs.

Packaged in an attractive box format, the new "bricks" are being marketed on a pilot basis in the New England area. And, if successful, they will be extended to outlets in Chicago, Boston, New York and Toronto, according to the board's marketing man John Foley.

The bricks, similar to briquettes on sale here, have already been test marketed in selected homes and more than half the households involved said they would be willing to buy.

"We are not selling the peat as a commodity fuel but as something for special use. We view it as a long-term project," Mr. Foley explained. People like the smell of the new bricks and their appeal is not confined to middle-class and upper-middle-class buyers, he added.

Initially, the board is planning to sell 50 tons of the product in the first phase of the US marketing campaign which followed consultations with Coras Trachtala and months of market investigation.

Dail offer to the new radio stars

By JOHN FOLEY

CHANGES are to be sought in Dail rules to enable newly licensed independent radio stations to broadcast proceedings from lively Dail committees.

The Committee chairpeople want invitations sent to Century Communications to cover the four major public committees because of RTE's persistent refusal to broadcast their proceedings. Angry deputies have accused the national broadcasting station of refusing to honour its contractual arrangements to cover the Dail or recordings of its related committees.

And because of RTE's refusal, there are growing demands that the CPP should now change its rules to extend to the new independent network the option of broadcasting committee proceedings or recordings.

Moves to involve the independent network are being spearheaded by Fine Gael's Gay Mitchell, chairman of the all-party Public Accounts Committee.

"Dail committees have continually been refused broadcasting facilities by RTE which maintains that it does not have the technical equipment or resources to extend its radio coverage.

"In the light of RTE's refusal to do what it has agreed, I will be asking the CPP to consider the position and invite Century Communications to take on the task," Mr. Mitchell said.

He added that all members of the various committees had been angered by RTE's refusal to cover their activities, despite several meetings with senior executives from the station.

Student fee row

THE UCD administration block on the Belfield campus was taken over by students yesterday protesting against college plans for a £50 capitation fee.

The college president, Dr. Patrick Masterson, briefly addressed the students explaining the university's financial difficulties — however, the students said they were staying in occupation and the administrative staff were sent home early.

Tug-of-love men 'home in 3 months'

By FRANK KHAN

THE Jordanian father of Nadine Nassir — the Dublin-born child at the centre of the tug-of-love drama — said last night the two Irishmen, jailed for attempting to abduct her, should be home "in three months".

And he added: "I've nothing against them."

Dr. Sameer Nassir denied, in an exclusive interview with the *Irish Independent*, that Gerard Flynn (26), of Knocklong, Co. Limerick, and Denis Dennehy (28), of Portlaoise, were being held in primitive prison conditions.

Dr. Nassir, speaking for the first time of his ordeal, revealed how he had visited both men with Nadine's uncle, Seamus McManus, and declared: "They are being treated very well. I've nothing against them."

He said: "I think they will be let out in three months with good behaviour. I'm glad the boys will be getting home soon." He expected both men would be transferred shortly to Sharjah prison where they would be entitled to buy food and have books supplied.

Dr. Nassir said Nadine, who will be six in April, was fine. "She is very well," and had spoken on the 'phone to her mother, Ann McManus, for 20 minutes yesterday.

Nadine's father, who spent 20 years in Ireland, said he would be prepared to let Nadine come back to Ireland to see her mother if sent an Irish court order giving him full custody. Nadine was under her mother's custody when she was taken by her father to Dubai last summer.

Under the "right circumstances", Dr. Nassir said he would return to Dublin with his daughter. Dr. Nassir, who is a surgeon at Khorfakkan Hospital, added: "I never wanted to deny Nadine her mother, or her mother Nadine. Under no circumstances would I allow them be separated forever." He said: "I did not kidnap my daughter — I feel she should be brought up here by me."

Dr. Nassir said he was disappointed by the way the Irish media had treated him, adding: "They tore my private life in pieces." Referring to the two-year sentences handed down by the court, Dr. Nassir said he had not been in favour of stiffer punishment.

Shares scam firms crackdown

A MAJOR crackdown on "share pushing" firms is being planned by the government as it emerged several such operations have set up here, with one Dublin-based scam now making more than £100,000 a month by conning investors overseas.

Industry and Commerce Minister Ray Burke admitted yesterday the so-called "boiler-room" operations are an international scourge and promised action to stamp them out.

By BRIAN DOWLING

There is mounting fear in legitimate financial circles that these firms operating from Dublin and Cork will damage the country's reputation and may cause major problems for the new Customs House Docks financial centre.

Already the Director of Consumer Affairs has taken steps to warn potential UK investors — one of the main target groups of the share pushers — to be wary about offers of shares or dealings in commodities markets by firms using telephone sales from Dublin.

In a circular to the British media, the Office of Consumer Affairs warned some of them have links to organised crime and international investment fraud. It says: "The office is concerned about the bona fides of these firms and about the dangers posed to inexperienced private investors by their marketing methods

The latest action follows a series of visits in the last week by staff from the Office of Consumer Affairs to a number of firms operating from Dublin and Cork.

One of them, selling shares in a Hong Kong medical supply firm, is running an elaborate scheme from Spain using Ireland as a covering address. Using a city centre office staffed by one person, share sales made on telephone through Spain are transacted via Dublin and investors' money lodged in a Dublin bank.

Once the investor agrees to buy shares, the Dublin office is contacted and sends out the share purchase form and invoices are then transacted here. Initial estimates are that the company is banking in excess of £100,000 a month.

Other firms under investigation are involved in selling shares in an Australian gold mining company and selling commodities — usually metals, which investors are told will rapidly increase their market value.

The Minister said he is examining regulatory structures to ensure such firms can no longer operate here. Asked in the Dail if he would set up a Securities Commission, as in the U.S., to police such operations, he replied this was like trying to "hit mercury with a hammer".

A golden welcome

• Coming home . . . Marcus O'Sullivan waves to the welcoming crowd at Cork Airport. Picture: TED McCARTHY

Homecoming of 'Magic Marcus'

By DICK CROSS

"MARCUS is magic", declared the schoolboy banner as Ireland's fast-track specialist, ex-Cork schoolboy Marcus O'Sullivan was given a triumphant homecoming with his world championship 1500-metre gold in his bag, yesterday.

The crowds thronged Cork Airport, then Carrigaline pipers played him and team mate Frank O'Mara down onto the tarmac and into an airport reception with speeches and presentations.

Then came the spectacular drive downhill through his native Turners Cross and past his old school, Colaiste Criost Ri, as friends and neighbours showed their pride in the local boy who beat the world's best.

Cork City Hall was on late opening as Deputy Lord Mayor, Mr. Corr, rendered honours on behalf of the city. Marcus rang his American-born wife, Mary, in New Jersey to tell about the reception. She stayed at home with two-months-old Laura.

His father, John (57), his mother, Elizabeth, brother Gregory and sisters, Grace and Lucia strove to hold back their feelings at the dimensions of it all. They were, clearly overjoyed.

"It is incredible", said his dad as he and Bishop John Buckley walked out towards the Aer Lingus plane just in from London.

The Taoiseach, Mr. Haughey, sent down a letter of congratulations and said: "It was a tremendous achievement and maintains the magnificent contribution which Irish athletes have made to sport at international level."

BRIEFLY

No bail on gun charges

A Belfast man who allegedly stored a large quantity of guns for the Loyalist Ulster Defence Association was refused bail yesterday by the High Court in Belfast.

The weapons were found during an RUC raid on the Rathcoole home of Leslie Mawhinney's girl friend last week. A lawyer said that after his arrest Mawhinney told police he had agreed to keep the arms because men had threatened to tell his wife about his relationship with the girl.

Not enough preparation

Progressive Democrat education spokesperson Mairin Quill claimed yesterday there was inadequated in-service training for the new Junior Certificate, due to replace the Inter and Group.

At present teachers are undergoing one day's preparation for the new syllabi which are due to be introduced in September but Mrs. Quill said this was not enough.

WP talks 'helpful'

Devolved Govt. for the North, security, education, economic investment and the promotion of a 'peace charter' were among the issues discussed yesterday when a high-level delegation from the Workers' Party met Northern Ireland Minister of State Dr. Brian Mawhinney at Stormont Castle.

A statement later from the Workers' Party described the meeting as being welcomed by the Minister as 'helpful'.

'Trade and Peace' talks

'THE ROLE of Trade in World Peace' will be the theme of the fourth annual international conference of the Shannon-based Centre for International Co-operation.

The event, from May 17-20 at the Limerick Inn Hotel, will be opened by President Hillery. Trade experts from the UN, GATT, the EC, Soviet Union and the US will be among the speakers.

Haughey to hire jet 'at full rate'

By DON LAVERY

THE jet which will take the Taoiseach and his entourage to Washington on St. Patrick's Day will be hired at full commercial rates, the Government spokesman said last night.

The use of a private jet should cut five hours each way off the trip, the spokesman added. The plane will probably be provided by the Jefferson Smurfit organisation.

Hiring an executive jet with the range to fly to the U.S. will cost about £10,000, and may even save the Taoiseach's entourage money when compared to the cost of executive class travel. The many landings and take-offs involved would also mean longer flight time for the party.

The use of the Government's own executive jet, the British Aerospace 125-700, has been ruled out. A spokesman at Hatfield, where British Aerospace produce the plane, said the 125 was excellent for trips around Europe by Ministers but it would have to make two refuelling stops at Iceland and Gander if it was used to cross the Atlantic.

Health hazard row on river water

By TOM SHEIL

AN UNHOLY water row has led to a rift between clergymen and some of their flock in a south Kerry parish.

Members of a newly established development committee claim that water which is being pumped from a nearby river into 123-pupil Killinliath National School, near Waterville, is a serious health hazard. But local priests are adamant that the supply is perfectly safe for human consumption and that frequent testing has proven this.

So strong are local feelings on the issue that a meeting organised by the development committee passed a vote of "no confidence" in the chairman of the Board of Management, Fr. Fergal Ryan C.C.

In a strong sermon on Sunday, parish priest Fr. Joseph Nolan, called for an end to the acrimony stating that he could guarantee that the water was safe.

Development Committee Chairman Donal O'Shea claimed yesterday that the servicing of the system was haphazard, and there was a danger of dead animals — some of them dogs which had been given strychnine — falling into the river. He said that his committee was prepared to raise the money to supply the school with water from a spring nearly two miles away.

School board chairman, Fr. Ryan told the *Irish Independent* last night that "one of the best pump and filter systems in the country" was installed on the school supply six years ago.

"The water was tested on Saturday and found to be perfectly safe for drinking," he added "I can understand the concern of parents but they have absolutely no need to worry."

In his sermon last Sunday, PP Fr. Nolan announced that he was having the system — which includes a chlorine treatment and charcoal unit — serviced tomorrow.

The £8,000 purification system installed in 1983 was "adequate".

37 Pictures on a broadsheet page – the *Irish Independent* crashed train coach being hoisted past a house establishes an instant eye-catcher, and takes the reader straight down through the headline to the intro. The tonal values are good and it benefits, with its left to right movement, by being placed on the left-hand side of the page. At the same time the two single column pictures of people involved give a human dimension to the text of the story and provide a middle of the page breaker. Panelling in the story with 2-point rules gives unity to the display and makes the page. The cropping in all cases is impeccable, accentuating in particular the composition of the main one. The picture in the advert adds to the visual balance of the page, and enables the chief sub to fill the remaining spaces with text and headline.

The broadsheet *Irish Independent* **(37)** has a bigger problem since the page lead has no picture. Here a virtue is made of an attractive picture of the homecoming of a boy athlete which is composed into a picture + headline + text module and used as a centre page fulcrum round which to wrap the lead. The end column of briefs on this busy news page serves as a barrier which prevents the boy from seeming to look out of the page. The remaining picture (top left), gives a necessary focal point to help balance against the headline, the boy picture and the prominent advert down the page.

The location of pictures in a design, it can be seen, draws the eye into and round the page. It is to achieve this effect unimpeded that both in location and subject they must not clash with, or repeat visually, material in the display advertisements on the page, or material on the opposite page. In arriving at the best effect from the materials allocated, taking into account the design style of the paper, the designer needs to ask: Is the page being over-pictured? Does the picture's quality warrant its size? Does the page contain unacceptable grey areas? Is the best use being made of the available pictures? The examples on pages 176-7 show some faults in picture use.

The many variables of size, composition and subject in pictures give variety to a newspaper's pages. There are, of course, other variables governing page design, and these will be examined in later chapters.

Picture desk

The picture input of a newspaper is channelled through the picture desk. This is controlled by the picture editor who performs a gathering and collating role similar to that of the news and features editors, briefing staff photographers on requirements of news and features pictures to be taken, and tapping other picture sources as necessary. The following **(38)** are the main picture sources.

Staff photographers

Newspapers, depending on their size and circulation, carry from three or four to as many as twenty-five staff photographers. Their work is integrated closely into the news and features gathering operation and staff photographers often work on assignments with a writer. They are aware of the paper's style and requirements and offer the best chance of exclusive pictures.

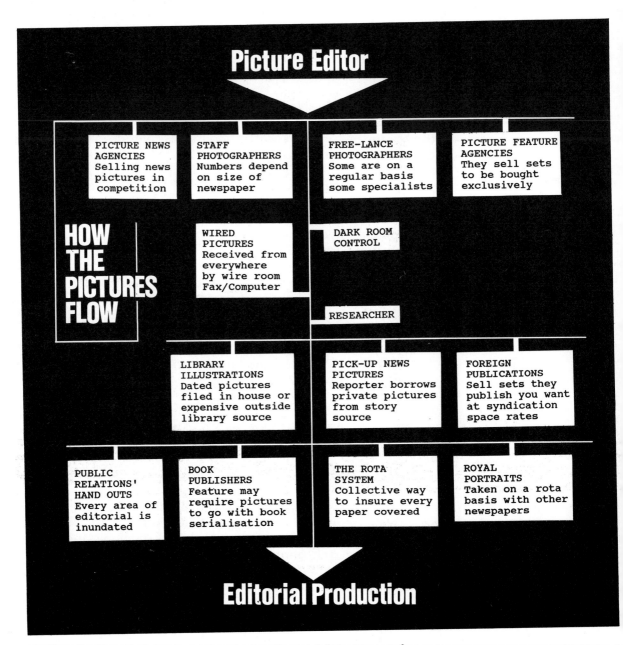

38 Picture sources — where the daily input comes from

Freelances

There are many freelance press photographers working in a variety of fields some heavily specialized into such things as glamour, fashion and industrial photography. They might be employed on particular assignments or on day-to-day or week-to-week arrangements, on retainer or fee, or particular pictures might be bought from them. Most freelances are used because of their special experience or reliability in certain types of work, or as holiday relief. Exclusiveness of work depends on the rights bought or the type of contract.

Picture agencies

There are a great many picture agencies serving both special and general fields. Some, such as the Press Association, circulate available pictures to subscribing newspapers to be selected and bought at whatever rights are appropriate. Some such as sports agencies rely on specific contracts for certain types of work, while others are used as required depending on their known specializations. Exclusiveness depends on the rights bought – first or second British, English language, book rights, world rights, etc.

Rota pictures

Major events, such as Royal occasions or celebrity picture calls, sometimes limit press photographers to a set number on the understanding that under the special rota system run by newspaper picture editors and news agencies the pictures taken will be made available to all papers subscribing to the rota. Photographers are usually chosen in turn from the various newspapers and agencies on the rota. The system rules out exclusiveness.

Pick-up pictures

Some news stories and, more especially, some features and series, depend upon pictures supplied by the subjects. They are often bought with the stories and are chiefly pictures of the subject taken on earlier occasions which might not otherwise be available. The question of ownership or rights should be checked before use.

Hand-out pictures

Showbiz pictures, including some glamour, or those from PROs or press officers are often available free because of the publicity value to the owners or subjects.

Picture library

The office picture files, going back in some cases as many as thirty years, are an important source of stock pictures for 'flashback' use or for head or 'mug' shots of politicians, sportsmen and other well-known people.

Briefing

The picture desk organizes the transmission and processing of live pictures and – through the picture library – their storage and retrieval for use. Techniques have greatly advanced in these areas. Film can now be processed on site and transmitted in negative form, in black and white or in colour, to be printed out at the receiving end and there, if need be, stored digitally for recall and selection. Portable transmitters have become miniaturized, long focus camera lenses reduced in size and increased in power, and cameras adapted for use for night photography.

Such things are peripheral to the design function, although they do speed up the availability of needed pictures, and – along with faster typesetting and page make-up – provide undreamt of facilities for getting the latest news coverage into the paper. Of more immediate importance is the skill of the photographer in getting the right shots and the right 'shape' of pictures, and of the picture editor in locating vital pictures from the various contact sources.

Staff work allows the advantage of a detailed briefing when pictures are being planned as ingredients of certain pages. The photographer might be told to include specific details, or to take particular people together, or to go for close-ups or shots that will lend themselves to horizontal or vertical shapes to fit planned slots on pages. An experienced cameraman (or woman), relying as they do these days on 35 mm film, will shoot off a sufficient variety of pictures to allow for such eventualities as a change of mind by the editor or page executive, a change of advertising shape on the page, or the transfer of story and picture for unpredictable reasons to a different page. It is possible that a shot tried on spec by the photographer might yield up a better picture of a different sort than was anticipated to the extent that the projection intended for the page is totally changed to fit it in – such is the balance between planning and pragmatism in picture use.

Picture editing

The task of editing pictures to size and subject falls to the art desk, or to the person drawing the page, and not to the picture editor, who is normally the executive in charge of picture procurement. A necessary preliminary is the choosing of the pictures and this is done usually by the executive responsible for the contents of the page, who might be the night editor, the features editor, the chief subeditor or even the woman's page editor (see Chapter 8). Under the art desk system the art editor would expect to be included at the picture tasting stage to give expert advice on a picture's possibilities and to relate it to the page design.

The main procedures in editing a picture are cropping, to give it the right printing image; scaling or sizing, to give it the right dimensions in the page; and retouching, to improve the quality.

Cropping

Few pictures are used in exactly the form in which they are taken or first printed. There are editorial reasons for including or excluding certain detail and artistic reasons for getting the best possible image out of the part that is to be used. Therefore the picture is cropped. This is done by marking the wanted part on the back of the print in pencil, while exposing it to a light source, so as to exclude unwanted detail and give the shape of picture needed for the page. This part of the picture is then 'shot' to produce a final print of the required image and size for the page. It can alternatively be done by pencilling in the cropped area as a tracing on the front of the picture **(39)**.

In most cases newspaper pictures are used for their functional role in providing a wanted image rather than being displayed simply for artistic merit, and this purpose can often be enhanced by cropping. The purpose might be to blow up part of the picture – perhaps one person in a group or one house in a terrace. Some pictures are cropped to improve the composition of the main image, or to exclude people or things that are not relevant to the story the picture is illustrating. Editorial purpose is the overriding thing. Pictures are not cropped to some abstract aesthetic standards. Some might not even be good pictures in the aesthetic sense; they might simply be the only ones available, with their usefulness depending upon right cropping and the improving of detail by retouching (see below).

What is a good picture from the photographer's point of view is not necessarily so when it comes to its function in the page. It must primarily serve the story it illustrates and the page design, of which it is a part, although it would be a foolish designer who ruins a good picture just to squeeze it into a preconceived slot.

There is usually a sound reason in the visualizer's mind for the way in which a picture is cropped, although this does not stop cropping being a subject of controversy among journalists. There is no doubt that bad cropping can destroy a picture's effectiveness, and the following guidelines should be considered.

A picture should be cropped so that:

1   The relevant parts of the picture's subject fill the main area to be printed.
2   Any distracting background or unwanted detail is excluded or minimized provided it can be done without damage to the picture.
3   People's features and other essential detail are preserved. For instance, in a 'mug' shot giving only a face the crop marks should leave in the whole of the chin, though they can come down on the

39   Cropping and scaling a picture. The dotted lines on the cropped image on the left – here shown as on a tracing – indicate how the required width measured across to the diagnonal determines the depth. The diagram on the right shows how the traced image is used to draw diagonals to determine the measurements for a step required top right of the picture

hair (unless the hair is a reason for using the picture); ears should be left in. Thus, while achieving the biggest image in the space, the essential features will not be damaged.

4   Any 'tilting' used in squaring off the cropped area to produce a more balanced picture does not create a nonsense by throwing verticals (lamp-posts, walls, fences, etc.) out of true.

5   Essential features or characteristics of a person or object are not misrepresented by excluding detail.

The example in **(40)** demonstrates cropping techniques at work.

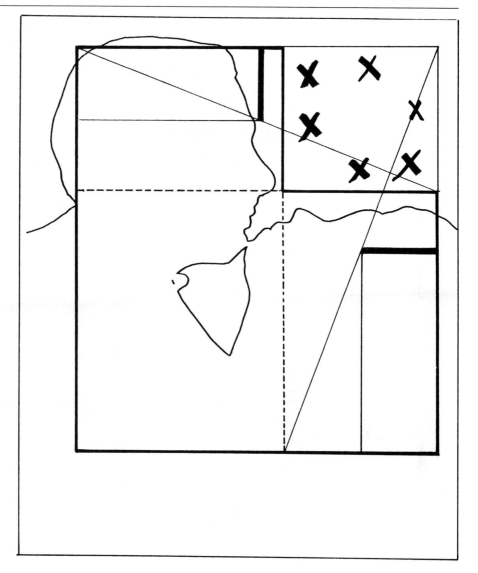

Scaling

The prominence to be given to a picture, or pictures, is a key decision
in formulating a layout idea. Having cropped the original to arrive at
the best image to print, the designer works out the size on the page by
scaling, or sizing, it. Invariably this means deciding upon a width
that suits the page – single column, double, four column, bastard
width or whatever – and then finding the depth by measuring from a
diagonal line drawn in pencil from corner to corner on the back of the
cropped area. The required width is measured across and the
distance from the point of intersection on the diagonal to the foot of
the cropped area gives the depth that the picture will make on the
page.

If for some reason, such as a proximate advert position, the depth is the critical measurement, then the chosen depth should be measured upwards to the diagonal and the picture's width will be the distance from the side of the cropped area to the point of intersection. The method works which ever way the diagonal is drawn, though the usual way is to draw it from bottom left to top right, as in **(39)**.

If the picture is intended to have a cut out edge or a sloping side to fit a montage or picture composite (see below) it should be squared off to its natural rectangle and the waste area removed afterwards. To scale the picture effectively the working area has to be a rectangle. If there is a difficulty scaling it to a size that will fit the space available, then the cropping should be checked to see if the picture area can be widened or deepened without damage to the image. In any case, cropping and scaling are usually done at the same time since requirements of size and space can influence how a picture is cropped.

BRITT'S IN FINE FORM

★ BLONDE bombshell Britt Ekland arrives for the premiere of the new Bond film Licence To Kill — and provides her own stunning double feature.

★ Sexy Britt, 46 — who played Mary Goodnight in the 1974 Bond movie Man With The Golden Gun — went on later to a private celebration party. Guests guzzled champagne and downed Mexican food. Hot stuff, Britt.

Picture: NIKOS VINIERATOS

A Britt of all write!

■ BLONDE bombshell Britt Ekland pops out for the evening — and shows why she's still a big draw for autograph hunters.

The sexy Swede may be 46 but she became a mum again last year and it's obviously keeping her young. Her nifty dance footwork was a real wow in the early hours at a London nightspot. Write on, Britt!

40   Actress Britt Ekland at a premier makes a striking picture . . . the cropping on the left shows her essential sex appeal; the rival paper's version, right, keeps in the pens of the autograph hunters, thus shifting the eye's attention

Calibrated wheels, or even a slide rule, can be used to do the job but the diagonal method is visual, simple, almost as quick, and avoids the danger of a mis-reading and is widely used even on the most sophisticated art desks.

Sizing pictures on screen

It is possible to crop and size pictures on screen where newspapers are moving into total screen make-up, although some problems remain. A machine called a Wisefax will show a picture editor all the day's input of pictures received by wire from every source in groups of miniatures. Individual choices can be blown up for closer inspection. The machine is one of a number that can be used to size the pictures stored.

This is achieved by the use of a mouse-operated cursor and an on-screen 'box' which can be moved by the cursor into any rectangular shape needed over the chosen picture. When the crop and size are right, a key command can send the marked-up picture to the Autokon laser printer to be made into a page-ready bromide.

One problem of this method is that no hard prints are available to the subeditors or caption writers until a screened Autokon print is outputted, normal computer print-outs from storage being generally poor. There can also be problems where a picture is required to be 'tilted' to get the best image or where a larger-than-screen reproduction is required, though the large screens available are overcoming this problem.

Retouching

The other important aspect of picture-editing, and one that causes almost as much controversy as cropping, is retouching. This is the improving of an original print by the use of a sable brush to sharpen detail or an air brush to blow back unwanted background, and it is done by specialist artists who should be under the control of the art desk since what is done to a picture is an editorial responsibility.

Retouching, which is carried out before the picture is shot for the page, is invaluable for pictures that for some reason are not of good reproductive quality. The general rule is that unwanted detail can be removed (provided the picture's purpose is not damaged), and poor detail improved by discreet brushing, but that absent detail cannot be created – or should not.

The essence of good retouching is that it is not noticeable on the printed page. Sharp visible lines or the working in of new detail can make nonsense of a picture and can also land an editor in legal trouble. The discreet removal of background can highlight people and features in the right picture, but retouchers should beware of 'fogging detail' so that the background looks unnatural, or so the subjects appear to be standing in a cloud.

A number of other things can be done to pictures to enhance them or the page.

Reversing

Reversing – known in computerized systems as *flopping*, from American usage – means simply shooting it for the page by using the negative the wrong way round, and is useful to avoid having faces looking out of a page or out of, for instance, a panelled-in features display. The device bristles with dangers such as a well-known person's hair being parted on the wrong side, a wedding ring on the wrong hand, and a jacket being buttoned up the wrong way round. It can be confusing to readers if an identical agency picture has the American President facing in opposite directions in the same pose in two different papers. More extreme dangers, if not spotted in time at page make-up stage, are cars turned into left-hand drive and number plates reading back to front. The device should be used only after a careful inspection of the original has ensured that no nonsenses are being perpetrated.

Closing up

Closing up people together by means of a scissors job on the original bromide is sometimes used to dispose of waste in the middle of a picture and can produce a satisfactory page image, but it is fraught with danger if, say, a couple are made to look so ludicrously close as to be out of character. It is a piece of editorial licence to be used with caution when an original is wastefully gappy and cannot be substituted. As with over zealous retouching it can lead to complaints to the editor, and is ethically dubious since once an original has been cut up its use is open to charges of fabrication.

Substituting backgrounds

Outdoor shots and seascapes are sometimes 'improved' by substituting different sky effects where this adds interest and does not clash with the circumstances in which the picture was taken. If this practice is extended to substituting more detailed backgrounds then the danger again is that it can lay the paper open to charges of tampering with a picture.

Montages

An enhanced effect of action or atmosphere can be gained by grouping pictures together in a block or pattern, where there is a linking theme. This is a useful ploy in a features layout where mood or a 'flash-back' element dominates a display. Flashbacks, (that is, happier days or earlier days shots or reproduction of a picture published previously) can look effective as *tear-outs*, or *rag-outs* with a black ragged tear line applied round them. Where, in a blurb or display, pictures are fitted together into a pattern along with type, sometimes in the form of WOBs or BOTs, the device is known as a *compo*, or composite.

Chapter 16 discusses aspects of editing colour pictures.

Legal aspects   It is possible to libel a subject by the way a picture is cropped or retouched and care should be taken that such work does not misrepresent anyone. And not only humans – a national daily was in trouble in the 1950s when an overzealous retoucher reduced the size of a prize bull's vital member and the owner, who relied on stud fees, sued.

6
The modern art desk

Modern newspaper design is centred more and more on the art desk, a production refinement at one time associated only with magazines. Here layout artists, or journalists whose speciality is layout, carry out a range of tasks to do with the presentation and projection of editorial material, ranging from picture editing to the preparation of graphics and the actual drawing of the pages and, nowadays, the utilizing of computer graphics both for paste-up and screen composition.

Many small papers still rely on the chief subeditor, or even the editor, to carry out such design work as becomes necessary, but the increased sophistication of materials and effects, and of computer capability, are resulting in more editors hiving off the design function and establishing an art desk, however minimal, within the editorial area. A common method is to have one art desk serving a number of papers in-house, although this tends to treat design as an assembly line process. Another is to have a suitably skilled senior executive, with the help perhaps of a trained graphic artist, entirely responsible for the design and house style of the paper, commissioning such extra art work as is needed.

On bigger papers a new breed of journalist/designer, professionally trained in graphic arts, is being recruited to staff art desks under an art editor. This arrangement takes the responsibility for design off the shoulders of hard-pressed chief subeditors who have enough to do with the actual editing. It also ensures that some regard is being paid to evolving a consistent and polished design style that will reflect the newspaper's character and make it attractive to readers. A third advantage is that it saves the newspaper's visual face from being at the mercy of a variety of hands, particularly at times of frequent staff changes.

The art desk system in no way diminishes the control by editors and senior executives over the planning and editing of material. Rather, if properly organized, it gives more scope and options to editorial decision makers and the means to more imaginative presentation. If, in the chapters that follow, the involvement of an art desk in the design process is assumed by the authors, it is because this is the way editorial practice is moving.

Origins of the system

An awareness by British newspapers of design as a distinct entity, rather than as a loose tradition, owes a good deal to the development of the so-called tabloid layout style by H. G. Bartholomew's *Daily Mirror* in the late 1930s. It was on Mirror newspapers that the first art desks appeared and functioned as central points for design. In the preparing of pages the duties of picture editor and art editor were initially blurred and newspapers suffered from neither function being performed properly. However, as awareness of the value of centralized design developed, a department gradually evolved that went beyond the simple scaling of pictures demanded by the shouts of a hard-pressed night editor.

The art editor, or with some grander publications the art director, became a powerful influence on the development of the paper's layout style. As the drive for higher circulations and more reader appeal grew in the 1950s and the system, with the easing of news-print restrictions, began to produce results in improved presentation, the art desk expanded into a fully manned department with a deputy and team of layout artists. The expansion of television at this time and of colour TV in the early 1960s made editors more aware of the need to compete visually with the rival medium.

Trust in the expertise of the art desk took time to develop. Senior editorial executives, dubious of the need for 'visualizers', went on putting their own pages together. Art editors would be thrown 'roughs' of pages by night editors and told to 'put that through the system'.

On the national tabloids the crucial development came in the early 1960s on the *Daily Mirror*, then reaching the peak of its success, and its sister papers. The method demonstrated its value in 1969 when Rupert Murdoch acquired *The Sun* and had it redesigned as a rival to the top-selling *Mirror*. By this time the Thomson titles at London's Gray's Inn Road, principally the *Sunday Times*, had moved into desk-based design, to match the paper's great rival, *The Observer*. The art desk had arrived.

As the method was seen to work other newspapers, particularly national ones selling in a competitive market, but also specialist ones and the bigger provincial titles, began to adopt it in the drive to give a professional look to their products. An important effect of the art desk system, with its integrated approach to design, was the teasing out of some of the faults that had bugged the old ad hoc methods in which layouts came with subbed copy from the subs' desk, and picture editors cropped and scaled pictures to their own fancy in between briefing photographers and running the picture library.

A trained visualizer could ensure that headlines did not run into each other from page to page, that editorial material on opposite pages did not fight each other, that pictures balanced properly one page against its partner and stories and pictures did not conflict with the surrounding adverts. Thus the piecemeal approach was replaced by design cohesion, with a working dummy of pasted up layouts or page proofs operating as a master blueprint.

Role of the art desk

Editorial production on a morning or Sunday newspaper is control-led by the editor or the night editor; on evening or weekly papers by the editor or deputy editor, and occasionally by the chief subeditor. For the purposes of this book these executives will be referred to as the back bench. Sitting with the night editor on a national paper (which is the model of this chapter) are the deputy and assistant night editors and sometimes a 'prodnose' whose duty is to read every word in the paper and query any suspect facts or grammar.

From the back bench comes the decision making – the selection of material and pictures that will make up the page contents – as the production cycle unfolds. Feeding into the system are the features from the features department, news stories from the newsroom and agencies, and pictures from the picture desk, with lists of forth-coming material being constantly updated in line with revised timings caused by various obstacles in the way of photographers, writers or machinery.

Production factors on any newspaper dictate that certain pages must be early on the processing list. Stock features pages, including TV listings, at the back of the paper come early, though on a tabloid paper pages at the very back must be kept open since they marry with the front late news pages on the final printing plate.

Now begins the first of the day's debates between back bench and art editor. It might concern a small news page at the back – small because the advertising space on the page happens to be heavy. Therefore the placing of the picture and disposition of stories is critical. The weight of advertising needs to be thought about for the editorial subject matter must be seen by the reader as reading priority. Should the reader's eyes swing to the advertising first, then the creative director of the advertisement is a bigger success than the newspaper's art editor.

As the debates proceed and layout sheets bearing squiggles begin to emanate from the night editor **(41)**, the art editor is roughly drawing ideas on a layout pad and amending them as back bench thoughts evolve. The art editor might suggest alternative ways of doing a headline to simplify the typographical approach or to carry the length of text better. The wording and general shape are quickly clinched, for time is the master. The chief subeditor is waiting for the page rough to be drawn in detail so that instructions can be passed to the subeditors on the treatment and length for stories and the setting and headline sizes.

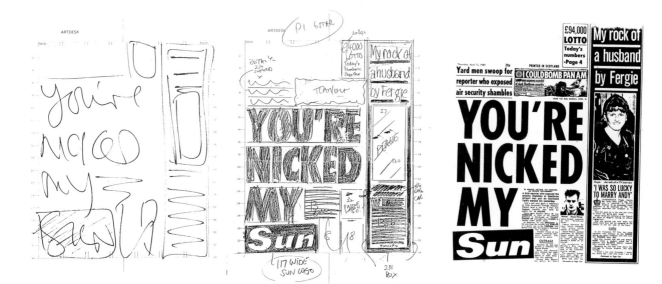

41 The three stages in creating a
page – the rough, the drawn layout,
and the ready-to-print page from an
edition of *The Sun*

The development from rough to finished layout (see also **Plates 2
and 3)** will test the accuracy and feasibility of the original concept. It
does not follow that because two 'great' minds have produced the
first page idea that it will work without some modification. The duty
of the layout person is to produce a finished design that will stand
several tests. First, the weight and lengths of stories dictated by back
bench decision should appear in correct relationship to the page.
Second, the type and setting used should come within the parameters of the house typographical style. Third, the page must be
given visual balance as well as a balance of contents. For accurate
visualizing, main headlines should be traced off from the type book
or, if in-house computer setting facilities exist giving instant outputs,
the heading should be set. The original setting can then be used in the
final paste-up or screen assembly.

The same care should apply to the chosen pictures which should be
blown or reduced to size on a Grant projector, from which the image
can be traced and applied to the finished layout. Trying a picture out
to size on a Grant can also reveal things not noticed on the original
print. There might, for example, be an area in a corner of a
photograph, which could take a caption or a chunk of intro without
damaging the picture, thereby helping locate the lead story better.
The Grant projector in which, by means of lenses and a screen, a
photograph can be inspected instantly at the size required, is the
work-horse of the art desk. Should a picture need to be used as a cut-
out effect, or be given overprinted type – common ploys in magazine
design – the accuracy of the Grant machine (see page 96) is vital.

The mechanics of the job

Pages, tabloid or broadsheet, are best drawn on full-size gridded sheets. The surface should be comfortable and smooth to draw on and the paper stout enough to withstand ill-treatment on the back bench, the subs' table and paste-up room as well as on the art desk where rubbing out and re-drawing of lines is not unknown. The sheets (they can usually be printed in house to suit) should be scaled in centimetres up one side and down the other side so that the stories can be measured in length downwards, and the adverts more appropriately upwards from the bottom. (See **(41)**)

Layout sheets should also be scaled across the required column widths of the paper, with a pica of white between columns, and show 18 points at the top of the page for the folio space enclosed in a parallel horizontal line running across the page. The sheets should be slightly transparent to allow show-through on a light box or Grant projector. For tabloid papers two sizes are required – one at single size and one at double-spread size with the grid showing a vertical centre gutter of appropriate width. Broadsheet papers need only their own single page size. In both cases it is possible to print the grids on A2 size paper.

Metric measurement is now universal in advert depths (that is, three columns by 20 cm; single column by 14 cm, and so on) while picture sizes, especially those not of standard column width are usually in millimetres (that is, single column by 36 mm; 48 mm by 36 mm, and so on) in place of inches. Page designers, however, still have to cope with traditional print measurements. Type sizes, as we have seen, remain in points. Although variation in size down to half a point is possible in computerized systems, most typesetting is formatted to give the standard series of sizes, which continue to offer the best guarantee of well planned type balance. Setting widths, as a result of American practice, are expressed in the systems in picas and points, and not in ems and ens. For precise calculation of measures when drawing the page, especially with bastard setting or non-standard picture widths, a print rule or gauge calibrated in picas and points remains essential.

The use of paste-up has made the eye more important in the absence of thick and thin metal *leads* (pronounced ledds), in assessing columnar space during page make-up, but the process is helped by the fact that make-up cards, as with layouts sheets, have the columns separated by a clear pica of space as well as being divided horizontally by centimetre lines measured upwards and downwards at the side to give text and advert depths. On the make-up cards these lines are in non-reproducible blue so that the grid does not show when the page is photographed to be made into a printing plate. With the simpler news pages the standard grid enables a page to be made up quickly. With features pages, where bastard measure, panel rules and non-standard picture widths are more likely, a trained eye is of the essence if white space is to be allowed to a consistent style.

Desk routine

As the page builds up on the layout sheet the smaller headlines are indicated by horizontal squiggly lines occupying the depth of the appropriate typeface – in perhaps 14 or 18 point. The main headlines, however, should be drawn to fill exactly the space they are to occupy in order to give an accurate depth for the stories under them. This information is needed by the subeditors handling the stories.

Attention is paid to 'colour' in terms of bold, roman or italic body type showing on the page. The layout person, with detailed knowledge of the paper's type style, will try to achieve a pleasing balance. Perhaps a column of briefs in column seven could be enhanced visually by alternating roman with bold items. A long single-column story could perhaps benefit by being set in reverse indent, with the first line of each paragraph standing proud on the left, a technique which gives variation in columnar white space but must be used sparingly.

When the layout is complete and the picture lightly drawn and identified in its rectangle, instructions to the subeditor/typesetter and to the page make-up person should be written on the margins of the page. Headline size and typeface should be indicated and any special setting commands such as 'set right' or 'centred', or an underscore or panel rule needed. Even if an instruction is obvious from the accuracy of the drawing it should still be marked on the layout, even down to sizes and widths of body type and – very important – the catchline of the story, by which it is identified in the setting system.

The more sophisticated the art desk operation the more in-depth are the instructions across the layout. Typefaces, for instance, might be indicated with computer command instructions with which the subeditor is familiar as he (or she) edits on screen. Picture widths and depths might be in millimetres, or inches depending on house style. Any step or slot in a picture should be marked precisely and nothing left to paste-up or screen operators' decision. All this saves delay in page make-up.

A check with facing pages to make sure duplication or clashes of typeface and pictures have been avoided should be second nature to an art desk person. Then the page number and edition are written at the head of the sheet and the top and photocopies are passed to the back bench to be circulated. No longer need there be an unlucky person who gets the barely legible fifth carbon. An important point here: a revised layout must be marked as such – if necessary as second or third revise – to ensure that the wrong version is not being used.

Meanwhile, on the art desk other pages are being worked on at different stages – a tabloid paper may run to as many as 64 pages – as the operation moves towards the final page of the edition, the front page, with its own special claim on the reader.

The routine on a broadsheet art desk is similar to that on a tabloid though, having fewer pages and often being less display-orientated, the pace is less frenetic. With some broadsheet papers the change to computer systems has led to design becoming more straightforward, with an accent on modular construction that lends itself to screen make-up. This means that items on the page will be put together in multiple column blocks that can be assembled into a page at paste-up or on screen, though the need remains to maintain a creative and integrated approach to design. Attention must be paid in modular patterns to type weight and balance as well as to size of item so that changes and replacement of story modules between editions can be effected without damaging the design (see Chapter 11).

Variations in headline size are not, on the whole, as pronounced in broadsheet styles as with tabloids. While imaginative changes have taken place in the design of many broadsheet papers, as will be seen in later chapters, some base their style on relatively few changes of type size so that the movement of the eye down the page is not so excited by individual treatment of stories. Perhaps a change in body type to bold or italic is permitted, or the panelling in of an item. Yet the technique of creative accuracy in page drawing is even more important on the relatively huge area of a broadsheet page. Picture size and cutting play an enormous part in keeping the interest of readers and helping them to choose what they should read first.

Tools of the trade

The Grant projector

Before the Grant projector's appearance in the late 1950s it was necessary to reduce or enlarge type or pictures for layout purposes by using tracing graph paper. One piece was laid over the picture or type and the other used to enlarge the image by increasing the tiny graph squares by an appropriate number. It was tedious and hard to get an accurate result. The Grant projector **(42)** has solved the problem.

There are several versions of projector marketed for this role but the Grant is undoubtedly the toughest. The principle is simple. Camera bellows and lens are suspended below a flat screen. The bellows contract and expand to give a focal point while a movable platform below the lens supports the artwork, pictures or type specimens. Two spindle handles, one on each side of the machine's front panel, control the two elements. Under a perambulator hood to keep out excess light is a glass screen on which layout paper or tracing paper can be laid. When the spindles have been adjusted together to give a sharp image on the paper, and regulated to give the size required by the layout, the image can be traced off directly on the paper. If needed, images can also be traced from, say, a parcel or a hand.

The original purpose of the Grant projector was for use in advertising studios. Some believe that newer technology will now mean the end of it. While this is unlikely in those offices that use one, there are available some very efficient rivals such as the high definition colour copying machines made by Konica and Canon. These will reproduce any flat original artwork or transparencies up to

42   Essential tool of the creative artdesk – the Grant projector

the percentage size required in less than the time taken to trace off an image under the hood of a Grant. But they cost nearly twelve times as much.

Others believe that large screen computer page make-up will render the Grant's operation redundant. It is worth noting that the projector makes possible the accurate marrying together of pictures to make one huge original simply by placing type, artwork or photographs on the movable table inside the projector and manipulating the lens bellows and platform. The image is then traced off on opaque layout paper on the screen at the top of the machine. This goes beyond the bounds of possibility in present pagemaker computers. The Grant also has the advantage of two lenses: long and short. It will blow a 35 mm colour transparency (which is illuminated by the built-in light box) with its long lens as well as it will reduce a 10 × 12 mono picture.

The light box

A free-standing light box on which pictures can be viewed face downwards on to a light source through a ground glass screen is another essential piece of equipment. Such boxes range from an A4 size with a handle to allow it to be passed round a busy department to a full-sized desk with a big light surface much favoured by newspaper art staffs. The facility to view mono pictures through their backs means that the editorial mark-up of picture areas to be used can be accurate. It also helps with composite picture work by allowing the operator to trace off the points where pictures overlap. Type overprints or white-out of words can be located correctly on the picture and, if needed, traced off in reverse on the back for even greater accuracy. Larger boxes are useful for see-through layout paper, which helps in complicated work, or when changes to drawn pages are called for. Type or pictures can be placed under the layout and be traced on to the sheet.

The light box has the facility, in the larger size, of allowing complete rolls of photographic transparencies, or contact prints, to be viewed at once – an important advantage in assessing fashion or big news picture coverage.

Pencils and felt-tip pens

Pencils – still the best tool for layout purposes – should be carefully thought about. Now that photocopiers have done away with multiple carbons, lines can be changed and rubbed out as the design comes together, so a soft eraser is a must, too. If all that is required is an accurate mechanical drawing for the make-up department or artist, then a 2H is the tool. It is precise because the hardness produces a very thin line. Remember, the thickness of a line can distort the finished total of millimetres even across the full width of a tabloid double spread or the depth of a single broadsheet page. If representation is needed on a layout then a full range of B (soft) pencils should be available. Large typefaces can be fully pencilled in with authenticity and a proper blackness. Where photographs have been traced off through a Grant machine to give a layout a polished and finished look, a range of pencils of varying softness will allow tone values to be copied at speed.

Felt tips in colour are dramatic to give visual effect to a finished layout but they should be used with care. The colour spreads and if a visual (as when creating a dummy) is used as a mechanical the calculations will not make sense. Some colours will not only spread but will penetrate the layout paper and ruin sheets beneath the one being worked on. A word of warning: this sort of pen can be dangerous when one is creating visuals under hot lights and a whole group of colours are uncorked at the same time. The headache that ensues can be the effect of the chemical which is the base or drying agent of the colours. Treat with care.

Tools of measurement

Every pencil and felt-tip pen feels at home running along the edge of a ruler – which happens to be the layout person's best friend. The ancient printer's gauge, made of dependable steel, is still the most reliable, usually with picas and 10 points on one side and inches and millimetres on the reverse. However, the shiny surface can reflect light, particularly strip lighting, and many mistakes have occurred through this. Another problem is that some are too comprehensive in print measurements, giving 5, 6 and 8 point as well as 10 points and pica. This can result in the user accidently reading off the wrong figure. The modern 18 in/45 cm rule is the best for drawing pages.

7
Graphics

Line drawings, scraper-board, charcoal and wash, even woodcuts, were among early forms of newspaper illustration that gave way to the photograph with the invention of the half-tone reproduction process at the end of last century. Since then the camera has dominated page design. Today there is a strong movement back into what has come to be called newspaper graphics. This does not mean that the photograph is in any way an endangered species – just that there is a new awareness of the potency of drawn illustration in conveying certain types of news and information.

Graphic artwork has never entirely been absent from newspaper pages. The big political cartoon of the Victorians stayed in fashion as did a variety of thumbnail cartoons by signed artists. Comic strips, both for adults and children, were increasingly used in the popular dailies from the 1930s as circulation pushers. Line drawings appeared with fashion articles on women's pages (43) and were resorted to when illustrating Sunday series, especially fiction, which was popular with 1930s newspaper readers. Yet, against the camera, artwork was not taken seriously in the main business of informing readers and illustrating the news and features of the day.

The change began with the Second World War in which maps and diagrammatic illustrations were devised to explain the fighting on the various fronts in a way that was beyond the camera. The chronicling of big battles in illustrated maps, with picture break-outs of the guns and tanks used became common in wartime newspapers.

One editor/strategist who was the 'officer in charge' at Kemsley's *Sunday Graphic*, which was noted for its picture coverage, had the entire North African desert war laid out on a sand table containing a whole cubic yard of sand. Models of German Tiger tanks and British Shermans, together with British 25-pounders and German 88-millimetre guns, were laboriously constructed and the battles, from El Alamein right up to the Mareth line, were fought out on the table

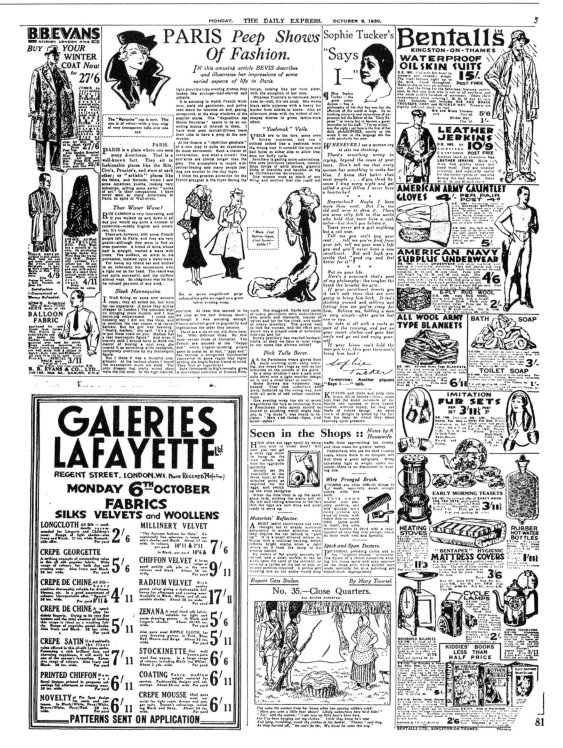

43 Fashion graphics in 1930 – the *Daily Express* looks at the Paris scene

week by week. Information was brought up to date each day and the contours of the sand adjusted to point up the difficulties under which the troops of Montgomery and Rommel were fighting. Early on Saturday morning the photographers would be sent into the huge 'war' room to photograph simulations of the latest battle scenes 'from the air'. Guns would be seen firing their puffs of cotton wool and bombs exploding. By this means, as they turned to the centre pages, the readers of the *Sunday Graphic* were given an armchair view of what it was like to be in the front line.

The *Daily Mirror* under H. G. Bartholomew, in its tight wartime format, pioneered the use of symbol graphics to explain simply to its readers the effects of government policy, of the latest budget, of the balance of armies in battles and the dietary value of wartime rationing, by presenting charts tricked out with little men and half men, guns, tanks and milk bottles.

Graphics generally means any non-photographic illustration, whether it be maps, diagrams, cartoons, comic strips or drawn symbols submitted or ordered, or provided in-house, used to illustrate the contents of a page. The days when a drawing or cartoon was chosen to lighten a page in the absence of a suitable photograph are a thing of the past. Today, graphic illustration is an art form in its own right that forcefully claims page space because it can do a required job better than any photograph. The rapid growth of the art desk system in newspapers is a recognition that there is more to artwork than drawing pages, scaling pictures and preparing blurbs. Newspaper artists skilled in diagrammatic reconstruction, 'exploding' pictures to simulate an event, caricature work, and the creation of ingenious information charts are in great demand. Nowhere is this more apparent than in the quality Sunday field where the interpretive approach to the week's news can be powerfully enhanced by graphics.

Cartoons and drawings

The use of stock symbols for charts and motifs has been made easier today by the many books of 'instant' **(44)** artwork and stored computer graphics. There is still a wide area covered, however, by traditional line work either submitted by freelance artists or agencies or drawn in house. This includes cartoons, full-size and thumbnail, comic strips and simple diagrams to go mainly with features, and drawn motifs for holiday pages and advertising and other supplements. The important thing in the drawing is that the lines be strong enough to reproduce easily on newsprint, bearing in mind that they are usually drawn to be two or three times reduced on camera. Problems of reproduction are likelier to crop up with work submitted on spec, staff artists and regular freelances being more aware of a paper's requirements. In the case of commissioned illustrative work the drawings must be geared to the mood of the words that are to accompany them and an artist should insist on

44 Instant art – what the stock books offer to enliven sports logos. An example from *Instant Art Book 1* (Graphic Communications Ltd)

being shown the text.

Contributing artists need to be aware of the need to enhance cartoons and strips with stick-on reproducible tints to give a drawing texture (easily available from art shops in sheets) and for colour washes to suit colour reproduction, now the thing with cartoons and strips in web offset-produced newspapers. A pressing demand exists, and a potentially high income, for comic strips with strong characterization and good gag lines, and an adult appeal, that will stand up to long-term publication in a regular slot.

Instant art

There are now many books of instant art available for a variety of editorial and advertising purposes. Simplicity in its use is essential. Symbols and little stylized drawings come in pages, catalogued by subject, to be traced off as needed for a quick chart or motif. Letraset and other art companies similarly provide stick-on art material **(45)**.

Art editors, and sometimes picture editors and advertising departments, usually keep a library of such books and materials, which are

45 Transfer graphics – some examples from Letraset's catalogue

particularly useful for smaller papers without skilled artists. They should be frequently updated since the artwork in them will reflect the trends in design at the time. Unless the journalist-designer is producing a vignette or dated effect, illustrations in a book even five years old can give an unwanted image.

A collection of previously used, or even rejected, illustrations is worth keeping around for copying on one of the sophisticated machines now in use when instant art is called for, although it must be regarded as a supplement to 'live' work produced in-house or commissioned.

Some companies specializing in the production of instant art offer only pieces in mono, though there is some sophisticated work around which is accompanied by colour separations for use in run-of-press colour should they be required.

For newspapers and magazines wanting to reproduce a period effect in a feature article there are compilations still to be found on the shelves of antiquarian bookshops. More modern authorities have made collections of ancient steel engravings and woodcuts culled from printers' stock rooms. These often include original swash and script illuminated lettering useful for ornamental drop letters and many other display applications. A monumental work was produced in 1973 entitled *Art For Commerce*, with the subheading *Examples from a valuable and curious book of engravings and designs the stock of a Victorian*

46 Samples from an old print specimen book

printer'. The Victorian printer was E. S. & A. Robinson, who flourished in Bristol during the late nineteenth century. The pages present a great range of period commercial examples which have the advantage being cleared for copyright purposes **(46)**.

A point to remember: where books contain variations on coats of arms (occasionally a useful motif in a feature) the publisher will warn that if the work is used in a heraldic fashion the College of Arms must clear the finished artwork before publication. It should be remembered, too, that care must be taken if British currency or notes are reproduced so that forgeries cannot be made from film or plates that ensue.

Type and half-tones in graphics

The main input of original artwork comes from a newspaper's own art desk and a good deal of it is concerned with the preparation of blurbs and compos (composites) specified in page designs in which a combination of typography, line work and half-tone might be used.

A *compo* is a useful device to set off a blurb or feature display by combining a type headline with elements of the illustration – a cut-out head or drawn motif, for example – often with the type reversed into a WOB or a BOT. The type can be the main headline or simply a label or logo. This device is used to provide a dominant focal point in all manner of newspapers **(47)**.

The commonest form of compo is the *logo* on a regular column or feature, which can consist simply of the writer's name and 'mug' shot in a type and tint panel. Such logos are most effective if the type and graphic devices are made appropriate to the person's style. The Philip Wrack column in the *News of the World* some years ago, which started as a half-tone full face shot with the name in type enclosed in a panel, became at one stage just the name and a stylized version of the writer's characteristic dark-rimmed spectacles. The *Daily Mirror*, too, used Marje Proops's exotic spectacles to good advantage in her long-running 'agony' series.

The quality dailies and Sundays and many of their European counterparts have pioneered the use of graphics in logos. *The Times*

47   *Top left*: the two blurbs – serious and popular – the aim is to catch the eye. *Below*: The use of type, line and halftone is shown to good effect in the selection of news and features page logos

identification logos use high quality artwork to give 'colour' to what used to be (not long ago) rather flat features pages, setting the mood and subject of text and writer. Even small support features below the fold have their own effective mini-logos.

Charts and graphs

Charts and graphs are a source of creative work for newspaper artists in which instant art symbols might be combined with stick-on tints or colour tones and line work to produce a main illustration for a feature with a strong statistical content. These can range from milk yields and baby booms to defence spending and soccer hooliganism. Tints from Letraset and other companies are an art desk stand-by in this sort of work and can give freedom and flair to the finished product.

Type

Dr Swee Chai Ang abandoned her NHS career to care for Palestinian refugees injured in Lebanon. More recently she moved to the Ahli Hospital in Israeli-occupied Gaza. She describes the squalor, brutality, terror – and determination – she has encountered.

Letraset stick-on (transfer) type is much used for effects calling for type outside the system's normal range of faces. Bizarre examples are available for special display calling, say, for stencil or cursive letters, or the bastardizing of letters to produce logos by ligaturing, or the altering of strokes to transpose type characters into eccentric designs. They give great freedom of thought and movement in one-off pieces of artwork and will always be more inspiring to a designer than using a keyboard, mouse or light pen for screen work. For quick results there is otherwise plenty of scope in modern photosetting systems for special typographical effects, such as condensing or expanding letters for a given result, provided that this usage does not spill over into the page's normal typography.

Pictures

The half-tone process allows pictures to be tampered with for graphic purposes. A dramatic effect can be given by coarsening the screen on a particular picture to emphasize its symbolic relationship to a story. Cut-out pictures will often enhance a feature display or a blurb compo, while a slightly distorted close-focus shot reproduced big will lend a touch of drama.

48 A bleached-out photograph can produce a dramatic motif to flag an important story as in these two examples

To give greater authenticity a *bleach-out* picture of a well-known face or landmark, such as a political figure, the clock of Big Ben or a pithead gear, can be used as a motif on a story or long-running series instead of commissioning a drawn one. The motif needs to typify the story to the extent that it does not need a caption. The effect is achieved by developing the picture on until all intermediate tones have been bleached out leaving essential detail in stark black and white **(48)**.

Computer graphics   Many pieces of artwork, especially logos, are in regular daily demand in a newspaper office and it is a good idea, in paste-up production, to keep a stock of copy bromides in a box file, and even to recover and keep usable artwork from finished pages. Types of original artwork which might be needed regularly can also be inputted and stored digitally in the 'pi' fonts of computer setting equipment and retrieved at will. In this way a library of instant art can become even more instant.

The advantages of using computer graphics, either supplied with the system or inputted from originals, are many. To be able to call up at any size a piece of graphics and superimpose it on screen on, say, a financial graph, or any other sort of overprint, has been the dream of designers for decades. The facility now exists.

The more sophisticated word processors have graphics disks of symbols and chart models the application of which can be extensive. If your newspaper cannot afford the more expensive on-screen make-up systems, then examine the possibilities of inputting Bit-stream software into word processors that are already in house. They may be able to supply sufficient graphics for the paper's general requirements either for partial or full on-screen make-up or for printing out for use with paste-up **(49)**.

Computer graphics can speed the work on a big occasion such as a budget or a general election. As Budget information is relayed from the Chancellor's lips to the copytaster's screen, graphics staff are searching their computer's memory banks for illustrations for the vital figures. Drink, cigarettes, motor cars and mortgages are high on the list. The prudent old hand will, in any case, have these symbols ready from instant art books, with drawn charts lying ready in permutations of column widths awaiting the figures that will bring them alive. With full screen make-up the corners have already been cut – the artwork is there waiting to respond to the artist's sizing and overprinting.

Laser graphics   The versatility of the Autokon laser graphics system **(50)**, now part of most computerized printing systems, should be another factor in the designer's pool of creative tools. Anamorphic sizing – that is, the

49   Computer graphics at work – how a page motif is created on screen

enlargement or reduction of an original along only one of its dimensions, or along both its dimensions independently – is of immense value. This controlled distortion in printing out material will allow a new range of thinking in areas of typography, line or pictures. The system's capacity to apply a wide range of tints and screens to order for use on charts and other artwork being printed out should be kept in mind. Special effect screens such as mezzotints, Greek maze, etch, brick, triangle, diamonds, rope and many line screens can be utilized in a designer's creative approach to a job. The capability of the Autokon needs to be carefully studied. Many of the eye-catching advertising illustrations on posters and magazines which appear to be handdrawn are 90 per cent Autokon productions.

The machine, through its special effects, offers an illustration facility which can produce a fast mechanical result when a tight deadline makes the use of an artist's illustration inappropriate. For example, by a method called solarization it can reproduce a section of a photograph or a piece of artwork as a negative image while at the same time increasing the contrast of the rest of the illustration. The screen repeat facility will increase the coarseness, either vertically or horizontally, of a photographic screen, which can be used to give an added dimension to a design. The control and shape of dot screens **(50(b))**, the ratio of black that can be allowed, the decrease or enhancement in a photograph's sharpness – all these give the journalist/designer access to a far wider range of tricks than ever before **(51)**.

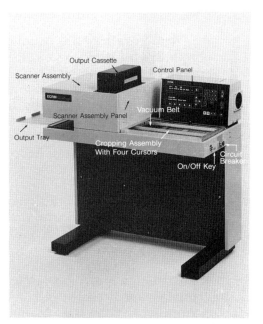

50 (a) The Autokon 1000 laser graphics system – principal parts

continued

50   (b) The range of screens available in the Autokon system

The accuracy of the Autokon makes it ideal in the preparation of bromides for colour work. Register will be perfect and the resulting openness of the finest dots will be reproducible. Solid types can be turned into an outline version and the thickness of the lines selected. This facility was originally built into the machine as a means of trapping a second colour but it can be used as a straightforward mono refinement. Even this variation can be achieved anamorphically inside the Autokon and distorted to the designer's command.

Operators of the Autokon in many newspaper plants are unaware of the capability of the machine they are using. Rarely is it in the hands of a journalist/designer who can use its design and 'editing' capability for artwork and pictures in the same way as the subeditor uses a monitor screen.

Information graphics

On-screen compilation of facts in the form of information charts is both fast and accurate and has become one of the great advantages of computer technology. The tedious and time-consuming beginnings of a chart that would require a ruling pen and a steady hand becomes a thing of the past. The keyboard and mouse will call up the lines, panels and boxes on screen with confidence that all the proportions

51   How dot control can change the emphasis when laser-printing a photograph

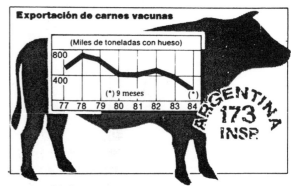

**Eliminan retenciones
a la exportación de carnes**

En medios allegados a la industria frigorífica trascendió que el ingeniero Roque Carranza, ministro de Obras y Servicios Públicos a cargo interinamente de la cartera de Economía, firmó ayer una resolución por la que se eliminan a partir del lunes los derechos de exportación que rigen para la carne vacuna refrigerada y que oscilan entre el 15 y el 20 %.

El documento, que sería publicado hoy en el Boletín Oficial, determinaría también algún nivel de reembolso para las carnes con mayor valor agregado incluido (cocidas y enlatadas). Si bien no trascendió este nivel, existía la creencia, con la consiguiente insatisfacción, de que no alcanzaría los porcentajes requeridos por la industria. El reembolso no sería mayor del 5 %.

De todos modos, y pese a la demora en el dictado de la resolución -la eliminación de las retenciones y el otorgamiento de reembolsos habían sido anunciados en Palermo por el doctor Raúl Alfonsín el 12 de agosto úl-

Exportación de carnes vacunas
(Miles de toneladas con hueso)
800
400
(*) 9 meses
77 78 79 80 81 82 83 84 (*)

timo-,la medida lleva cierta tranquilidad al sector industrial, ya que precisamente en estos momentos se encuentra en puerto un buque que viene a cargar aproximadamente 800 toneladas de cortes Hilton para la Comu-

nidad Económica Europea. El incumplimiento de este embarque hubiera puesto en peligro la continuidad de la cuota de 12.000 toneladas de ese tipo de cortes que la Comunidad tiene asignada a la Argentina.

52   A simple information graphic about beef exports prepared by Rolf F. Rehe for the Argentine paper *La Nacion*

will be accurate. When the basic frame is in place, the pieces of artwork required can then be called up and imposed at the point selected by the designer.

With the correct graphics disk programmed into the computer this will allow a wide variety of possibilities. Rolf Rehe's example **(52)**, used in the Argentine newspaper *La Nacion*, shows how the country's meat exports are declining. In it he boldly uses the facts reversed on to a large symbol of a bull, a concept that is a classic of its kind.

In most systems, however, the more advanced and complex charts benefit from paste-up being brought in to refine the end product. The computer is used as a tool on the understanding that at any time during the production of the artwork the designer can take a print-out so that embellishments can be applied by hand to the computer's part of the operation. In adopting this method, the chart, when complete on screen, is sized, printed out, and the print applied by paste-up to the page. Creativity can be improved by this combination.

Sophistication has grown in information graphics in recent years. The *Daily Star* in 1984, in its hot metal days, was concerned about the traffic of radioactive materials through built-up areas of Britain. It would have been easy to have written a simple news piece about the facts that had been uncovered but the editor knew that a graphic approach would push the story home more effectively. The feature was headlined THE ATOMIC DUSTBIN and the basis of it was that

53   A tabloid spread projection by Vic Giles on the perils of the 'atomic dustbin' (from the *Daily Star*)

54   Graphic treatment for a Live Aid campaign feature from the *Daily Star* – artwork and finished page

atomic waste from nuclear power stations, foreign as well as British, was being transported by rail and sea to the nuclear disposal site in Sellafield, Cumbria. The journalist/graphic artist team produced the double-page spread map **(53)**.

It had to solve two problems: to allow space on the map for text and headlines dealing with the different parts of the story, and also to allow for the presence on the double-page spread of a large advertisement consisting mainly of text. The shape of the available space precluded the first idea of superimposing the map on a black dustbin. Also time was short. The verdict on the spread as it appeared was that it could have been stronger in illustration, and that more could have been made of the shadow on the bottom of the map. Yet, in the short time available, the device achieved the editor's aim of riveting the reader's eye on the subject.

A double-page spread devoted to pop star Bob Geldof's campaign for support for the Ethiopia famine appeal, also in the *Daily Star* **(54)** showed an advance in technique. It was based on a huge surrealist guitar as a vehicle for a map of the world showing how countries were responding. At the same time the spread was packed with information for the paper's young readers – an important part of the projection. There can always be criticism: the elements across the top of the page, as can be seen, are fragmented, but the two halves of the spread are held together by the strip of pictures across the bottom.

USA Today, which sells widely in Europe, is a notable exponent of the mass readership graph. In fact, the idea of the paper is to provide the reader with eye-catching pieces of dressed up information. An example is the regular page one colour feature, USA SNAPSHOTS – A LOOK AT STATISTICS THAT SHAPE THE NATION **(Plate 4)** with its dramatic background cartoon work. Figures on pay for nurses in different cities, in this example, reach readers who are drawn to the feature by the humour of the artwork and then find themselves hooked by its geography.

USA Today using keyboard, mouse and light pen, deploys colour cleverly, placing tints to give an impression of a greater range of colour. Yet one of its most successful graphics effects in the edition illustrated, the artwork for the Super Bowl battle between Cincinatti Bengals and the San Francisco 49ers **(55)** relies only on mono. The projection, because of the three-quarter overhead view, enables the graphic artist to avoid giving the impression of players disappearing into infinity. The simplicity of the concept is continued into the descriptive captions, each one connected to the appropriate player by a fine pointer line. This is a good example of complicated factual information laid out in such a way that enthusiasts can relate the graphic details with the actuality of the television screen and almost forecast the players' moves.

News graphics   Schooled in the actuality of wartime graphics, postwar editors in

USA TODAY/International Edition • FRIDAY, JANUARY 20, 1989 • 15

AN IN-DEPTH LOOK AT THE MATCHUP

Keys to when Bengals have the ball

▶ **Line of scrimmage:** even. Bengals blockers are disciplined. A running team that believes in tight end offense (Holman and Riggs). Center Kozerski needs help on Carter, and Reimers (left guard) and Montoya (right guard) will have to pitch in. Munoz at left tackle will have to have a great day. He's big and strong.

▶ **Rushing:** slight edge to 49ers. Bengals will seldom see same defensive line faces in the same place during a series except for Carter. 49ers react well to run, but Woods will be a real force to contend with.

▶ **Passing:** edge to 49ers. Esiason is mobile — and will have to be — to avoid Haley. 49ers' corners are not great, but Lott and Fuller from their safety spots are solid contributors.

▶ **Kicking and kick returns:** edge 49ers. Both teams average on execution and coverage, but Taylor is a more dangerous runner than Jennings.

▶ **SUMMARY** — edge to 49ers' defense

Bengals strengths
Line overpowering, big, physical. . . . quarterback Esiason can throw long, throw short and scramble.

Bengals weaknesses
Lack of proven backups in all areas except running back and tight end. . . . Lack of a big-play receiver like Rice. . . . Can Bengals neutralize 49ers in various areas of either strength or speed?

How to defeat Bengals' offense
Pass rush: Because Esiason has so many options in his passing scheme, defense must be well-schooled in reading on the move. . . . Do a lot of stunting to interrupt quarterback rhythm.

How to beat 49ers' defense
Wyche must use all of his offensive guile and cunning and hold nothing back. This isn't the time to be timid or afraid to go for broke. Quick-hitting passes over the middle could cause the 49ers real concern.

Cincinnati's play-action pass

Because of its solid running game, Cincinnati can be especially effective with play-action passes. Quarterback Boomer Esiason fakes a handoff to the running back, forcing the defense to hesitate momentarily. Keeping the ball, Esiason drops back or rolls to his left and looks downfield for a receiver. He could throw to the tight end Rodney Holman. Or, he could go deeper to wide receivers Eddie Brown or Tim McGee who have time to get free because of the running fake.

1 Esiason fakes handoff to Woods

2 Esiason rolls to left and looks for Holman or Megee

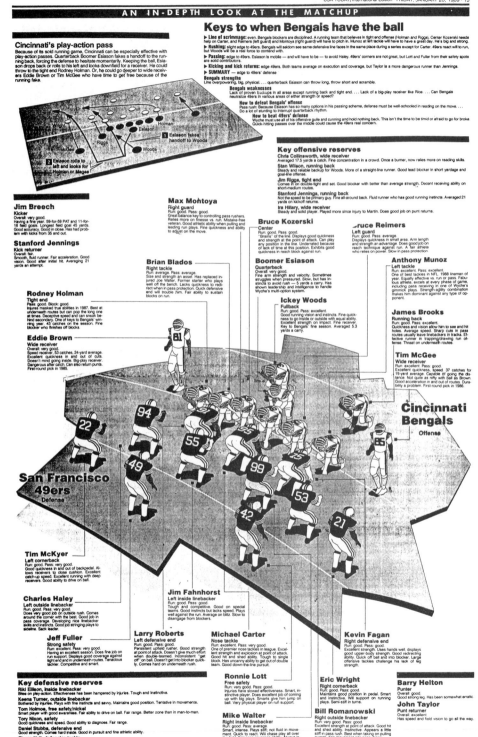

Key offensive reserves

Chris Collinsworth, wide receiver
Averaged 17.5 yards a catch. Fine concentration in a crowd. Once a burner, now relies more on reading skills.

Stan Wilson, running back
Steady and reliable backup for Woods. More of a straight-line runner. Good lead blocker in short yardage and goal-line offense.

Jim Riggs, tight end
Comes in on double-tight and set. Good blocker with better than average strength. Decent receiving ability on short-medium routes.

Stanford Jennings, running back
Not the speed to be primary guy. Fluid all-around back. Fluid runner who has good running instincts. Averaged 21 yards on kickoff returns.

Ira Hillary, wide receiver
Steady and solid player. Played more since injury to Martin. Does good job on punt returns.

Jim Breech
Kicker
Overall: very good.
Having a fine year. 59-for-59 PAT and 11-for-16 field goals. Longest field goal 45 yards. Good accuracy. Good in close. Has had problem with kicks from 35 and out.

Stanford Jennings
Kick returner
Overall: fair.
Smooth, fluid runner. Fair acceleration. Good vision. Good after initial hit. Averaging 21 yards an attempt.

Max Montoya
Right guard
Run: good. Pass: good.
Great balance key to controlling pass rushers. Relies more on finesse vs. run. Mistake-free veteran. Good athletic ability when pulling and leading run plays. Fine quickness and ability to adjust on the move.

Bruce Kozerski
Center
Run: good. Pass: good.
"Brains" of the line. Displays good quickness and strength at the point of attack. Can play any position in the line. Underrated because of lack of time at this position. Exhibits good quickness in reach block against run.

Bruce Reimers
Left guard
Run: good. Pass: average.
Displays quickness in small area. Arm length and strength an advantage. Does good job on reach technique against run. A fair athlete who relies on power. Slow in pass protection.

Rodney Holman
Tight end
Pass: good. Block: good.
Injuries masked true abilities in 1987. Best at underneath routes but can pop the long one at times. Deceptive speed and can sneak behind secondary. One of keys to Bengals' winning year. 43 catches on the season. Fine blocker who finishes off blocks.

Brian Blados
Right tackle
Run: average. Pass: average.
Size and strength an asset. Has replaced injured Joe Walter. Former starter who plays well off the bench. Lacks quickness to redirect when in pass protection. Quick defensive end will trouble him. Fair ability to sustain blocks on run.

Boomer Esiason
Quarterback
Overall: very good.
Fine arm strength and velocity. Sometimes struggles when pressured. Slow, but has instincts to avoid rush. — 5 yards a carry. Has shown leadership and intelligence to handle Wyche's multi-option system.

Anthony Munoz
Left tackle
Run: excellent. Pass: excellent.
One of best tackles in NFL. 1988 lineman of year. Equally effective vs. run or pass. Fabulous athlete, excels at every phase of game, including pass receiving in one of Wyche's gimmick plays. Strength-ability combination makes him dominant against any type of opponent.

Eddie Brown
Wide receiver
Overall: very good.
Speed receiver, 53 catches, 24-yard average. Excellent quickness in and out of cuts. Doesn't mind going inside. Big-play receiver. Dangerous after catch. Can also return punts. First-round pick in 1985.

Ickey Woods
Fullback
Run: excellent. Pass: excellent.
Good running vision and instincts. Fine quickness to go inside or outside with equal ability. Excellent strength on impact. Fine receiver. Key to Bengals' fine season. Averaged 5.3 yards a carry.

James Brooks
Running back
Run: good. Pass: excellent.
Quickness and vision allow him to see and hit holes. Average speed. Sharp cuts in pass routes usually leave linebackers in tracks. Effective runner in trapping/drawing run offense. Threat on underneath routes.

Tim McGee
Wide receiver
Run: good. Pass: good.
Excellent quickness, speed. 37 catches for 19-yard average. Capable of going the distance. Not quite as nifty with ball as Brown. Good acceleration in and out of routes. Durability a problem. First-round pick in 1986.

Cincinnati Bengals
Offense

San Francisco 49ers
Defense

Tim McKyer
Left cornerback
Run: good. Pass: very good.
Good quickness in and out of backpedal. Allows receivers to close cushion. Excellent catch-up speed. Excellent running with deep receivers. Good ability to drive on ball.

Charles Haley
Left outside linebacker
Run: good. Pass: very good.
Does very good job on outside rush. Comes around the corner with the best. Good job in pass coverage. Developing nice linebacker skills and instincts. Good job stringing plays to sideline. Sack leader.

Jeff Fuller
Strong safety
Run: excellent. Pass: very good.
Having an excellent season. Does fine job on run support. Displays good coverage against tight end and in underneath routes. Tenacious tackler. Competitive and smart.

Jim Fahnhorst
Left inside linebacker
Run: good. Pass: good.
Tough and competitive. Good on special teams. Good instincts but lacks speed. Plays well against the run. Average on blitz. Slow to disengage from blockers.

Larry Roberts
Left defensive end
Run: good. Pass: good.
Persistent upfield rusher. Good strength at point of attack. Doesn't give much effort when double-teamed. Inconsistent "get off" on ball. Doesn't get into blocker quickly. Comes hard on underneath rush.

Michael Carter
Nose tackle
Run: excellent. Pass: very good.
One of premier nose tackles in league. Excellent strength and explosion at point of attack. Good hit and shed ability. Tough to single block. Has uncanny ability to get out of double team. Good down-the-line pursuit.

Kevin Fagan
Right defensive end
Run: good. Pass: good.
Excellent strength. Uses hands well, displays good upper-body strength. Good redirecting ability. Quick off ball and into blocker. Large offensive tackles challenge his lack of leg strength.

Ronnie Lott
Free safety
Run: very good. Pass: good.
Injuries have slowed effectiveness. Smart, instinctive player. Does excellent job of coming up with big plays. Smarts give him jump on ball. Very physical player on run support.

Eric Wright
Right cornerback
Run: good. Pass: good.
Maintains good position in pedal. Smart and instinctive. Will support on running plays. Semi-stiff in turns.

Barry Helton
Punter
Overall: good.
Good strong leg. Has been somewhat erratic.

Key defensive reserves

Riki Ellison, inside linebacker
Bites on play-action. Effectiveness has been hampered by injuries. Tough and instinctive.

Keena Turner, outside linebacker
Bothered by injuries. Plays with fine instincts and savvy. Maintains good position. Tentative in movements.

Tom Holmoe, free safety/nickel
Smart player with good awareness. Fair ability to drive on ball. Fair range. Better zone than in man-to-man.

Tory Nixon, safety
Good quickness and speed. Good ability to diagnose. Fair range.

Daniel Stubbs, defensive end
Good strength. Comes hard inside. Good in pursuit and fine athletic ability.

Pierce Holt, defensive tackle
Power rusher, exhibits good quickness. Good strength at point of attack. Competitive. Good pursuit. Problem redirecting.

Mike Walter
Right inside linebacker
Run: good. Pass: average.
Smart, intense. Plays stiff, not fluid in movement. Quick to react. Will chase play all over the field. Fair pass coverage ability. Always in good position. Overreacts in play-action pass.

Bill Romanowski
Right outside linebacker
Run: good. Pass: good.
Excellent strength at point of attack. Good hit and shed ability. Instinctive. Appears a little stiff in pass rush. Best when taking on pulling guards. Fair movement into pass drops.

John Taylor
Punt returner
Overall: excellent.
Has speed and field vision to go all the way.

14 · FRIDAY, JANUARY 20, 1989 · USA TODAY/International Edition

AN IN-DEPTH LOOK AT THE MATCHUP

The information on this page is provided by Media Sports Research, Inc., based in Lake Oswego, Ore. The company's president is John Ralston, a former NFL head coach who led the Denver Broncos to their first Super Bowl appearance in 1978. Larry Bryan, a former scout in the NFL and USFL, conducts its football research. MSR was founded in 1987 by Jay Baldwin, a clothing manufacturer, to provide a handy, insiders-like guide for the pro football fan.

San Francisco's 'pick' play

San Francisco uses its "pick" play to get receiver Jerry Rice free against man-to-man coverage. Rice will line up in the slot with cornerback Lewis Billups in single coverage. Rice goes in motion, with Billups following him across the field. Rice will break upfield and cross behind Craig, the halfback, who picks (or screens) Billups. Rice then is open for the pass.

Keys to when 49ers have the ball

► **Line of scrimmage:** slight edge to 49ers. The 49ers must do a job on Krumrie who is the heart of the Bengal efforts up front. Bengals' Fulcher can disrupt any plan of attack if allowed to do so. 49ers must know where he is at all times.

► **Rushing:** even. Buffalo, a solid if not spectacular rushing team, could not run against Bengals. Krumrie once again anchors everything. Craig has the ability to battle anybody. This could be one of the game's top confrontations.

► **Passing:** edge to 49ers. In his last two outings, Montana has been amazing. During the same span, Rice has caught five touchdown passes. But Montana is not as mobile as he used to be and must be protected.

► **Kicking, kick returns:** even. Cofer has had a fair year. Return men favor 49ers (Taylor) with coverage for each about the same.

► **SUMMARY: Edge to 49ers' offense**

49ers strengths
Quarterback Montana is outstanding at executing the Walsh offense. . . . Running back Craig is a hard worker can make big plays. . . . wide receiver Rice is the best in the business.

49ers weaknesses
Line is young and inexperienced at present (except for Cross), but could develop rapidly. . . . Tight end Frank an exceptionally good blocker, but there is quite a drop off to Ron Heller and Brent Jones. . . . Fullback Rathman can block but is an ordinary ballcarrier who simply relies on the defense being surprised when he gets the ball.

How to defend 49ers' offense
Must interrupt the rhythm of Montana's passing. . . . Use four-man rush; blitzing is not generally effective against this team. . . . If too much blitzing or use of "46" defense, Montana will counter with short drops or sight adjustments. . . . Gang tackle Roger Craig, who is a high-knee, strong-as-a-bull runner.

How to beat Bengals defense
Attack deep: Montana and Rice might have great success against man coverage. . . . Sweeps and off tackle: Craig has to get off the mark again after frozen Chicago field. Be patient: Montana can hit with Craig, find Rice on short post patterns, and take advantage of average linebacking.

Mike Cofer
Kicker
Overall: good.
Beat out Ray Wersching, 15-year vet. Gives team better kickoff strength.

Harry Sydney
Kick returner
Steady player. Has good inside running vision. Good strength after initial hit.

Key offensive reserves
Steve Young, quarterback: Has knack of moving out of the pocket to make the big play. Best in play-action, half-roll, short game.
Doug Dubose, running back: Tough and competitive. Good burst up the inside.
Mike Wilson, wide receiver: Press technique bothers him.
Ron Heller, tight end: Displays good quickness in pass routes. Tough and determined blocker but lacks strength.
Bubba Paris, offensive tackle: Has ability, size and strength. Speed rusher a problem. Lacks redirect quickness. Former starter.
Bruce Collie, tackle/guard: Fine strength on running plays. Uses hands well in pass protection. Will finish off blocks.
Harry Sydney, kick returner/running back: Steady player. Good strength after initial hit. Lacks speed to be true threat.

Harrison Barton
Right tackle
Run: very good. Pass: good.
Very good strength and power at point of attack. Displays quick pass set ability and footwork. Has problem with speed rusher on outside shoulder. Hard worker and determined. Very good sustain ability on run blocks. Has good movement on cutoff blocks.

Joe Montana
Quarterback
Run: good. Pass: excellent.
Very good mobility in pocket. Excellent vision and instincts. Quick to find and hit secondary receivers. Excellent mechanics and ball-handling. Competitive. Throws well on rhythm routes. Very heady player; seems to make big plays when needed.

Randy Cross
Center
Run: good. Pass: good.
Instinctive player. Gets most out of his ability. Positions well and uses hands well in pass blocking. Not an overpowering player. Has problem with stronger pass tackles when athletic ability cannot overcome lack of strength.

John Frank
Tight end
Run: average. Pass: good.
Fine quickness and strength. Blocks high and settles. Competitive but lacks punch on drive blocks. Smart player. Good receiving on short and medium routes. Good run after catch.

Tom Rathman
Fullback
Run: good. Pass: good.
Does good job on inside running plays. Very good lead blocker with power and strength. Fine receiving skills out of backfield. Competitive player. Straight-line runner. Excellent strength and effort after initial hit.

Jesse Sapolu
Left guard
Run: good. Pass: good.
Displays good quickness in cutoff blocks. Fine athletic ability when pulling and leading. Gets overextended at times when pass protecting. Tough and determined player. Has overcome many injury setbacks.

Roger Craig
Running back
Run: very good. Pass: good.
Excellent leg and hip strength. High stepper. Good vision and acceleration. Excellent effort after initial hit. Highly competitive. Fine running vision inside and out.

Guy McIntyre
Right guard
Run: very good. Pass: good.
Very good strength and power at point of attack. Good pass set quickness. Good balance and base on drive block. Sustains his position well. Has good ability to adjust on the move.

Steve Wallace
Left tackle
Run: good. Pass: good.
Keeps good position in pass protection. Fast inside rush bothers him. Good work habits, ability to sustain on the move. Positions well on running plays. Fine strength at point of attack. Arm length on pass protection is an asset.

Jerry Rice
Wide receiver
Run: very good. Pass: excellent.
Premier receiver in the NFL. Excellent ability by all measures. Very deceptive speed. Benefits from playing in Walsh's system. Can go the distance on any play. Has some problems when pressed up close.

John Taylor
Wide receiver
Run: good. Pass: very good.
Excellent athletic ability. Smooth and fluid runner. Good acceleration in and out of routes. Can do the distance. Not quite as disciplined in routes as Rice.

San Francisco 49ers Offense

Cincinnati Bengals Defense

Eric Thomas
Right cornerback
Run: good. Pass: good.
Excellent speed and burst to ball. Vastly improved over rookie season. Fine instincts and awareness. Good run support. Loses his position on receiver at times. Leads secondary with eight interceptions.

Solomon Wilcots
Free safety
Run: good. Pass: average.
Smart and competitive. Good run support. Displays range and movement to ball. Has good burst. Lacks burst. Former college corner with good awareness.

Reggie Williams
Right outside linebacker
Run: good. Pass: good.
Leader and stabilizer. Good instincts and movement. Lacks burst in pursuit. Maintains good position and leverage. Steady and instinctive. Quality person, dedicated, highly competitive.

Joe Kelly
Right inside linebacker
Run: good. Pass: excellent.
Pursuit ability more suited to playing outside. Excellent quickness and movement. Good change of direction in pass coverage. Makes some big plays. Injuries have hurt his development. Displays good burst when blitzing.

Jason Buck
Right defensive end
Vastly improved from '87. Good movement and instincts on pass rush. Does good job in down line pursuit. Lacks quick burst to ball. Needs to disengage from blocker quicker. Good work ethic and attitude.

Lewis Billups
Left cornerback
Run: good. Pass: good.
His development is one of '88 keys for success. Good speed and quickness. Good change of direction. Plays better up and pressing receiver. Lets cushion grow at times. Overruns receivers on deep routes. Good run support.

Lee Johnson
Punter
Overall: average.
Versatility an asset. Can kick off and punt. Acquired from Cleveland. Displays fine touch and strength.

Ira Hillary
Punt returner
Overall: average.
Good hands and makes good decisions. Has better-than-average escape ability.

David Fulcher
Strong safety
Run: superior. Pass: good.
Linebacker in secondary. Excellent run support. Quick to find and hit secondary routes. Has fine speed and athletic ability. Might be heavier than listed weight. Has problem with covering lighter and quicker tight ends.

Leon White
Left outside linebacker
Run: good. Pass: good.
Intense and dedicated player. Good quickness and strength at point of attack. Good in pursuit. Has pass-defending ability. Good instincts and reactions. Comes hard on blitz.

Jim Skow
Left defensive end
Run: good. Pass: average.
Fine strength and quickness. Deceptive pass rusher who can apply pressure. Intense worker with fine instincts. Has filled in at left end for injured McClendon. Gives away 30 pounds against most opponents.

Tim Krumrie
Nose tackle
Run: very good. Pass: average.
All-Pro for second consecutive year. Highly productive. Excellent strength at point of attack. Determined and relentless. Maintains fine balance. Tough to handle one-on-one.

Carl Zander
Left inside linebacker
Run: good. Pass: average.
Steady and competitive. Tough against run. Displays good lateral movement. Fair range and movement in pass coverage. Rarely out of position. Good straight line speed.

Key defensive reserves
David Grant, defensive end Comes in on pass downs. Good takeoff on pass rush. Has improved steadily in his rookie season.
Rickey Dixon, free safety Excellent speed and movement. Displays good burst to ball. Late to training camp has hindered development. Capable of some big plays.
Leo Barker, linebacker In on passing situations. Fine movement and speed. Good situation player.
Barney Bussey, strong safety Nickel and dime defender. Solid player against run. Does good job on underneath coverage. Lacks speed and range. Fine player on special teams. Former USFL starter in Memphis.
Ray Horton, free safety Good instincts and movement. Lacks speed to play corner. Good awareness as free safety. Plays well on special teams.

55 The big show – a double broadsheet spread in *USA Today* given over to the Super Bowl final Copyright 1989, *USA Today*. Reprinted with permission

Fleet Street began to employ art school graduates to help make news events 'leap' out of the page. An earthquake story would show how villages at the epicentre were affected and the artist would put himself (or herself) inside the event and show landslides tracking across the page. A big robbery would conjure up a map of the robbers' tracks through the streets with actual photographs combined with drawn work reconstructing the event. Or a drawing would reconstruct from an eyewitness's account thieves making their snatch, then killing and injuring. Often the headline would integrate with the drawing, while accentuated shadows would increase the drama for the reader and give the eye an impression of leaping from the flat plane of the newspaper's surface.

In news graphics, the computer can give a quick response but the result, however well manipulated, will always appear mechanical against the work of the professional graphic artist. This is why the most effective newspaper artwork can be found in such papers as the *Sunday Times* and *The Observer* **(56, 57)**. When a big story breaks mid-week, by Saturday night there has been time to produce a researched inside page story based on a detailed and sophisticated graphics centrepiece.

This approach to news is gaining more followers, especially in areas where news pictures are impossible or not allowed. Court room

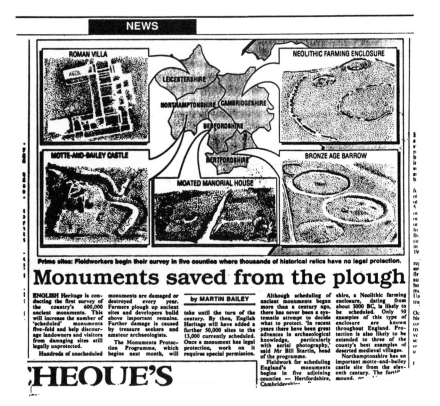

56 Archaeology in graphics – a novel application by *The Observer*

scenes in noted trials are a first favourite, with even television leaning to this technique. The artist attends with the reporter and notes the positions and facial characteristics of people and the surroundings of the dock and witness box so as to give authenticity. Care must be taken about the laws of contempt. Juries' features must not be shown. The artist should consult the reporter on legal protocol. The likenesses of well-known people can be researched from stock pictures. Artists who can produce this kind of work at speed can command a high fee and are invariably sought-after freelances.

Political controversy can be pictured in this way, with reconstructions of Cabinet room rows and dramatic debates beyond the presence of the camera. Again, surroundings and well-known people's features must be authentic, with even the kinds of drinking and water glasses on a table under scrutiny.

An effective example of a news graphic occurred in the *Daily Express* in the edition of July 7, 1978 **(58)** when the situation on board a wrecked night sleeper could only be truly rendered by a piece of graphical artwork. The headline INSTANT DEATH BEHIND CLOSED DOORS told the essence of a story which was that people could not break out of their blazing coach. While inside page pictures developed the detailed coverage, the artwork on page one posed the vital question: Were the carriage doors locked? The graphic reconstruction, while something of a comment as well as a question, had hit the point that became most relevant in the subsequent inquiry.

57 Highlighting a food controversy – emotive use of graphics in *The Sunday Times*'s New Society section

58   News in graphics – *Daily Express* handling of a rail crash in a Vic Giles projection

The movement into news graphics to give an extra dimension to illustration has been most pronounced in national newspapers where there is the stimulus to get a step ahead of a rival paper in big stories. How the terrorists got aboard . . . how the ship came to capsize . . . how the bank robbery was set up . . . how the police rescued the hostage. In stories like these a skilled artist can construct and reconstruct so that known facts are brought more vividly to the reader, often through montages in which half-tone combines with line drawing.

Let us look at a typical situation. A jumbo jet with hundreds of people on board has crashed after what is believed to have been an explosion. The picture editor gets from the library stock pictures of the sort of aircraft involved – say, a Boeing 747 in flight – preferably carrying the logo of the airline. The night editor alerts the art desk and calls for a map to indicate the flight path. A designer's plan of the aircraft's interior, it turns out, is available from file. This could help in rendering authentic detail although for the moment the cause of the disaster is conjecture.

Gradually, incoming copy indicates further details – where and how the wreckage fell, the position of the aircraft on the ground. Did it disintegrate in the air, and how?

By this time the artist has been given a new briefing. A decision has been made that the map must include an aerial drawing of the actual explosion, which is now known to have occurred. From crumbs of information in copy of the way the wreckage is lying on the ground, the artist forms a view of the likeliest scene. Should time be short, use will be made of an actual photograph printed to the size needed for the artwork and processed on the Autokon (see page 109) in such a way as to look like a drawing. The next step will be to literally tear the aircraft artwork apart at the points where it is assumed the explosion happened. The pieces are stuck down on the art board in their assumed order and position. The explosion is then drawn on to the board over the aircraft's flight path on a topographical impression of the town or country beneath. The disintegrated image will show pieces below or well away from the main structure in keeping with the information available.

While the artwork is put together, the subeditor is preparing the story from incoming copy sources, at the same time supplying bits of information to attach to the drawing. Meanwhile the overall dimensions of the job are given to the night editor so that allowance for the shape of the picture, when sized, can be made on the page rough.

Correct sizing and choice of size are the vital keys to the layout. It is better, in a case like this, that the shape of the artwork govern the page design rather than an arbitrary shape cramp the artist's ability to render the scene properly. Each happening demands different considerations of space. In some cases, allowance for sky is important to give correct proportion. Once proportions and effects of distance are lost the reader becomes confused. The design must also make correct allowance for captions and name tabs, which will need to be set separately, perhaps reversed as white on black (WOB) and imposed on the work. Drawn lines and arrows help the reader here. Tabbing and captioning artwork properly is also important to draw the reader's eye to the significance of the drawing. Applied tints can enhance part of it and give it 'lift' from the page through the subtlety of shadow.

Colour applications require even greater care because there will be

Philip Howard

Times Roman centurion

Today is the centenary of the birth of one of the oldest and most influential of the noble army of *Times* men. For 30 years he was the *éminence grise* of Printing House Square, and keeper of the conscience of *The Times*. A slight figure, in thick, steel-rimmed spectacles, dressed invariably in a black suit with a white shirt and black tie, and outdoors with a silly little black hat, he struck strangers as looking like a Jesuit. He referred to his paper with affectionate mock depreciation as "the sheet", or in the style of an old-fashioned citizen of London, "the House". They say you could hear the capital H.

Stanley Morison was a mess of contradictions: devout Roman Catholic and Marxist and conscientious objector; austere and a keen clubman; shy and a show-off; learned and silly; humble and vain; enjoying pantomime songs and Gregorian plain chant. But the oddest thing about this archetypal *Times* man was that he was not a journalist at all, but a typographer. He introduced the revolutionary notion that *The Times* should be good to look at and a pleasure to read, even if you disagreed with what it said.

The story starts on September 10, 1912, when Morison, a disgruntled clerk at the London City Mission, read *The Times* printing supplement. This was his vision on the road to Damascus, and concentrated his mind for the rest of his life on the study of letters, written and printed.

He became Britain's greatest authority on letter design, and freelance typographical consultant to several publishers, including the Cambridge University Press. He came to *The Times* as the result of rude remarks he made in 1929 to a *Times* rep about the paper's drab and old-fashioned appearance.

In those days, if you wanted actually to read the paper rather than merely to be seen carrying it under your arm, you needed

keen eyes and dogged determination to plough through the unbroken furrows of inspissated thin print, broken rarely by a plonking headline across one column. The rep reported Morison's remarks back to the manager, and the manager appointed the whizz-kid of print as typographical adviser to *The Times*, and asked him to devise a new typeface for the old paper.

In a characteristic memo, Morison wrote (in very small part) that a new typeface had to be "worthy of *The Times* — masculine, English, direct, simple, not more novel than it behoveth it to be novel, and absolutely free from faddishness and frivolity". Typography is a cannibalistic art, feeding off previous types, since only a finite number of faces to represent letters is available to human ingenuity.

Nicolas Barker, Morison's biographer, concluded that the original model for Times New Roman was the "Gros Cicero" type of the French punch-cutter Robert Granjon, dating from about 1568. Whatever its origin, Morison's new typeface became the most widely used typeface of the 20th century, still used *passim* in books and magazines.

The change of type at *The Times*, made over a weekend with no loss of production, involved bringing in 35 tons of new metal and many thousands of new matrices for the machines that set the type. But on Monday morning readers were amazed (and on the whole gratified, except for those who grumble at any change in anything) to see white space around the words, making the page more attractive, and even readable without a magnifying glass.

There were still only single-column headlines, of course; but the new type led the eye easily along the line, yet was strong enough to withstand the pressures of mass production printing. And, good grief, what was this? The Gothic

title-piece at the top of the front page had been replaced by Times New Roman. This was the holy of holies, because traditionalists regarded it, together with the Royal Arms (to which, incidentally, the paper is not entitled) as immemorial hallmarks of *The Times*. Morison outflanked them with tradition, by demonstrating that the earliest issues of *The Times* had Roman, not Gothic, title-pieces. He was not allowed to bring the Royal Arms, still quartering the Arms of France and Hanover, up to date.

Morison's position at *The Times* developed into something much more than adviser on printing. He edited and largely wrote the four-volume *History of The Times*, and was for two years editor of *The Times Literary Supplement*. He became the unofficial adviser to two successive editors on organization, appointments of staff, and even for a time about editorial policy. Morison himself spoke (rather too much for his own good) of his "occult influence" on *Times* editorial policy.

After the war, scarred by its

support of appeasement, *The Times* had lost its traditional function as noticeboard of the Establishment, without finding a new role. The paper's first (top-secret) management survey by a firm of chartered accountants recommended popularization to attract a larger and broader circulation, including women, the young, and other outsiders. The traditionalist Morison criticism of such a policy was pungently expressed in an outraged anonymous memorandum of 39 pages, labelled "To the Chief Proprietors only" (and

written in Morison's fine italic). It was trumpeting stuff: "Obviously Great Britain cannot function without a strong, educated, efficient, informed governing class. *The Times* is the organ of that class. It remains, and for all we can see to the contrary under a non-capitalist economy, must remain absolutely necessary to that class . . ."

When William Haley became editor in 1952, with instructions to modernize the paper for the new world, he at once removed Morison (without his feet touching the ground) from his position as unofficial guardian of *The Times* tradition. Haley later said: "Sad as it was that Morison so much resented being shut out from anything to do with the editorial side of *The Times* during the last 15 years of his life, the fact is that he should never have been allowed in."

Much turbulent water has flowed under the old bridge since Stanley Morison was keeper of the sacred flame at the House at Printing House Square. But his influence is still potent. You do not have to agree with or even like everything that you read in *The Times*. It would be a very peculiar paper if you did. But the revolutionary idea that it should be a pleasure on the eye and easy to read you owe directly to Morison.

He was the most influential typographer this century, and an endearing eccentric. Lunching a guest at his beloved Garrick Club one day, when the soup (Brown Windsor) arrived, he exclaimed: "To lunch at the Garrick is an act of Christian charity at the best of times, but this is going too far," and swept his guest off to the Savoy Grill.

The great man of print, the true *Times* man, was born on May 6, 1889 — appropriately the feast of St John *ante portam Latinam*, the patron saint of printers.

Commentary • David Hart   MAY 6   ON THIS DAY   1955

OBSERVER

▶ PROFILE

YITZHAK SHAMIR

Israel's stone-faced stonewaller

LIKE Margaret Thatcher, Yitzhak Shamir, the Israeli Prime Minister who arrives in London tonight on an official visit, is a conviction politician. He is as likely to lecture as be lectured, to hector as be hectored.

He will listen to what his host has to say, but he will insist on delivering a message of his own. Yes, of course, he wants peace with the Palestinians ('the Arabs of the Land of Israel', as he prefers to call them, at least when he's speaking Hebrew), but on Israel's terms, not Yasser Arafat's, not George Bush's, and certainly not Margaret Thatcher's. What he is seeking is diplomatic support for his Government's peace initiative, not gratuitous advice.

If it's up to Shamir, once described in these columns as 'a small, hunched, almost frog-like man who exudes an air of deep suspicion', the

secret service and politics says: 'He has nerves of ice. He never makes snap decisions. He thinks that time is on his side. His adversaries usually make the first mistake while he waits.'

Two years ago, he killed an opening to Jordan, engineered by his own Labour Foreign Minister, Shimon Peres, by a mixture of attrition and arithmetic. He knew Peres could not command a coalition majority. King Hussein was ready to negotiate. The Americans were pushing. But Shamir sat tight, and prevailed.

The full emotion of his commitment to Eretz Yisrael, the ancestral Land of Israel, emerges most frankly when he is addressing his own, the Likud faithful. 'A foreign State will not arise here,' he promised a party rally in February. 'A Palestinian State will not arise here

Behind barbed-wire eyebrows, he calculates, sticks to essentials and bides his time.

estine mandate must take precedence, even trying at one stage to make common cause with Germany and the Italian Fascists. After Stern

known is that their son Yair, an air force colonel, does not vote Likud.

Shamir's last escape was

mind that it doesn't pay to underestimate.

He is fallible, none the less. For months before the

---

59 Portraiture in line – Stanley Morison in *The Times,* and Israeli politician Yitzhak Shamir in *The Observer*

separations to consider so that the colours can be printed in register. Preparing the separations will need the attention of the processing department. An early copy of the artwork should be available for checking by the back bench for accuracy of names and information, and for instructions on possible updating of detail or text from edition to edition, or even for changes of page layout in later editions. If the finished drawing splits easily into two pieces the night editor might consider running it across a spread. In this way the shape and character of the artwork can influence the final page design.

As with chart graphics it is possible to achieve the laborious and less creative part of the work on screen where computer graphics are in use and the outputs transferred to the artist's drawing. Where an advanced graphics facility exists, and where this is the normal entry into the sytem, it is possible to create the entire job on screen. If the computer's instant art library is comprehensive a reasonable likeness of the aircraft might be featured, explosive symbols utilized, and the topography accurately traced by light pen or mouse. This could cut down time in the hands of a skilled operator but it has to be said that the finished product would appear mechanical compared with the refinement and actuality of a professional graphic artist's work.

Caricature and portraiture

There is a new trend in newspapers towards using graphics for portraiture, some of it stylized into caricature. American papers frequently rely on the artist's pen to devise portraits of their celebrities as fun comments that are also works of art. They are more than cartoons since the work is carefully and artistically executed and generally needs no caption. The distinctive work of Gerald Scarfe is an international example.

In Britain, *The Times*, *The Observer* and the *Financial Times* in recent years have brought cartoon portraiture to an art form in its own right. Peter Brookes's drawing of the great typographer Stanley Morison, commissioned by *The Times* to mark the one hundredth anniversary of his birth **(59)**, is a notable example of this. Brookes is a superb exponent of the cross-hatch style reminiscent of the copper and steel engraving techniques used in late nineteenth century illustrated newspapers. His method, however, is highly sophisticated and is linked closely to, and extends, the story that goes with the picture, in this case a piece by Philip Howard about Morison's achievements as a designer and typographer. Brookes embellishes the subject by pointing up Morison's splendid Times Roman type and weaving it into the drawing as a pair of spectacles resting on Morison's nose – a lesson to all journalist/designers and cartoonists in the use of caricature and visual graphics.

A similar technique is used by Trog (Wally Fawkes) to give enormous vigour to his drawn portrait of the Israeli politician Yitzhak Shamir in *The Observer* **(59)**, while the *Daily Mail's* amusing bicycling drawing of the Labour Party's Neil Kinnock and John Smith **(108)** on page 202 partakes of both portrait and political cartoon.

8
Essential page planning

Deciding what goes into the paper on a weekly or daily basis is the crux of the editing process and the essential preliminary to designing the pages. The readership market having been defined and accepted, it is thereafter the editor's role to provide the right staff and the content to fill the paper. To this end the news and features coverage are departmentalized **(60)** and the work planned so that the input of text and pictures is available in the right quantity and at the right time. Less easy to guarantee is the quality. There are good days and bad days for news, even for specialist papers, and there are great features and not so great features, and features that have to be found space because they fill a guaranteed regular slot. Come what may, out of it all a newspaper has to be produced; it is not the job of design to reflect some absolute standard by which the content is judged but rather to do the best possible job with the material that is available on the day.

The organizing and processing of this material ensures that a flow of copy is constantly entering the production system where the text is being edited and the pages put together. Despite the ongoing nature of all this (some news happenings, for instance, being unpredictable) decisions have to be taken sufficiently early about the overall balance of content and the placing and handling of the main stories and pictures, available or expected, to enable the work of editing to be pegged out to some sort of time scale. In fact, information in the news room, features and picture desk work schedules (though expected stories can fail and better ones crop up) enables an outline plan of the paper to be devised by the late morning conference on a daily paper and by the Thursday conference on a Sunday paper. The actual decison making at this stage is the responsibility of the editor, influenced to a greater or lesser degree by conference discussion. As production unrolls, the changes and modifications to pages neces- sary in the light of the day's events are usually left to the executive in charge of them, although a major shift in events can lead to the editor

BACK Bench

BACK BENCH
A Night Editor who controls the day by day editorial sits with his deputy & assistants on the traditional Back Bench where he is responsible only to The Editor of the newspaper.

ADVERTISING
Every issue will have a dummy to be started with blank pages in which advertising spaces are drawn. Better if actual proofs are stuck down to enable page comparison.

NEWS EDITOR
He will maintain news contact with the Night Editor at all times.

ART EDITOR
He consults the Night Editor on each page in the paper to provide rough layout ideas for the Night Editor's approval.

ART & DESIGN DESK
The Art Editor runs the group of layout artists and graphics people. He will ask someone to reproduce his rough in a finished form and brief a graphics or illustrative person, should it be necessary.

PICTURE EDITOR
He will keep the Night Editor supplied with the day's picture flow.

CHIEF-SUB EDITOR
Page designs are passed to the Sub-Editorial and the Chief-Sub hands out indivual stories to be fitted into the spaces allotted to them.

SCREEN and/or PASTE-UP ROOM
Layouts or machine commands will be passed from Art Desk on a strict time schedule.

FEATURES EDITOR
The Night Editor must be given constant confidence by the Features Editor that all his pages are in order and up to date. He must also provide blurb material.

PLATE MAKING and PRESS ROOM
These departments depend on the smooth timing of all the other elements, relying, as well, on the marrying of pages at the front end of a tabloid with those beyond the centre pages.

60 Planning the paper – the flow of ingredients into the editorial production system and out to page make-up and printing

calling a further meeting of executives and reshaping the outline of the paper.

Contents planning

The edition dummy supplied by the advertising department discloses the volume of advertising, the number of pages to be filled and

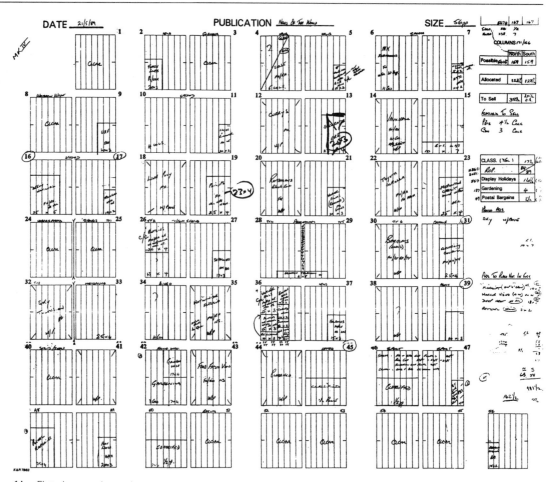

61   Flat plans, as shown here, are used by many advertising departments to indicate pagination and position of adverts. From these, editorial dummies are devised for detailed planning of the edition

the advertising spaces that have been sold. Some newspapers have adopted the magazine practice of displaying all the pages and their advertising on one sheet, which is called a flat plan **(61)**. While this gives useful at-a-glance information and is easy for ticking off pages completed, it is no substitute for an actual size dummy in which layouts and proofs of advertising can be pasted and kept handy to help in establishing visual balance as the designing and making up of pages proceeds.

The general balance of editorial contents – the amount of space allocated to news, sport and features – is fixed in most newspapers on a broad percentage basis to suit their market irrespective of pagination so that increases or decreases in size day-by-day do not fall unfairly on any one section. A departure from this would be if a heavy sports coverage such as the Cup Final, or a General Election or similar big news story demanded a more than average amount of space.

News pages

Balance of content within the news pages depends on the paper. While most newspapers are general newspapers – that is, as opposed to specialist newspapers – they carefully balance out their news space to suit their readership. For instance the national quality dailies such as *The Times, The Guardian* and *The Independent*, give particular pages or groups of pages to home news and foreign news and, in some cases, to political and industrial news, giving the pages a label or tab at the top. Usually the subediting is carried out quite separately. Financial news has its own pages, as does sport. Town evening newspapers sometimes separate national and local news, while many evenings and local weeklies have special pages for area news.

Not all newspapers have this precise compartmenting. The popular tabloids and more popular based evenings use broad readership appeal as their yardstick for allocating news and pictures to pages, though a balance will be struck on a page between human interest stories and more serious ones so that a page's news 'feel' is not too weighted, and it is not either too serious or too frivolous. Equally, running two stories on a similar topic will be avoided, unless there is merit in tying them in together as a news peg.

In quality dailies and Sundays, where there is less use of what the populars call human interest stories, a balance is struck between 'spot' news and interpretation. Here it is possible for the fine line between news and features to become blurred as byline writers lace their reportage with comment and background.

The planning will have to take account of stories that turn from the page to continue on other pages. Turned stories can be a nuisance to readers and it is best to have a regular system. *The Times*, for instance, carries all turns of page one stories on the back page of the main section. Other papers avoid them as a matter of policy, although it is hard on a tabloid-sized page one not to use them. A way out is to carry a taster of a story on page one with a cross-reference to the full story inside. A design feature can be made of a cross-reference so that, perhaps tied to a small picture, it becomes a blurb of what can be found inside the paper. Such treatment can contribute vividly to the page.

Turn heads should be in a type that connects with the stories' main headline for easy recognition. It is unwise, for the same reasons, to continue a story on another page in a different body type or setting width. Non-standard setting would make it hard to accommodate the turn, particularly at short notice on screen. The lines TURN TO PAGE . . . or CONTINUED FROM PAGE . . . should be in a distinctive type from the body face for easy recognition. Such usage should be regular in the paper. The story should ideally turn in the middle of a paragraph so the reader does not assume the item has ended.

Where news summaries or a story index is the practice on page one, which is the case with many broadsheet papers, a useful design ploy can be made by choosing and sticking to a distinctive type and format and locating it in the same position each day, with perhaps the weather forecast under. Here it can be easily located by readers who want to find something and are short of time.

Features pages

The term features encompasses a wide range of non-news content from the editorial opinion to cartoons and horoscopes and backgrounders by specialist writers. The design approach is correspondingly wide, ranging from formularized familiarity for name columnists to the lavish display given in the popular Sundays to the confessions of the famous. Unlike news there is more identity between the display and the point of view or mood of the writer. Where news pages are made up mostly of unconnected items, features pages on the whole are built around a deliberate projection of headlines, pictures and text, with the subeditor seeking to bring out the essence of the writer's point of view.

Most newspapers keep features and news pages separate, although there is a tendency to mix them more and more. This is acceptable provided the typography of a feature makes it distinctive from a news story so that the reader is enabled visually to separate fact from comment. A panelled-in regular feature column with a logo, for example, can acceptably fill an end-column position on a news page in the same way that a column of news briefs is used in an end column on a features spread in a popular tabloid.

One thing that keeps features separate from news is the longer time span that goes into their planning and the fact that as ordered material, often of a specific length, features are usually ready earlier in the day. Routine ones such as listings and home and beauty columns, often with stock logos, are among the earliest copy into a newspaper office. It is thus that features pages are planned first into the production cycle.

The main difference at the layout stage is that features pages, even in newspapers with a fairly tight design formula, are distinguished by a freer use of pictures and typography, and by more varied layout devices. The broad type format remains, but one or two extra types are introduced for display purposes, and pictures are often chosen and cropped for mood rather than for actuality, and the generally longer texts are lightened perhaps by drop letters, highlight quotes or more elaborate crossheads.

Scheduling the work

Once the editor has decided on the overall plan for the edition and laid down any policy involved, the detailed production work falls to the various executives in charge of pages. On the average town evening or weekly paper this usually means the chief subeditor in the case of the news pages, the features editor in the case of features pages, and the sports editor for the sports pages. With national papers, both morning and Sunday, and the bigger regional ones, there is more likely to be a night editor in charge of overall editorial production, and an involvement in origination of pages by, perhaps, a foreign editor, city editor, women's page editor, or even by assistant editors with overlord responsibility for sections of the paper.

Where there is a variety of hands concerned in originating pages, the art desk system performs a useful function in producing a uniform and acceptable standard of design for the finished product, and the art editor (sometimes the art director) of a big national paper can have a powerful voice in the discussion that goes into the planning of the paper.

The broad blueprint having been set, the drawing, editing and making up of pages is then arranged so that those for which text and pictures are likely to be available first are attended to first and the rest slotted in as the ingredients come to hand. This, as we have seen, usually means that features pages, other than the one containing the editorial opinion, are the earliest, including such areas as the TV and radio programmes, women's pages and serialized material. By the same coin, page one and usually one other news page, plus the main sports page, go to press last so as to include the latest and most up-to-date information.

From this work pattern a production schedule is devised giving nominated press times for each page, ending in the final 'off stone' time for the edition. This scheduling is not only for editorial purposes but to give an orderly plan to other pre-press work such as page make-up and platemaking. An essential from the production point of view is to stage this work so as to avoid delays to press times than can arise from 'bunching', when too many completed pages are waiting to be readied for platemaking .

Drawing the pages   A page begins life as a 'rough' prepared by the executive concerned. It might consist of a 'lead' headline with an approximate note of story length and a main picture which at that moment is still a briefing in the cameraman's head, perhaps one other story that would make a half lead, with a couple of stories still to be found, and perhaps room for another picture. To the outsider it would look like an indecipherable squiggle.

With news pages, particularly papers using high-speed computerized systems, it is possible to alter or switch stories up to just before press time in the light of developments that can outdate decisions taken earlier. A much vaunted exposé story turns out to be worth only half the space; a 'dead cert' vertical picture turns out, on being printed, to be usable only in a horizontal shape; a promised 'pick up' picture, it seems, is not available. There might (although less likely) be a late change of advert shape. There might even be a change of mind by the editor or the executive concerned about the weight to be given to a certain story, or about using it at all. If the page layout has been finished and distributed, a revise has to be prepared, or even a substitute layout drawn. If the layout person is still drawing the page, then either part of the page is erased and started again, or it is cut away and a new piece of drawing grid attached with gum.

With a running news story of, say, a disaster or an election, a good deal of pressure falls on the art desk to amend the layout right up to the last possible minute to accommodate extra text or late pictures, although a truly flexible news page, by the nature of its design, should allow for these contingencies. For these reasons it is a good idea to build in flexibility as well as balance so that last-minute changes can be made without delaying the edition.

With features pages such dramas are less common, though disagreements and second thoughts on projection can still result in the page being drawn several times. In place of the hassle of speed and revision endemic in news pages the layout artist has to meet the need for sophisticated and detailed presentation of longer texts, and often more complex picture editing.

Once the page shape is finalized, subeditors are expected to edit precisely to the space allocated to stories and headlines so that make-up, either with paste-up or on screen, is not delayed by late cuts or extensions to text. For this purpose, the chief subeditor, who supervises the actual editing, works from a copy of the layout and sees that headlines and text are set in the right type and measure, captions prepared for pictures and any remaining places on the page filled up with edited items of the right size. While this is being done the layout person is editing the pictures to the required shape and size and preparing any artwork needed.

Column formats

The discussion over what is the ideal number of columns from the reader's point of view is now largely a thing of the past. Tabloid papers over the years have been four, five, six and seven columns wide, and broadsheet papers eight, nine and ten columns. Today there are few broadsheet papers that do not print in eight columns, and fewer still tabloid ones that do not print in seven columns, the flexibility required by modern design techniques being best served by these sizes. A factor towards uniformity has been the need for advertisers to have the minimum of variety in advert widths and depths to which to work so that the same, or similar, adverts of the same size can be used in campaigns spread across different newspapers.

Newspapers have always been printed in smaller type than books in order to get the maximum text into the space available, and they adopted a columnar format at an early stage, as we have seen, as an aid to the scanning eye. The 7 point or 6 point across 11½ to 14 picas favoured by the well-filled Victorian papers would have been hard to

62　Some papers dispense with a rigid column format when possible. Here, freedom from adverts on page two allows the *Daily Mail* to set variously in 8 picas 3 points, 9½ picas, 11½ picas and 12 picas …

read across a book's width.

While there is no dispute that narrower columns are easier to read, the limit becomes reached if the column is so narrow – 5½ picas for example – that the words begin to break badly in setting or have to be spread out to justify lines. On a seven-column tabloid paper, panel setting can reduce the lines to 7 picas, but setting of less than this is usually used only in bastard measure caption spaces alongside pictures where problems of bad word breaks can be solved by setting the type ragged right **(75)**.

With advert widths as a built-in factor on pages there is a strong case in design for sticking to the paper's standard column format, although there is no reason why this should not be varied to permit special effects. If, for example, adverts can be contained in a block across the bottom half of the page, a seven-column tabloid paper could set a special feature across five wider legs in the top half. Where a features series is being carried across a two-page spread it is sometimes the practice to ask for the adverts to be arranged so that the designer has the option of varying the column format, while for design purposes any page setting can be rearranged across legs of bastard measure to fill a given width. Some papers – the *Daily Mail* is an example – vary the column format from page to page to differentiate between news and features pages, or when freed from advert shapes **(62)**, but this can involve a complicated juggling of advert positions to avoid setting anomalies.

In the debate that raged some years ago on column formats in design, various aesthetic and practical reasons were adduced as to why a particular number of columns was the right one. On grounds of readability of the text there is no evidence that the eye, scanning and dropping line by line through a story, encounters any greater or less difficulty in an 8½-pica column than it does in an 11-pica column. The only difference is that the narrower measure is read faster because it contains fewer words. Of greater note in the choice of column format, as with the choice between broadsheet and tabloid size, is its applicability to the paper's readership market and design style. The practice that has grown up in recent decades is that papers that run their stories at greater length and with less display, such as the quality dailies and Sundays and some regional morning papers and county weeklies, use the wider columns in broadsheet size because more words can be got into a given measure, while papers in more popular markets and running shorter items for readers with less reading time, opt for the narrower columns of the seven-column tabloid format. In each case the chosen size and column width suits the display techniques adopted for the length of items and type of readership market – a reminder that content and market shape design techniques.

Column rules

Tabloid papers use fine column rules to separate stories more than do broadsheets. While white space, as style, can look effective and sufficient, fine rules dividing the stories do give the impression on the smaller size that the pages are exceptionally full of things. Strictly, there should be no rule through the centre of a two-leg story. While a cut-off rule should mark the end of a story, it is usual where several stories descend a column to separate each with a half centred rule. Where, on features pages, a thicker 1-point or 1½-point separation rule is used as style more white should be left on either side.

The layout

In creating the page pattern, or layout, the designer is imposing a style of presentation on the materials of which the page is to be composed – the text, headlines, pictures and supporting page furniture. Only in the preparing of a dummy newspaper for a new product or a relaunch will the designer have a relatively free hand to try different design approaches and type formats. In the daily task of designing pages for a newspaper running perhaps to scores of pages the parameters are dictated by the paper's accepted style as well as by the number of columns. Thus the designer will know the sorts and sizes of types that can be used and the approximate amount of space on a page that can be given over to display, and even certain things that are permitted or not permitted. Some papers might forbid cut-out pictures; others might allow special types to be introduced for certain feature stories; some styles forbid the use of cross-heads or drop letters or keep them only for features pages, while a common practice is to have all headlines set lowercase or to banish the use of italic type. These are style conventions whose purpose is to give continuity to the paper's appearance.

Yet whether the designer is producing a page within an agreed design format or setting up an entirely new format, and irrespective of any design style or conventions, the page must obey certain guidelines if it is to be successful. It must, for instance, have the following:

Balance

The idea of a page with equal proportions, with left balancing right and top balancing bottom nurtured by some design faddists over the years is a dead letter in modern newspaper design. The arbitrariness of advertising placement always militated against it, but even with a page clear of adverts, or having a block of them across the page, to compel the contents into a symmetrical pattern of 'perfect' balance would lead to distortion of text and headline values and would impose restriction on content selection in addition to those already existing. Instead of the pattern and distribution of highlights being decided by the contents, the contents would be forced into artificial relationship with each other. The result would be a dull page of monotonous appearance.

Thus when we say balance we mean the distribution of headline and picture highlights – of display ingredients – that takes best visual advantage of the page, whatever its shape, and in a way that responds to editorial values. To this should be added that the editorial contents must take account (that is, not clash in shape or mass) with the advertising on the page, and must also create a balanced effect against the opposite page even, and especially, if it is a full-page advertisement **(63)**. In fact, no page should be consigned to platemaking until it has been checked in good time against its partner. It is worthwhile pasting not only page layouts but page proofs or photocopies into the working dummy of the day's edition. It can save a clash of similar types or half-tone (and even headline words) jumping out at you when you thumb through the first copies off the press.

Variety

Too much variety of type or effect on a page is bad for the eye, which is drawn hither and thither, not knowing where to look first. Yet too little (of type choice and size, for instance) can lead to dullness so that the design fails in its purpose of attracting and holding the eye. Variety is thus a necessary but subtly used weapon – a Century bold page varied by the odd Century light headline, or sans kicker; a deep single-column picture livening up a news page that might otherwise be trying to say too much; a long column pierced by a carefully placed cut-off; the bottom of a page saved from fragmenting into bits by a

63 Balancing an editorial page against a full page advert opposite – an example from *The Daily Express*. Note how a column of body type separates the two display areas

30-point caps headline across columns that catches the eye just when it thought it had run out of page.

All these are devices that can be used to flesh out the page once the initial balance of materials has been achieved.

Emphasis

The visual highlights of the design should reflect the relative importance of the items. Thus the bigger headlines, pictures and panelled-in stories are not just 'look at me' devices but clear signals as to how the page should be read, how the relative importance of the various items is being conveyed to the reader – in a word, how the page is given emphasis. A page in which the visual highlights that first hit the reader fail to respond to the worth of the items they cover has failed.

Points to watch

To say that good design arises from the nature of the editorial content rather than from the content being submitted to a preconceived pattern is a truism, yet it is not the whole picture. Obstacles, particularly those arising out of advertising, crop up however, well-intentioned the designer and can undo all the work:

- *Advert coupons.* Cut-out reply coupons for adverts selling goods and services are sacred. Woe-betide the page that has cut-out editorial material such as recipes or competition entries backing on to one, or if one is moved from an outside page edge where it can be easily cut. It can be a clear excuse for a demand by the advertiser for a refund or a free advert.
- *Clash of interests.* The general charge that advertising influences editorial policy has failed the test of proof in the three post-war Royal Commissions on the Press, yet day-to-day influence of advertising on page planning is inescapable. For example, stories containing criticism of a company or the armed services should not appear on the same page as an advert for the company or for recruitment in case the purpose of the advertisement can be claimed to have been frustrated. Clash of interests detrimental either to the editorial content or an adjoining advert where there is a common subject can be a reason for redrawing a page or moving an advert – for instance to avoid a cosmetic surgery advert appearing next to a story about a bust enlargement that went wrong.
- *Stolen style.* Some adverts, to draw custom, are designed deliberately to look like an editorial item in the style of the paper. These are disliked by editors and sometimes banned as policy or, if used, they must carry a line of type at the top saying 'advertisement'.
- *Edition traps.* Edition area advert changes with entirely different

words and display even for the same product, can throw out carefully designed page balance or – if anticipated in time – lead to the same page having to be drawn in two different ways.

- *Spreads.* They should be checked carefully at the make-up stage to see that strap-lines and rules leaping the central gutter are aligned at the exact level to give 'read across' – it will not arise, however, on the centre spread, which allows print-over.

Planning and the computer

The page designer is less affected in working procedures by computerized editing and typesetting systems than are the writers or subeditors since pages, even those made up electronically, begin life as drawings and are carried to a precise stage of design and measurement before being committed to paste-up or screen. There is a notable effect, however, on the style of design practised by a paper where screen make-up has been adopted. Here, a modular approach to page patterns has to be accepted even with the latest high-speed computers with full graphics capability (see Chapter 11).

The main advantage of the paste-up operation, which is the method generally used for page make-up under computerized systems, is the flexibility it allows designers in achieving, with camera and scalpel, sophisticated effects with type and pictures involving such things as overprinted headlines, elaborate montages and composite artwork, and the facility of 'bending' type to suit special purposes. Among other spin-offs for the art desk: headings can be precisely cast off on screen before being consigned to the typesetter; changes of setting within a story can be precisely calculated; formatted panels (even with rounded corners) can be achieved on screen to a precise size and depth; simple graphics effects such as white-on-black type, or 'reverse video' can be achieved from the keyboard. The general speed of typesetting and halftone production enables headlines to be set and pictures shot in time to be superimposed on page layouts, where special effects are being prepared, while the text is still being subedited. Where the photo-retouching operation is conducted from the art desk – which it now mostly is – it allows, in addition to the other factors, a measure of fine control to be achieved over the picture content of the pages.

9
Markets and style

Various experts have tried to classify newspaper design into a series of set patterns, or layout fomulas, but the dynamic nature of newspaper content and the variability of readership markets (not to say advertising placement) have always proved stumbling blocks.

Layout patterns   Edmund Arnold, a leading American expert, defined six basic layout shapes into which all type styles fitted: symmetrical; informal balance; quadrant; brace; circus and horizontal. Symmetrical – a page of evenly balanced proportions – is, as we have seen, unmanageable and a non-starter in the modern newspaper. Quadrant involves, according to Arnold, treating the page as four quarters and assigning a main display element to each quarter. In the brace, the headlines are arranged, in effect, in steps, with each headline and chunk of text supported by the headline below it, as with a pantry shelf, a feature 'resulting from the very mechanics of newspaper make-up'.

Circus is a layout style which, according to Harold Evans's description, appeals 'to the visual senses, emphasizing appearance over content. Circus . . . aims for layouts with variety, contrast and movement, and are happily prepared to let order and a scale of values go to the lions. The drama or comedy of the layout is as much part of the message as the news'.

Horizontal layout has the text presented in a series of multicolumn units descending the page, and giving – in reaction to the old vertical approach – strength below the fold and the facility of hiding longish texts in a series of easily readable legs (which can be a useful ploy in certain situations). This method is now regularly used in American papers, although being horizontal merely for the sake of it can lead to pages as dull as the uncompromisingly vertical ones.

Of the six layout formulas, informal balance, in which the items are placed in relation to each by means of a series of strategic focal points arising out of the content and shape of the page, has the merit of general application, even if it departs from the notion of precise shapes. In fact, it is not surprising that Arnold, in a later work on newspaper design, went off the idea of six basic formulas. The American Bruce Westley's view that layout is based on the four key elements of balance, contrast, focal points and motion is a more valid summing-up and is closer to the views of the authors of this book which are that design, provided that certain general principles are understood and applied, and the skills properly learned, requires a pragmatic approach depending on content and readership market.

The yearning for pure form which some of the American designers, such as Peter Palazzo with his revamp of the *Sunday Herald Tribune* in the 1960s, have shown in their dummies is perhaps an unconscious wish to elevate newspaper design to an art form of balanced shapes – which it is not. However sophisticated the system and imaginative the designer, projecting the material has to do with selling the paper and attracting readers within its market. A page pattern must relate to editorial purpose, which is geared to this function, and the ideas that go into layout must start with this in mind. Text length should relate to story value, headline size to importance on the page; a picture should have editorial usefulness as well as being an eye trap; a piece of rule or type decoration must have some demand to make; the size, or variation in size, of column setting a purpose.

In all these tasks – which are carried out within the newspaper's type format – the reader must be drawn in and guided round the pages without being aware of the psychology at work. To be successful a page pattern cannot be a case of anything goes. Nor can it be a rigid geometrical shape. It requires the skilful use of visual devices to achieve the designer's end.

Editorial targetting

We have emphasized the importance of market and content in newspaper design. The precise 'feel' of a paper, although its design is a contributory factor, has to do with what it contains, what it has to say, what package the editor has been able to put together. Most of all it has to do with whether these things are in keeping with what, from your experience of it, you as a reader expect to find in the paper. The way in which a newspaper's content and opinions are put in tune with its readers is the principal aim of its editorial policy; and in its turn it is editorial policy that governs the targeting of the paper on to its readership market.

Few papers share an identical market; some give greater weight to news of the day, some keep the needs of women readers in mind, some go for the younger reader (a diminishing percentage of the population statistically but one still much sought after by editors); some stay up-market with news coverage, giving a wide segment of political, cultural and world news and detailed background features; others go for quick easy-to-read titbits on familiar subjects for readers with little interest in the big world outside. Town evenings go for local news and features primarily with perhaps a bit of national news at the front of the paper and some pages of sport at the back. Free newspapers have a special task of persuading readers that the paper is not just being run entirely on behalf of the advertisers. Quality Sundays, tailored for a day of leisure, go for the long read, plenty on the arts and lengthy pieces of investigative journalism, all of which can find good space on a Saturday production day when there is little hard news about; the popular Sundays solve the problem with double-page exposés or revelations about the stars.

The proportion of its space that a paper gives to news and features, and the way these are presented, depend on these variable factors of readership targeting, and they are an explanation of the variety of layout devices that are used in newspapers as designers try to develop styles of presentation that correspond to a paper's editorial aims.

Typographical style   The principles of design (which we examined in Chapter 1) might be universal but, for the reasons we have just discussed, typographical style can vary a good deal, as can be seen by looking at any newsstand. It would be convenient for textbook writers if it divided into two main sorts – into popular and quality, for example; or tabloid and broadsheet. Unfortunately there will always be titles somewhere that cut across such neat theories: a broadsheet that has adopted tabloid ideas; a tabloid that has gone upmarket in presentation; a quality paper that has thrown away all the rules and struck out into new territory. So in examining typographical style, we are looking at *trends* to be found in contemporary British papers rather than seeking to put newspapers into stylistic pigeon holes. It is possible, with this caution in mind, to isolate a number of current trends in type style and relate them broadly to markets. For example:

Traditional

The nineteenth century journal of record – *The Times* and *The Daily Telegraph* are surviving examples – bequeathed to the twentieth century an austere, orderly style of presentation based on seriffed headlines of a modest 14-point to 36-point size, mostly in Bodoni or Century; sparing use of pictures, with the headline weight mainly at the top of the pages in the old vertical fashion. The concentration on text was ideal for readers seeking a wide and detailed account of the day's news. Today, with discreet innovations, this type style enjoys a continued use in *The Times* and *The Daily Telegraph*, the *Financial Times* and a number of regional morning papers such as the *Western Mail*, *Northern Echo*, and *Eastern Daily Press* and also London's *Evening Standard* **(64)**.

The principal innovations are that bigger pictures now compete for

64   Traditional type style at work – the more imaginative use of pictures has given it a new dimension

space and focal points, intros are wider than in the old days, though still of standard measure; the odd wide headline is used down page to give 'strength below the fold', and body setting is varied by the occasional use of a panelled or bold item.

The traditional type style does not have to be static. With careful use of a good stock type face such as Times New Roman type or Bodoni, the designer can combine authority with elegance, preserving the best of the traditional form on the news pages while introducing discreet typographical novelty on features pages. Eye boredom on the news pages, always the danger with this low key approach, can be averted, as in the examples above, by the careful balancing of main headlines and pictures as asymmetrical focal points, the use of artistic white space and of graphics as breakers.

Though mainly a broadsheet preserve, the traditional type style has remained popular with many city tabloid evenings, of which the *Evening Standard* is an example.

Tabloid

The most commonly used alternative to traditional type style is the tabloid, so-called not because it is used by all tabloid papers but because it originated in the typographical and display ideas first introduced by H. G. Bartholomew in the tabloid *Daily Mirror* in the late 1930s and 1940s. Its characteristics are the use of big sans caps headlines for the main stories, bold picture display, liberal use of print rules, panels and reverse WOB and BOT type headlines to emphasize selected stories, and a general shortness of items and

65 The tabloid type style with its heavy sans headlines has reached far out from Fleet Street as this selection shows

strong magazine content to suit a popular readership not looking for detailed news coverage.

Leading examples are the popular national dailies *The Sun*, *Daily Mirror* and *Daily Star*, together with the popular Sundays, *News of the World*, *Sunday People* and *Sunday Mirror* **(65)**. In a modified form the tabloid style has been adopted by a wide range of regional evenings selling to a broadly down-market readership in industrial conurbations, of which the *Liverpool Echo*, and the *Irish Press* are examples. As can be seen from the pages shown in these chapters, the tabloid type style does not necessarily mean less news but rather shorter items selected more specifically for the paper's readership market, whether national or regional, and more boldly displayed with bigger headlines than in papers of traditional format.

Sunday quality

From the mid-1960s the *Sunday Times*, under the Thomson owner-ship, and also *The Observer* began a series of changes in typography and layout which took them away from their modified traditional and mainly vertical type format into new page shapes dominated by well-whited square and expanded types, of both serif and sans families, horizontal single-deck headlines and multileg setting separated by heavy solid horizontal rules. These changes were accompanied by a bold close-cropped 'artistic' treatment of pictures, chosen more deliberately for design purpose, with fine black border lines, and an increased use of symbol and working graphics slotted into design shapes. By the 1970s both papers, followed in style by *The*

66   The Sunday quality style as seen in *The Sunday Times* and *The Observer*

Guardian, had moved into a wholly lowercase headline format, eschewing italic type and the use of cross-heads, and relying for eye comfort on shallower horizontal shapes, and on a mix of bold and light versions of their stock types of up to 72 point, with built-in strategic white space.

The pages, and sections into which quality Sunday papers had now divided, were flagged with matching WOB motifs, often sandwiched between 2-point rules at the tops of pages, while bleach-outs or drawn motifs were used as labels for special presentations.

The components of this type style, which might usefully be called the Sunday quality style, and their uses are demonstrated in the titles shown above **(66)**.

Transitional

Typography, as can be seen, knows no boundaries. Serif or sans serif type families can be utilized for either tabloid or broadsheet design styles, with both families offering a wide range of condensed and

67   The tabloid shape but with bold display clothed in traditional dress – what might be called the transitional style

expanded variants, and bold and light versions. With some regional titles going for a sans format in broadsheet or a serif in tabloid and some, in recent years, switching from one to the other and even back, it is not difficult to find examples that fit into none of the above categories. Uncertainty of, or changes in, readership market, or worry over falling sales, can be reasons for type format changes, although it is wise to precede a drastic change of type style with some detailed research into market, since this should determine content which, in turn, should determine style.

Nevertheless there are papers undergoing no such trauma which draw successfully from several typographical trends to create something distinctively their own, and which present to the eye a style which, for want of a better word, one might call transitional. Such a paper is the *Daily Mail*. Declared a 'compact' paper by Vere Harmsworth in 1971 when it became the tabloid-sized successor to the old *Daily Sketch* and the broadsheet *Daily Mail*, it opted for an elegant mix of Century Schoolbook type, the legacy of the old broadsheet dailies, and of Gothic and Rockwell slab-seriffed type. With items not quite as short as the popular tabloids and a strong features content it was able to combine elegance and busyness in a handy page size which suited its middle-of-the-road readership – middle of the road socially, that is. Following closely alongside it in content, its market rival, the *Daily Express*, a reluctant convert to tabloid size after its successful years as a Century bold broadsheet, adopted a similar approach with a mixed Century and sans type format which avoided what some considered to be the 'poster page' excesses of the tabloid style **(67)**.

This middle-of-the-road approach has also suited the content and market of a number of regional evenings who favoured the handy tabloid shape, though not the tabloid style of journalism and presentation.

Design – the creative basis

A discussion on typographical style is to some extent a statement of the obvious since the differences in type use between papers can be quickly demonstrated by a few illustrations. More fundamental to an understanding of modern newspaper design is an awareness of the creative parameters underlying it. We now come to this important aspect.

Whatever the type style in use, design can be reduced in its essentials, to two sorts:

1   The static approach.
2   The dynamic approach.

The term *static* broadly covers the patterns established by many older newspapers in which an 'informal balance' on a page is achieved by locating headline mass and pictures as assymetrical focal points within a routinized design formula. It is an approach dominated by the use of accepted headline and picture shapes. This does not mean that it is confined to a series of fixed page patterns. The patterns can be varied to suit story length, picture size and advertisement shape and position, but only to the extent that they comprise the same basic headline and picture shapes and the same standardized body setting. Nor is the static approach confined to any particular type format or page size.

Stories, under this method, are placed in the page position and given the headline size that suit their importance or length, these matters being determined by the editor or chief subeditor. If a story grows in importance from one edition or another, then it is moved to a bigger or more important spot, thus taking the place of another story. Yet the concept in this sort of page display remains static in that the headline is written to fit the type and measure, and the story (unless other items have been cleared out to make way) is cut to fit the space on the layout, the page pattern being more or less preserved. Obviously an unexpected picture would require some reorganizing but the simplicity of static layout usually allows even this intrusion to take place without too traumatic an effect.

Static layout need not be dull. There is always room for a bigger than usual picture, and writing headlines to fit the type and measure need not rule out good headlines – the discipline can be even a spur to some subeditors. The routinized shapes are also handy for quick edition changes, when there are minutes to get a story in and out and away. And if the static approach has come under threat on newspapers faced with the tempting freedom of electronic editing and typesetting and the flexibility of paste-up, it has also had a new lease of life on those newspapers taking the next technological move into full page composition. For it is but a short step from the static shapes of traditional layouts to the modular shapes of mouse and screen.

The *dynamic*, or what is sometimes called the *freestyle* approach, is a relative newcomer in newspaper design in which headlines and picture shapes – and therefore page patterns – are created in response to the words and content of the material. In other words, the headlines are written first and the cropping and placing of the pictures decided upon before the page is drawn.

It is still done within an accepted type format, and the freestyle element tends to apply mostly to main stories and 'projections', but it does result in more varied and 'visual' pages than the static approach, and in a more deliberate targetting of material at a paper's readership. It is an ideal way to get the best out of the bigger story and the out-of-the-way picture. It makes greater demands on editorial skills and judgement, but it can bring a story – and a page – alive. It also does not preclude keeping slots and positions for easy edition changes. In fact a freestyle projection works better in the context of typographical familiarity, and is as dependent on typographical and visual balance as is any other sort of layout.

In the next two chapters we consider the creative effects of the two approaches to newspaper design and look at some examples.

10
The dynamic or freestyle approach

The spread of dynamic or freestyle page design can be traced back to two quite different sources: the new tabloid journalism of the *Daily Mirror* of the late 1930s and 1940s under H. G. Bartholomew, and the reborn *Sunday Times* in the 1960s under the Thompson ownership.

Two more different papers could not be imagined. The *Mirror* was slugging out war news and virtual propaganda material for the troops in great poster headlines, with readership stunts and hectoring features by flamboyant columnists; the *Sunday Times* was creating news in depth with its Insight column, and presenting significant 'long reads' in two and three-page spreads, while moving over to an elegant version of the great American sectional newspaper. Yet both, in their use of headline type and page shapes, were breaking out of the old up-and-down 'mortice and tenon' mould and letting the material call the typographical tune. Both were discovering how to project stories using the full resources of typography, pictures and graphics, instead of just getting the material into the paper.

On the *Mirror* in the brilliant 1950s the marriage of words and typography, and the combination of easy reading and earth-shattering events, was creating a new world for subeditors who were being hired not only for their ability to write headlines that fitted, but ones which shouted 'Read me!' The *Sunday Times* began using type to project and extend the text and not just to provide a comfortable format in which to drop the stories. Each paper in its way was turning upside down stock notions of what a newspaper should look like. And each, in its field, was to become a topseller.

The original concept behind freestyle thinking in newspaper design was to stretch the visual parameters of the page, to break out of shapes made by horizontal and vertical lines in which every story began with a short double-column intro turning into single column, witl. the adjoining story fitting neatly into the shoulder, as if put together by a carpenter. Down-page multiple stories were introduced to break up the verticals. The hatchet-shaped headline appeared with one long top line and a second deck of three or four short lines underneath. Pictures were used to give a feeling of display down page. Variable and bastard setting was tried to break the tyranny of standard measures. Headlines reversed as white-on-black or as black-on-tint were introduced. The full area of the page began to be used.

The freestyle method is far from a licence for anarchy, and bears no relation to the contemptuous term 'circus' layout given to it by some American newspaper designers. It is not an 'anything goes' ragbag of type and pictures but a considered technique of presentation working within a typographical framework of chosen faces and sizes and an accepted columnar format. Its practitioners are aware that a newspaper needs to have a continuity of style and appearance that makes it instantly recognizable to its readers. Yet within these parameters it uses the deliberate projection of selected stories as a pivot round which a twin assault of surprise and familiarity is launched upon the reader.

Each page is built round one or two main ingredients, whether it be a features or news page. In the case of a news page the ingredients might be the lead and the half lead, or the lead and the main picture (which may or may not be connected to it) which are the natural focal points of the design. But instead of the designer/journalist roughing out a banner head, an intro running round the main picture and a half lead with three lines across two columns, or some other such basic layout shape, the lead story is weighed carefully by the page executive in terms of angle and projection, and might be discussed with the art editor. The headline is then written first. The words of this are the main selling lines for the page (if the story is properly chosen). The main picture, whether connected with the lead story or not, is likewise considered as a piece of projection in its own right, and its position based upon its composition, required size and best shape. The news value of the half lead might also be considered similarly and the headline written first.

The projection might call for an explanatory strap line for the lead story, or for a deliberately wordy headline that takes several lines of a smaller type size than usual. The headline might need to closely integrate with the picture, or the picture might have its own headline and caption. Perhaps an exceptionally wordy second deck is needed to exploit an important quotation that is the fulcrum of the story.

The lead story, alternatively, might consist of three distinct elements with a main statement backed up by separate headlines on the other aspects which need to be knitted together by panel rules – or the story might have good pictures that demand to be run across a spread of two pages. A quick chart or map might have to be worked in. The required length of the story and how it can best be run in relation to the pictures and the space available on the page has to be considered. It might demand a more than average length, while at the same time be lacking in suitable pictures. A separate picture with self-contained material might therefore be allocated to the page to give the layout visual balance.

Whether there is an art bench involved or the page is being drawn by a designer/journalist, the essence of the freestyle approach is that the shape the page takes on the design pad is dictated by the material. This means that time must be allowed for discussion and evaluation. The best projections are often the product of a committee of minds, but essentially imagination and a knowledge of design techniques must play some part in the solution.

Out of this discussion a rough, or several roughs, is drawn to test the projection against the advert shapes and content. On an important page a change in advert shape and position might be negotiated to help the display, although there is usually time for this only in the earlier part of the production cycle. Once this initial idea-juggling has taken place and the rough pattern approved, the page is then drawn in detail with appropriate type and lengths marked in. Any single column tops, lesser important doubles or fillers needed for the rest of the page are tasted and slotted in by the chief subeditor in the normal way. Some papers, intent on story balance as well as visual balance, scheme down to the smallest one-paragraph filler.

In the case of features pages, freestyle projection has more obvious advantages since it enables the page executive and subeditor to base a whole page display on an amalgam of text, headlines, pictures and quotations. On a page or spread consisting of one or two stories this makes for very unified treatment with type and picture effects not to be found on news pages. Dramatic or very personal material gives the designer a unique opportunity to 'sell' a page visually to the reader. Even here, however, an element of continuity is helpful to the reader, and it is customary to place stock ingredients such as regular columns and service features in their fixed format alongside a freestyle display, where they help to provide context for the rest of the page.

The virtue of pages conceived in this way is that, far from showing untrammelled freedom, they display deliberate purpose instead of looking like a couple of galleys of type have been dropped in to fill the spaces left by the adverts.

Disadvantages?

The freestyle method might appear time-consuming, especially for evening papers, or those with limited staff and facilities, or on any paper where edition deadlines are near. Can an editor afford to carefully project particular material as an integrated design when stories are waiting to be placed and subedited?

The answer to this is that it can take more time to think up a headline of perhaps two decks to fit an arbitrary type size and measure and to edit a text to a fixed slot than it does to properly assess a story and 'see' it as a projection comprising a given headline/quote/picture/length. If the back bench is geared to the freestyle approach rather than to filling 48 pages of set patterns and news slots, the projection of main page elements will come naturally and effortlessly as part of the cycle from copytaster to make-up. Each page will take shape round a given projection that stems from the headline, text and picture shape of the main ingredients. If time and page material are properly allocated to take account of edition deadlines there is no reason why a newspaper should not use a dynamic approach to news and to features. The bonus will be pages that tease and excite the reader's eye. Computerized facilities have made the mechanics of this approach a lot easier.

The modern tabloid

The Sun has been the most successful example in Britain of the popular tabloid approach to freestyle and the lineal heir, in this sense, of the *Daily Mirror*, which started it **(28)**. Its readership market is suited to the boldness and inventiveness of this method, and its vigorous page layouts, even if the contents are criticized by some purists, are backed by tight subbing based on a terse distillation of the written word, and a willingness to descend to the colloquial and sloganizing when necessary to communicate. The aim is not only to display big and hit the reader hard but to fill up every last corner of the page with material in which every word counts. Story counts per page are examined at 'morning after' conferences, and the bold simplicity of the concept belies the careful planning of content and projection that goes into each edition.

The purpose at its relaunch under the Murdoch ownership in 1969 was to go for the readership being vacated by the *Daily Mirror*, which was then going through an up-market phase. The typographical approach was derived from the ideas of H. G. Bartholomew to which was welded a flair for self publicity that would have delighted Lord Northcliffe, whose life-long aim was to get his papers talked about.

Its type style and layout ideas have been refined since then rather than changed. The page one in **(68)** is typical of *The Sun*'s back-slapping approach in connection with a campaign for the overturn of a particularly bad court judgement. The elements of projection are all there. A quote from a prominent MP who has been induced to congratulate the paper is immaculately displayed and spaced, the attribution prominent yet not too big, the underscores subdued and neatly cut into the descenders, the quotation marks big enough to impart a feeling of confidence. The headline is the correct weight for the type of layout, so as not to overpower the repeat *Sun* masthead that completes the phrase 'Thank you my Sun' – a flashback reminder to the paper's story that began the campaign. This gives a feeling of authenticity for the reader who has joined the story late. An appropriate subheading in four lines of 42-point Futura/Tempo underscored with a 6-point rule rounds off the page, and the whole story is contained within panel rules. There is nothing haphazard or rushed about this approach. The Bingo blurb is a typical *Sun* art desk

68 *The Sun* page one celebrating a campaign triumph

compilation of devices that are guaranteed to excite the more competition-minded readers.

The Sun, despite its boldness, is closely conscious of the need for continuity and manages to combine free-style thinking with formula. An ideal arrangement with a spread **(69)** is to have a good photographically supported feature flanked by a column of news on the right with a secondary four-column news or features piece on top of the advert on the left-hand page, thus getting the advantages of

69　Combining boldness with busyness – a *Sun* centre-page spread

display width on the main subject, while keeping up the story count and trapping the extra reader looking for snippets.

A particular creation that has lasted has been the Sunspots, tiny tightly subbed pieces of spot news contained in milled rule boxes a paragraph long, which can be used potently as cut-offs between stories. Its pages are also helped by the sharp headline writing in which story points are well taken in the paper's own style, and the lines filled out to the allotted space so that it all looks easy.

The paper has been particularly careful not to change its typographical style following the trauma of the switch to computerized setting at its new plant at Wapping, in London's East End. If there is a criticism to be made of its approach to design it is its reluctance to make use of the improved computer graphics facilities now available to give an extra dimension to its pages. Its graphics look old-fashioned compared with some papers.

The *Daily Mirror*, which invented tabloid journalism, and moved confidently into web-offset colour on news and features pages under the editorship of Richard Stott in 1988, showed no such inhibitions as *The Sun*. In its search for new layout shapes embodying both mono and colour elements the *Mirror* displays the dangers as well as the excitement of the freestyle approach when the aim to grab the

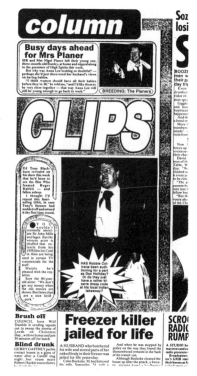

70   A misreading of the freestyle method – convoluted page design in Eddie Shah's ill-fated daily, *The Post*

reader's eye is freed from the constraints of an accepted type formula. The integration of the subjects into the page illustrated in **Plate 2** is cleverly executed. The separations of items are clear enough, defined by liberal use of solid and tinted rules of varying thickness, yet the eye is in danger of being dazzled by competing claims for attention.

Mr Eddie Shah's national tabloid *The Post*, produced in Warrington, in North-West England, which had a short life in 1988, shows a misreading of the freestyle approach. It is rendered almost unreadable by its convoluted page design **(70)**. Its failure to attract readers is also a reminder that the athletic power of the design-and-production machine is not enough if a paper has not got something to say and compelling words in which to say it.

A number of provincial papers have successfully adapted the freestyle tabloid approach. The *Kent Messenger*, which circulates in the conurbation of the Medway towns, won the *UK Press Gazette* British Regional Weekly Newspaper design award in 1989 with a 116-page edition containing the pages illustrated in **(71)**. Page one is built around a brilliantly cropped and displayed picture of a baby boy who has had his sight restored. The bold masthead, which prints in yellow and black with the white county heraldic symbol, enables an important local story to be given top of the page treatment without detracting from the eye-catching splash. The contents index-cum-

71 Three pages from an award-winning edition of the *Kent Messenger* show freestyle methods used effectively in a provincial weekly paper

blurb in column seven, also printing in yellow and black, links the two focal points together. The inside news page is an example of how a panelled-in picture story, in this case in double fine rules, can help a page in which the splash has no illustration. The down page single column picture is correctly placed visually to break up the legs of reading matter across the page, the only discordant note being the unnecessarily heavy three-column rule under the splash headline.

The sports page is an object lesson on how to let the contents dictate the design when the picture desk has turned in a brilliant set of action shots of a local boxing hero. This visually effective spread still leaves room for five sports stories down page. The pages show effectively how a Century bold and light lowercase type style can be made to work in the tabloid format.

The double page spread from the *Liverpool Echo* (**72**) shows how a successful town evening paper has harnessed the freestyle approach on its features pages. An all lowercase sans dress in Futura bold and Helvetica light is used cleverly in a well-balanced display of four items, of which the main one, an interview story, SHOWBIZ IN THE BLOOD, is keyed together across the two pages by an effective 18-point tone rule. The eleven-line set-left standfirst in Helvetica, bastardized to about 33 point to fill out, acts both as an effective break between the two main pictures and as a lead-in to the main headline which is used to tie in the spread across mid-page.

The lack of adverts and the need to give length to the feature on the left has resulted in a daring decision to turn it to run under the first three legs of the main story. The text pivots on another Helvetica

A grand life for Stan and his piano

Showbiz in the blood

Tony Austin meets a rising star from Liverpool hoping for his biggest break so far . . .

Danger from the deep

Graeme Kay discovers that Emmerdale's old Seth is not the country clod he appears

Golden rule

Gerard Henderson reports on the Irish Sea controversy

Wargames

Janet's diary day in the life of TV

By Judith Moss

72 Letting contents shape design – a fine example of the freestyle approach in this double-page spread from the *Liverpool Echo*

lowercase headline which provides correct eye contrast with the main heading, but the master stroke in this risky typographical ploy is to run the text against a beautifully cropped picture of the subject of the piece, Stan Richards, standing up from the bottom of the page in columns four and five. This totally convinces the eye of the cleverness and logic of a design idea that could have failed.

Both wings of the spread in this wholly freestyle concept are well supported without the display detracting from the impact of the main story. The map on the right gives ideal contrast against the five halftones, the only visual blemish on the page being the shy second line of the headline DANGER FROM THE DEEP. As is generally the case with the `Echo, the pictures are particularly well cropped to achieve their maximum purpose as focal points.

Sunday quality

What could be called the Sunday version of freestyle is rooted predominantly in the use of seriffed types and artistically cropped pictures and it tends to rate elegance above boldness, while being otherwise just as free-ranging. The *Sunday Times* fashion page **(73)**

73 Giving pictures their head – a striking fashion page from the *Sunday Times*

74   How the freestyle approach copes with a long read – a *Sunday Times* News Focus special on Winnie Mandela

8

GLASGOW HERALD WEDNESDAY MARCH 5 1988

THE THINKERS AND THE THISTLE – Day Three of the series presented by Harry Reid

A case for Scots to return to their egalitarian roots

DR TONY CARTY is an international lawyer whose specialist interest is nationhood and how it can be achieved and fulfilled. He analyses the current constitutional imbroglio in Scotland thus: "The Scots joined themselves into the British nation in 1707. Up till now the Scots have generally been passive about their nationhood, but now they are being forced to confront it, to decide if they wish to return to their pre-Union roots.

> ' The Scots would be best to let the English drive them out — that would make it much easier in the European context, to have been pushed out of Britain by the English. '

CARTY: Scots are reacting negatively to what they distrust, but they have as yet no clear vision of what they want.

THATCHER: "A genuinely revolutionary politician, hacking away at the British identity."

Ireland's honorary Scotsman

TONY CARTY was born in Belfast and brought up in Dublin, then the family moved back to Belfast, where he studied law at Queen's University. His father came from Wexford, his mother was an Ulsterwoman. He thus knows Ireland — both parts — intimately, but he now regards himself as an honorary Scot.

Harry Reid

JONES: It is false that if we do nothing, nothing will happen — something will happen, but we shall lack influence.

Let's not be afraid to be a nation of intellectuals

By PETER JONES

TOO often to outsiders, we in Scotland appear as bronchially berating, sour souls, myth-laden in grievances.

TOMORROW: Thursday is traditionally Education Day in the Herald, and our series concludes with some outspoken remarks from Professor NIGEL GRANT on the assault on Scotland's education system, as well as the pertinent thoughts of WILLIS PICKARD — the man who prompted the Government's attempts to try to emasculate the rights of Scotland's university rectors.

75 Dynamic yet elegant – a features page from the *Glasgow Herald*

with its well-balanced interlocking pictures dominating the page, is a vintage specimen. The headline consisting of the simple legend SALE AWAY! is given interest by being mounted neatly on a drawn carrier bag slung through the first 'O' of the word LOOK, which establishes the page, and is an example of the paper's technique of integrating graphics into its display. The pictures help by being superb photographs in their own right. The fine keyline round them protects the low-key backgrounds from fade, while the typey adverts down page act as a foil to the design, at the same time containing useful information for the readers. Like all good freestyle design the page scores with the bold simplicity of its concept.

The front page of the *Sunday Times'* News Focus **(74)** shows how an old-fashioned device like a cut-out fist can be pressed into service to produce high drama against a heavy seriffed 84-point lowercase headline DOWNFALL OF A BLACK EVITA in Clarendon bold. Overprinting the fist on to the lower part of the 'C' in FOCUS creates an almost three-dimensional effect. This freestyle display with the two contrasting pictures carries a page that is otherwise routine by *Sunday Times* standards, with two long reads schemed horizontally across the page without crossheads, relying on secondary halftones and standfirsts to give focal points.

The *Glasgow Herald's* broadsheet page eight **(75)** is built around two atmospherically cropped pictures and the elegant use of white space. The fine detail of the lower picture benefits enormously from the space left above the caption. The thistle graphic and the quote lighten

76   Six specimen pages from Vic Giles's 48-page revamp of the *Sunday Sun* carried out for the Thomson Organisation at Newcastle-Upon-Tyne in 1989. The designs are a rework, with new headlines and pictures, of material in an existing edition, with body setting 'junked' in the columns to fill. They are intended to demonstrate how the freestyle approach to headline and picture use can be used to give vigour to both news and features pages of a provincially based Sunday tabloid competing with national tabloids in an industrial conurbation.

the centre of the page, while the whole concept is saved from modularity by the effective use of keylined pica toned rules and a jauntily tilted picture of Margaret Thatcher in column eight – a rare exception to the rule that tilted pictures seldom work and are best avoided. The long texts are in 8 point with 15-point gutters, which give a lightness that compensates for the lack of crossheads, now generally unused in Sunday quality style design. Another recognition motif of this genre of design is the thick and thin rules topping the page.

11
Static and modular design

The shift towards freer design influenced by the tabloid poster styles and the revamping of the quality Sundays in the 1960s still left a large section of the press, particularly in the provinces, committed to traditional presentation. Worries over circulation in the 1960s, however, and concern about increased television viewing, spurred some papers to try to make themselves more attractive and eye-catching. In the main the movement was towards modular patterns, experiments with lowercase type formats, a greater magazine content and the more imaginative use of pictures.

It is tempting to attribute these changes to the expected availability of full page screen composition as a result of the computerized printing systems which began to be introduced in regional production centres from the early 1960s. Yet full page composition, apart from the union problems of job allocation, aroused little enthusiasm at first. The problems of graphics generation looked to be insoluble except possibly in the long term, and even in America the method was not making a great deal of progress. In Britain in the late 1980s after two decades of 'new' technology, only a handful of papers, national and provincial, had moved into screen make-up and even they were printing out on to bromides to take pictures and adverts by paste-up into the 'windows' that had been left.

Two things influenced the move towards modular design in the more traditional papers. First, once pictures began to be a more highly rated part of the mix, the old established styles of papers like *The Daily Telegraph, Yorkshire Post, Birmingham Mail* and *The Scotsman* lent themselves easily to modular pattern-making, with headlines and pictures sharing the role of focal points formerly occupied almost exclusively by the headlines. Pictures, in fact, rather than headline shapes have become the key in modular design. Second, the fashion for lowercase type formats, fanned by the successful re-styling of *The Times* and *The Guardian*, required a more segmented page to gain the best eye appeal from headline location (see examples in this chapter). It also required some care to be given in the pages to the juxtaposing of different weights and sizes of the chosen headline type.

A third factor probably weighed with some provincial editors. Where a paper's traditional appeal was valued, the move towards an imposed modular or semi-modular type style with defined parameters gave protection against the dangers of excessive innovation unleashed by the freedom of cut-and-paste make-up. Some of the early examples of web-offset-produced local papers were unbelievably garish and messy as papers cut loose from the restraints of hot metal, and young journalists with little training and a determination to experiment were given their head on paste-up pages.

What happened as systems improved was that those with the more modular formats, led by *The Times* and *The Guardian*, provided a growing number of candidates for the switch to full page composition (FPC) once companies were satisfied that the systems could deliver. As a result, medium-term planning in offices which were totally computerized was towards the changeover to FPC where this could be accomplished without damage to the design format. Influential in these plans was the fact that the two new national titles that came out in 1986, *Today* and *The Independent*, both settled for FPC from the beginning and committed themselves to modular design, though hedging their bets by laser printing their pictures and pasting them and the adverts on to the page print-outs.

Modular patterns

Modular, an old word given new currency by computerspeak, simply means in segments – in this case geometric shapes devised from rectangles. In full page composition in those systems that have the capability such shapes can be edited and set as complete text + headline segments, within panel rules if need be, and moved into position on a make-up screen by mouse or key controls. The stories are given to a subeditor to edit to the required length and shape to fit the layout – say, a headline across five columns with five legs of text running under it to fit a panel 14 cm deep – the same way as with any other layout. The editing screen shows when a precise text length and fit has been achieved and the story then passes through the revise subeditor and is sent to join the queue for the given page. The method imposes no greater burden on the subeditor, once keyboard commands have been mastered, than in subbing an ordinary story on screen to fit a column space on a paste-up page.

The simple logic is that having been edited, headlined and stored in the computer, the stories might just as well be kept there and fitted into the layout on screen for printing out as a page rather than be taken out of the photosetter piecemeal by the column and pasted on to a card, and then photographed as a page.

The ultimate logic is that pictures and adverts, having been created, sized and shot, should be entered into the computer along with the text to be likewise moved into the page on screen. It is here, however, that problems arise with full screen composition, for though computer graphics have made great strides in availability and flexibility in recent years, the digitized storage and manipulation of halftones is still a slow process. Hence the practice of printing out full screen pages as bromides so that adverts, halftone photographs and hand-prepared graphics can be shot separately and pasted into their spaces before conveying the page to camera and platemaker.

Despite the hybrid nature of this way of doing it, it does do away with the expense of a labour-intensive paste-up operation and allows fuller utilization of the systems' capabilities. Moreover, to print out the page as a bromide before consigning it to platemaking is necessary in any case if a proper editorial check is to be made on how it looks as a finished page as opposed to an image on screen – despite the fact that modern systems allow a page to be processed straight through from computer to platemaker.

There are other advantages to modular layout as well as its suitability for the computer. It means a good deal less difficulty for editors with small staffs. It makes page changes simpler since it allows module-for-module replacement. Stories of appropriate shape as well as length can be prepared and held for fitting at edition or slip changes. Where used in conjunction with stored computer graphics it is user-friendly to a newspaper with minimal art desk facilities. Above all, once mastered it gives the comforting impression that it is easier.

The disadvantages are that unless a determined effort is made and creative use of type and pictures brought to bear it can cause a newspaper to degenerate into formularized pages in which familiarity triumphs over any attempt at surprise. Dull, boring, repetitious design can be the result. This makes it particularly suspect to an editor who is running a successful newspaper that has been built up boldly on the freestyle method, or who is locked in competition with an enterprising rival.

Yet there is no reason why modules, given the use of a reasonable type range and well-cropped pictures of good size, cannot be the basis of imaginative page design. The need for effective focal points to grab the reader's eye remains and it is up to the visualizer, within the parameters of a paper's typestyle, to make the modules work for the page. Pictures are the vital ingredient, even though they may be unconnected with the main stories. They give essential contrast to the vertical and horizontal elements in the design, and against the size of the stories. Columns of briefs flanking or centring on the page can give the eye some relief from setting that might otherwise look grey. It is thus the way the modules are put together that really matters. There are plenty of good examples of how this can be done.

Updating the traditional

There have been three revolutions in the twentieth century at *The Times*. The first was the commissioning in 1931 of a new typeface for the paper from Stanley Morison which presented to the world the now familiar and much used Times New Roman. The second was the

Thursday August 5 1976
No 59,774
Price twelve pence

THE TIMES

Time to dump
the import
dumpers, page 21

Police open fire in new Soweto rioting

Police opened fire yesterday on a crowd of 20,000 blacks, mostly students, in the South African township of Soweto, scene of one of the riots in June in which 176 people were killed. Eyewitnesses reported three deaths yesterday, but this was denied by the police. The students were marching on Johannesburg to protest against the detention of colleagues.

Lord Thomson of Fleet dies in London hospital after chest illness

By Roger Berthoud

Lord Thomson of Fleet, joint chairman of the Thomson Organisation Limited, which owns *The Times*, *The Sunday Times* and *The Economist*, died yesterday in the Wellington Hospital, St John's Wood, London, at the age of 82. He entered the hospital a month ago with a chest infection resulting from a cold contracted on an Easter holiday in Tenerife. A day before he was due to go to Canada for three months, he suffered a severe relapse.

20,000 blacks march on Johannesburg

From Nicholas Ashford
Johannesburg, Aug 4

Violence erupted in the African township of Soweto again today. Police opened fire on a crowd of about 20,000 blacks, most of them students, who were making an eight-mile march to Johannesburg's police headquarters to protest against the detention of some of their colleagues.

Chemical company takes poison precautions

By Pearce Wright
Science Editor

The biggest manufacturer in Britain making a compound that could produce the poisonous chemical that has isolated the village of Seveso, in northern Italy, has temporarily closed a plant to make "110 per cent sure" there is no danger.

Women's day: The Oldest Member puffed reflectively at his memorandum. "Nippy fielders. Good discipline. Some nice copybook strokes. Can't say much for the bowling. Don't mind them being here as long as they don't come too often." (Marcel Berlins writes.)

Government to stock swine flu vaccine

By a Staff Reporter

The British Government is establishing a reserve of a million doses of vaccine against swine influenza. It will be stored at public health laboratories and probably kept for essential workers, according to the Department of Health and Social Security.

Employers and TUC settle differences in talks on economy

By Malcolm Brown

The National Economic Development Council yesterday endorsed a growth projection by the Chancellor providing average output growth rate by the manufacturing industry of 3 per cent between 1975 and 1978.

Loophole closed in benefit pact with Spain

By Pat Healy
Social Service Correspondent

The Government acted swiftly yesterday to close a loophole in a reciprocal social security agreement with Spain which could, in theory, allow an employed people to claim unemployment benefit for the period they were on holiday in Spain.

Five students reported shot in Uganda

From Our Correspondent
Nairobi, Aug 4

Five students at Makerere University, Kampala, were shot dead, more than 30 wounded, and several hundred arrested yesterday, according to reliable reports from Uganda reaching Nairobi today.

81 executed in Sudan over abortive coup

Sudan executed 81 men by firing squad at dawn yesterday for their part in last month's abortive coup against President Nimeiry, Omdurman radio announced.

Dr Kissinger's visit

Wounded evacuated

'Torture' in Ghana

Teenagers blamed for resort bombs

Eight bomb explosions that devastated the centre of the small Ulster seaside resort of Portrush on Tuesday night are thought to be the work of a gang of teenagers, some no more than 14 years old.

Councillors criticized

Drink-driving law

'Arms minister' is suggested

The Commons Expenditure Committee today recommends that a new junior minister is needed at the Ministry of Defence to take charge of the development and procurement of equipment for the Armed Forces.

77   *The Times*, August 5, 1976 – before the changes of the 1980s

78   *The Times* of 1989 – two examples show the splash headline type doubled in size and the royal coat of arms restored

removal in 1966 by Sir William Haley, the then editor, of the classified adverts that had filled page one for more than a hundred years. The third was the updating of the paper's type format in the 1980s in a bid to widen its readership under Rupert Murdoch's ownership and the editorship of Charles Wilson.

A comparison of the two page ones in **(78)** with the edition of August 5, 1976 **(77)** shows the visual effect of the changes that took place by slow stages through the early 1980s, not the least of which was the restoring of the Royal coat of arms to its position in the title piece. More dramatic, as can be seen, has been the increase in size of the splash headline type from 36 point to 60 point and sometimes to 72 point, and setting headlines centred instead of nearly all being set left.

The sectioning of the paper on American lines and the use of preprinted gravure as part of the modernization have been success-fully used to draw in both new readers and new advertisers. Most impressive of all, however, has been the way the paper has been able to retain its authority while undergoing progressive changes in type and picture use by which it has merged its traditional approach to page patterns with the best of modern modular design.

An effective part of the modernization was the reduction of the type area width from 92 picas to 81 to align production with the company's other titles when the paper was transferred from Gray's Inn Road to the new plant at Wapping in 1986. The number of columns remained at eight but came down to 9½ picas wide, with a subtle gain in readability. The changes have entailed a bolder use of pictures and the clever placing of graphics both as page decoration and as breakers. Generally there is an attempt to connect the main page one picture with the splash or half lead. While lengths in relation to the pattern, and the placing of items, have remained broadly traditional there is a willingness to break out of this in type and picture display on the day a big story breaks.

The broad format is well developed for ease of reading and finding for busy readers. The three-column three-line splash headline is now usually in 60-point Times bold lowercase, with the reader being offered a fast summary of the splash story before the eye arrives at the real intro. Within the changes and bolder type and picture use, an essential discipline of placement remains, with the maximum effect being derived from varying sizes and weights of headline type. The splash standfirst invariably consists of four paragraphs of 10-point Times bold, usually across a column and a half, each paragraph leading off with a 10-point blob, and all the same length. The extra white enclosing the paragraphs enables the reader to digest the summary without the main story diverting his attention, and is typical of the careful use of white space to lead the eye throughout the paper. A feature of *The Times* is its decision to solve the old problem of stories turning inside from page one by continuing them all on the back page of the main section, thus giving room for more on page one without upsetting readers by having them dive all over the paper to find story continuations or – worse still – giving up and not bothering to look.

The two pages illustrated **(78)** show how *The Times*, despite its discipline and move into modular segments, prevents a general format from becoming a formula and lets content dictate design in the handling of the bigger stories. Length is used as much as headline to signal the importance of an item. The interesting thing is how, apart from standfirsts and cross-references, sufficient weight is given to each story without the use of bold or italic setting variants, or even reverse indent, although bastard measures are now deemed acceptable both up and down page. The column one blurb and inside story index are drawn to the eye with neat graphics or a repeat masthead logo and offer an essential page one service to the reader. The index is more extensive for the five-section Saturday or weekend issue and is a worthwhile ingredient for a big busy broadsheet.

On its features pages *The Times* shows the extent of the revolution that has been wrought in recent years. There is a wider use of large sizes of Times Roman, four- and five-line drop letters as eye breakers, charts of all sizes with neatly tabulated information but, above all, a determination to make modularity work by the bold use of graphics. Demonstrating this is the brilliant harnessing of caricature on the Spectrum page illustrated **(79)** with the support of a chart, elegant rulery and a down-page logo.

The *Northern Echo* page one produced by the team commended in the 1989 UK Press Gazette awards **(80)** is an example of how a leading provincial morning paper has utilized graphics in adapting its traditional format to modular design. Here, an information chart is used as a centrepiece in the paper's coverage of the US Presidential election enclosed, with text, in a huge 8 point black panelled-in segment resting on top of its down page selection of national and regional news. Its double column News in Brief display in columns one and two enables it to get nineteen items on the page, the 24 point sans headlines serving a useful foil to the otherwise all-lowercase serif format.

The election graphic, inputted from the Press Association picture service, and enhanced by the *Echo*'s graphics artist shows the state-by-state results and is a good example of how graphics can be substituted on big page one stories when pictures are either unsuitable or unavailable and, by so doing, give a modular page almost the freedom of freestyle design.

The page four and five examples from the *Manchester Evening News* **(81)** show a busy evening tabloid paper that is thriving on a serif lowercase type format and modular design. The discipline and requirements of both approaches in no way diminishes the *Manchester Evening New*'s traditional vigour and determination to pack its pages with stories and pictures. The modules are boldly put to work in the cause of readability and eye appeal.

12 THE TIMES THURSDAY JANUARY 26 1989

SPECTRUM

Leading the case for the Bar

THE TIMES PROFILE

DESMOND FENNELL, QC

The Green Paper issued yesterday by Lord Mackay, the Lord Chancellor, heralds radical changes in the traditional structure and work of the legal profession. The prospective loss of the barristers' monopoly of arguing cases in the higher courts, and of their exclusive right to be eligible to be High Court judges, are only two aspects of the package which will transform the Bar.

Barristers are bound to be the losers in the legal reshuffling to come, but exactly how far the Lord Chancellor's revolution will go is not yet certain. There is still a lot for the Bar to fight for, and Desmond Fennell, chairman of the Bar Council, will be its protagonist.

There was a time when being chairman of the Bar was, in the description of one past holder of that office, a doddle. It meant, in theory, being the head of your profession; but it was an honour without too many responsibilities. There were committees to be chaired, social and professional functions to host and attend, and a couple of overseas trips as the guest of lawyers' associations abroad.

Occasionally the Bar chairman had to turn his attention to serious professional issues, but on the whole his dinner jacket was exercised more often than his ability. And at the end of a pleasant and ego-satisfying year, he could usually expect the offer of a seat on the High Court bench.

Three years ago, Robert (now Lord) Alexander, QC, ushered in a new era for chairmen of the Bar. Where his predecessors had been secretive and defensive about the Bar's affairs, Alexander was open and positive. Where they had mistrusted the media, rarely and reluctantly exposing themselves to public gaze, Alexander was always available and frequently seen, heard and read. From being a part-time honour, chairmanship of the Bar was becoming a full-time job.

Desmond Fennell's stint as chairman for 1989 offers even more frenetic prospects. It will be his duty to preside over what might turn out to be the most momentous year in the Bar's history. For the next 12 months he will be subjected to a degree of media and public exposure such as no chairman of the Bar has endured before; and within the profession his every move as its head and figurehead will be critically scrutinized. It will be no year for the faint-hearted.

Until a little more than a year ago, Fennell was well-known and highly respected within the profession, but virtually unknown to the outside world. He had not starred in any spectacular cases (though he was a junior member in the team that prosecuted the Great Train Robbers). He had written no books, did not appear on television, and was never the subject of newspaper articles.

The King's Cross fire changed all that. It was assumed at first that the inquiry would be chaired by a High Court judge, as the Zeebrugge ferry disaster inquiry had been, and there was some surprise when the appointment went to a QC who had never come close to handling anything of similar scale, complexity and importance.

His uncompromising report attracted an unusual unanimity of praise both for its findings and for the rare fact, for an official report, that it was written in intelligible English. According to a barrister involved in the inquiry, Fennell was extraordinarily quick to grasp the complicated scientific evidence. He said: "Desmond Fennell marked the inquiry with his authority from beginning to end. He was tolerant, courteous and considerate but he was also firm and fearless. He didn't hesitate to criticize where he felt criticism was necessary."

Fennell found the challenge "a fascinating puzzle", but emotionally gruelling. The day after his appointment as chairman he went to the scene of the carnage. "It's something I will never forget. It sounds a dreadful cliché but I can't think of a better description: it must have been the nearest thing to hell on earth. The feeling of claustrophobia, the stench, the burning, the devastation; thinking of the panic that must have gripped the victims trying to scramble for safety. But they were going up, which was precisely the wrong thing to do. It was terribly emotional and it made me even more determined to find out what had happened and to do what I could to make sure it never happened again."

The King's Cross inquiry was also a valuable introduction to becoming a public figure. He learnt to cope with the demands and the attention of the media. Colleagues say that King's Cross visibly boosted his confidence and air of authority. It also made him more relaxed about facing the pressures of publicity which his year as Bar chairman would bring. The superficial awkwardness with journalists which occasionally used to mask his amiability and humour has disappeared.

Only once before King's Cross had Fennell troubled the headline writers, in the unlikely role of protest-leader. The Wing Airport Resistance Association, of which Fennell was chairman, had its moments of glory in the late Sixties and early Seventies when the Roskill Commission into the siting of London's third airport sat for two years and recommended Cublington – Wing by another name – only a few miles from Fennell's home.

Fennell is proud of his group's resistance. "It became the blueprint for the future," he says. Tactics included the burning of an effigy of the arch-villain Lord Justice Roskill, later to become a law lord. The Cublington option was eventually abandoned and Lord Roskill was heard to refer to Fennell as the "man who wasted two years of my life".

The rest of Fennell's career has been covered by respectability and a steady but unremarkable rise, coupled with a quiet and obviously contented home-life with his wife, Susan, and three children, two at university and none showing any signs of entering the law.

The surprise is that Fennell's impeccably English manner and demeanour conceal entirely Irish roots. His mother was a Dubliner, his father a doctor from Cork who had settled in England. Fennell was born in Lincoln and took the conventional path for a son of a comfortably-off Catholic professional family: Ampleforth, Cambridge (economics and law) and two years in the Grenadier Guards. It was his father's disenchantment with the fledgling National Health Service that persuaded him to pursue the law rather than medicine. He had the good luck to become the pupil of Geoffrey Lane, another Lincoln lad, a high-flying criminal barrister and now Lord Chief Justice.

Fennell's style in court is solidly persuasive rather than flamboyant. As a barrister on the Midland and Oxford circuit, where he has spent much of his career, he was known for his meticulous preparation and total command of his brief, and as an advocate with the ability to put to the jury the most complex case in a way which they could understand.

A single interruption to his inexorable professional progress came within a touch of becoming permanent. When Dick Taverne, the Lincoln MP, left the Labour Party and resigned his seat in 1972, Fennell's links with the City got him on the Conservative candidates' short list for the by-election. He lost the nomination narrowly to Jonathan Guinness, who went on to lose the election to Taverne, standing as an independent democrat. Pundits at the time blamed Guinness's loss on a misguided right-wing campaign which included a policy to leave razor blades in the cells of prisoners. Fennell – "I'm dry on economic policy, in the centre on social issues" – thinks he might have fared better, and Lincoln has subsequently become Tory territory. He would have enjoyed being an MP, but never put his name forward again.

The skills he will need to deploy this year on behalf of the Bar are not too different from those that Desmond Fennell, MP for Lincoln, would have required. He will need to be advocate, negotiator, counsellor, fixer, marketing manager and advertising executive in one. It is by far the most difficult brief of his life.

Marcel Berlins

The author is a former Legal Correspondent of The Times.

BIOGRAPHY

1933: Born Lincoln. Educated Ampleforth and Corpus Christi, Cambridge
1956-58: Served with Grenadier Guards
1959: Called to the Bar
1966: Married, one son, two daughters
1969-71: Leads resistance to Cublington as London's third airport
1974: Becomes QC
1982: Awarded OBE for political services
1987: Appointed chairman of King's Cross inquiry
1988: Inquiry report published
1989: Chairman of the Bar

Caught in a cult of copies

artfile

A weekly look at the art world

Sarah Jane Checkland

We have adjusted to the "Shock of the New" – the thesis of the Australian critic Robert Hughes that, over the last century, the more significant the work, the greater has been its shock value. Now Channel 4 is about to advance the "Shock of the Neo", a far more chilling proposition.

A programme next Wednesday suggests that our culture is at risk from two contradictory obsessions: the cult of the original, and our acceptance of the "neo", or copy.

We see that Leonardo da Vinci's "Last Supper" has been reduced by the centuries to a faded ghost. And Rembrandt is dubbed the "Disappearing Master" now that a team of Dutch art historians and scientists has reattributed a number of his works, reducing his accepted *oeuvre* from 700 works to less than 300.

Further shocks follow. Because we are obsessed with Leonardo's cult status, we refuse to acknowledge or admire anything less than the genuine article. The multitude of later "Last Suppers", copied from Leonardo (including the stained glass rendition at Forest Lawn cemetery and the 19th-century version at the Royal Academy), do not therefore rate, although they might more closely resemble the original than the original itself. Also shunned, are the "faithful copies" of great paintings, currently touring Europe in a special exhibition, even though the French theorist Jean Baudrillard points out in the programme that they were painted as "an act of faith, an affirmation of the original".

Another pundit appears, comparing our reverence for "original" works of art to medieval relic worship. "If the saint did not personally touch the cloth, it is no longer of interest," he says.

The market is seen as both catalyst and culprit, prepared to milk any potential source of revenue. Julien Stock, a specialist on Old Masters at Sotheby's, argues on behalf of a daub he hopes is by Titian. If it is "right" it will be worth between £15,000 and £25,000. (The price would have been more than £1 million had it been in better condition.) If the concensus among academics is against, the price will be nearer £1,000.

Stock says that in his quest for authenticity, he trusts that "first feeling, which is either good or bad. This one has a good feeling". On the subject of Rembrandt, he says an "accepted" example can fetch £7 million at auction, while a "doubtful" portrait raised only £400,000 last year. He advises anyone who happens to have one to postpone sale.

Of the Dutch project, he says: "The Rembrandt chaps are making a lot of mistakes and eventually no one will take them very seriously."

So much for the art of the past. The programme now confronts further shocks in the contemporary art market. The American painter Mike Bidlo is discovered studiously copying Picassos and Kandinskys from photographs. The results – ambitious, if only in terms of scale – have been the subject of an exhibition at the Leo Castelli gallery in New York. Bidlo says: "They are other people's paintings but they become mine through osmosis . . . In some strange way I have been able to take possession of them.

"My Kandinsky can function as a Kandinsky but it has another level of meaning because it is a Bidlo. In other words, two for the price of one. I have people buying them because they think I'm an interesting artist."

His words are a nightmare amalgam of two lines of thought: the cult of the original and what Baudrillard calls "the culture of the copy".

We have two 20th-century artists, now dead, to thank for this last affliction: the Frenchman Marcel Duchamp (1887-1968), and the American, Andy Warhol (1928-1987). In 1913, Duchamp expanded the concept of "originality", which had emerged in the 19th century, by presenting his *objets trouvés*, or mass-produced "ready mades". His argument was that his powers as an artist transformed the most mundane of items into art works (when Duchamp is quoted on the programme, a predictable multitude of now famous urinals floats around the screen). This conceptual advance, valid at the time, has become the plague of contemporary art.

Warhol's contribution to the culture of the copy, approximately 50 years later, was to comment on the mass media and its icons, by reproducing famous "Pop" images.

The programme offers no resolutions to the impasse, only gloomy predictions of what is to come. Baudrillard reckons we are heading for a time when "everything will have the same value – the original, the copy, the fake".

That might be true, were it not for the existence of the art market. For experts such as Julien Stock and Leo Castelli will always find ways of grading and evaluating their products, in order to make a living.

• Signals: The Shock of the Neo *will be broadcast on Channel 4, next Wednesday at 9.15pm.*

79 Modular yet strikingly bold – *The Times*'s Spectrum page

BRITAIN'S REGIONAL NEWSPAPER OF THE YEAR

The Northern Echo

No. 36,750   Founded 1870   WEDNESDAY, NOVEMBER 9, 1988   STILL ONLY 18p

4 a.m. EDITION
★★★ Presidential Election Special ★★★

NEWS BRIEF

Grange Hill actress found

TV actress Penny-Belle Fowler, 16, who plays schoolgirl Tracy Dean in Grange Hill, was found wandering on railway lines in Swindon last night after going missing for 24 hours.

Police had said they were "very concerned" about her safety. She was said to suffering emotional problems.

'Ogling' strike

MORE than 300 council workers struck in Liverpool after women workers complained an area housing officer was ogling them.

Escape scare

THE Princess Royal's son, Peter Phillips, was at the centre of a police alert when three teenagers on the run from a youth custody centre broke into his exclusive Dorset boarding school.

Pay up, please

THE RAC is fed-up with being summoned constantly by a minority of members, and in future they will be allowed ten emergency calls a year. More, and their membership will be doubled.

Marcos boost

AN American Supreme Court justice last night granted deposed Philippine President Ferdinand Marcos and his wife Imelda a temporary stay of an order requiring them to produce bank records and other evidence demanded by a federal grand jury.

Death charge

A FATHER and son were remanded in custody last night, accused in connection with the death of four-year-old Irene Morgan in a road accident in Glamorgan.

Walesa crisis

SOLIDARITY leader Lech Walesa faced a rebellion by hundreds of union militants who went ahead with a strike at a Gdansk shipyard, after he decided there should be no showdown with the Polish government.

Bomber crashes

A UNITED States B-1 bomber crashed last night in Texas. Four people were reported to have parachuted from the plane.

IN THE NORTH

Robbery charge

BROTHERS Brian and Ronald Robinson, aged 18 and 25, of Rothsay Terrace, Bedlington, were remanded in custody at Sedgefield yesterday, accused of the robbery of the North of England Building Society office in Church Street, Shildon, on October 28.

Crossbow horror

AN open verdict was recorded at an inquest yesterday on a Wheatley Hill man who shot himself through the head with a crossbow. Page 7.

Memorial row

PEOPLE in Chester-le-Street are enraged by a new, modern £3,500 war memorial, which the local council provided in time for Remembrance Sunday. Critics say it is an insult to the dead.

Pigeon eviction

THOUSANDS of pigeon fanciers in Easington may have to get rid of their birds if the council goes ahead with a plan to ban back-garden lofts. Page 10.

TODAY'S CHOICE: The Echo TV Editor makes these selections for the next 24 hours' viewing. — Tyne Tees TV's series using private letters, diaries and photographs to tell the story of ordinary people during World War One Voices of War (C4, 6.30pm) earns a network screening; it's Mavis and Derek's wedding day in Coronation Street (ITV, 7.30pm); one of the year's best drama series Blind Justice (BBC2, 9pm) bows out with the radical lawyers in direct confrontation with the State; and Desmond Wilcox begins a new batch of documentaries in The Visit (BBC1, 9.30pm) by looking at a controversial therapy for autistic children.
● TV schedules — Page 2.

ECHO COMMENT ON . . .
The next president of the United States, setting off the water board land and picking on the pigeons. Page 2.

RING US

You can ring a Northern Echo reporter or head office DARLINGTON 381313; AYCLIFFE 311312; BARNARD CASTLE (Teesdale) 38029, or Teesdale 38584 (answering machine); BISHOP AUCKLAND 602232; DURHAM 3842251; HARTLEPOOL 272576; MIDDLESBROUGH 247645, 247647; NEWCASTLE (Tyneside) 281 1744; NORTHALLERTON 3510; RICHMOND 5281; STANLEY 280613; 232929; STOCKTON 675578, 671375; SUNDERLAND (Wearside) 567 3422 or 567 9155; YORK 655476, 34683.

Fax Number: (0325) 380539

WEATHER

Today

FORECAST: A few showers are likely, an odd one of which may be on the heavy side, and the day will be generally cloudy with nothing more than an odd bright spell during the day. Winds will be light, mostly at first, but will tend to become south or southwesterly. OUTLOOK: Showers will die out by morning but rain will return later in the day.
WEATHER PLUS: Page 3.

Duke left reeling as Republican sweeps back

By George — it's President Bush

By PHILIP YOUNG

GEORGE Bush will be the 41st President of the United States of America.

But Democrat Michael Dukakis gave him a harder run than anyone expected. Mr Bush won a solid block of support throughout the conservative South and mid-West, but there was no sign of the whitewash some Democrats feared just a week ago.

Riding on a higher-than expected turnout Mr Dukakis picked up significant popular support in many key states but at the end of the day came second in the winner-takes-all system.

★★★ Went down fighting

Late predictions showed Mr Bush's winning margin to be less than 10 percent of the popular vote. And the Democrats were set for victory in the prestige states of New York, Illinois and Washington DC.

An early result showed a Republican victory in Indiana, the home state of Dan Quayle who will become Vice-President when Mr Bush is inaugurated in January.

Mr Bush the winner to become the first sitting vice president since 1836 to be elected to the presidency.

But the Democrats went down fighting. Even as the polls were closing on the East Coast, Mr Dukakis was claimed: "It's a fight to the finish, a cliff-hanger all over the country. It's going to go right down to the wire.

★★★ Surprise a few people

"I think we're not only going to surprise a few people, but we're going to be doing the celebrating," he said.

Black civil rights leader Jesse Jackson, who had fought Mr Dukakis for the Democratic nomination, was among the first to recognise Mr Bush had won: "George Bush is to be congratulated. His basic projection of a kinder, gentler nation must be a commitment that both Republicans and Democrats rally to because the campaign is behind us now," he said in an interview with CBS.

Many Americans told pollsters they were not greatly attracted by either candidate — raising questions about the strength of the popular mandate Mr Bush will be able to call upon in any battles with the Democratic Congress.

Surveys of voters leaving polls suggested Mr Dukakis was doing well in several Western states, including California, Colorado, Montana and Missouri. But losing running mate Lloyd Bentsen's home state of Texas was a major blow

— no Democrat has ever made it the White House without the Lone Star state.

The Democrats were pinning their hopes on reports of much heavier than expected voting in many states. Nationally the party has the most supporters, but they are traditionally more reluctant to vote. A big turn-out by East Coast Jews and blacks could have rocked Mr Bush and Mr Dukakis a chance of victory.

And Mr Bush's celebrations were dampened

by the prospect of both houses of Congress remaining under Democratic control. That would force him to compromise and bargain to win approval for legislation if he wins.

The Presidential candidates were chasing a 270-vote majority of the 538 "electoral votes" cast by each state. The winner of the popular vote in each state receives all of that state's electoral votes.

Profile of a President — Page 8

1988 US PRESIDENTIAL ELECTION - RESULTS   POSITION AT 4.00 am

KEY TO MAIN MAP
Republican won state
Democratic won state
P Projected result
YX. State abbreviation (See table below)

% VOTE   1980   1984
REPUBLICAN   50.7%   58.8%
DEMOCRATIC   41.0%   40.6%
OTHERS   8.2%   0.7%

KEY TO STATES

VOTES CAST BY STATE

KEY TO SMALL MAPS
Republican won state
Democratic won state

File on fans is favoured

ENGLISH and Welsh football fans will have to join a nationwide computerised membership scheme before they can go to matches if a Government working party has its way, Whitehall sources said last night.

The working party's report, to be published later this week, also suggests setting up a football membership authority to administer the scheme as part of the Government's war against soccer hooliganism.

The Prime Minister has been urging such a scheme on Britain's soccer clubs for the past years.

But the football authorities have, in the minds of the Government, been dragging their feet, claiming that such a scheme would be unworkable and too costly.

Mrs Thatcher has warned them that unless they adopt a scheme voluntarily, she is prepared to make it compulsory through legislation. This is what will almost cer-

Colin Moynihan report urged national computer for fans

tainly happen following the report's recommendations.

The working party is chaired by Sports Minister Colin Moynihan and its membership comprises representatives of the police and the football authorities.

Those who have argued against membership schemes have been told by the Prime Minister that Luton Town has been successfully running one for several seasons, while other clubs operate 20 per cent membership schemes without any particular problems.

Most people expect the Government to introduce legislation in the next session of Parliament.

1,000-job hope from new units

UP TO 1,000 jobs may be created on a Spennymoor industrial estate following its purchase by London-based developers.

The scheme, claimed to be the first development of its type in the region, is on the former Courtaulds factory and is due to be launched on November 18.

Pavedelta Ltd, a subsidiary of London-based property company Smithfield Developments plc, recently purchased the former Sedgefield Enterprise Centre from Sedgefield District Council for more than £2m.

Pavedelta's sales and marketing manager Ray McMillan said last night that up to 60 companies would be housed in a variety of units at the centre and estimated 500-1,000 jobs would be created in the 300,000 sq ft factory.

Two units have already been let, to Bootie the Chemist and Rothmans International. Sedgefield District Council's deputy leader Fred Chaplin yesterday said he was delighted at the news.

Lords rebels lose eye vote

THE Government last night finally won its battle to introduce a £10 charge for eye checks.

The House of Lords voted 257 to 207, majority 50 to defeat a Tory rebel bid to scrap the charges, which, with the planned £3.15 fee for dental examination, has caused a major political storm and a serious Commons revolt.

Shortly after, ministers were victorious again when the House rejected a "fall-back" amendment by former Labour Health Secretary Lord Ennals, to exempt pensioners from the eye check charge.

But their majority was slightly trimmed to 41 — voting 227 to 190.

The Lords was packed, following frantic activity by Government whips to bring in "backwoods" supporters from the shires for one of the biggest roll calls this century.

Clear relief could be seen on the face of Health Secretary Kenneth Clarke as he sat on the steps of the Throne to hear the result announced by Government whip Lord Denham.

A revolt on dental checks was

Health Minister Kenneth Clarke: I'm extremely relieved

avoided after the Speaker of the Commons, Bernard Weatherill ruled that this was a financial measures, technically precluding the Lords from maintaining their opposition.

As the debate started, a concession was announced by Lord Privy Seal, Lord Belstead, who promised the Government would consider exempting poorer pensioners from the dental charge.

Health Secretary Mr Clarke said of the defeat of the rebel amendments: "I am extremely relieved.

Permissive price

Kenneth Baker

EDUCATION Secretary Kenneth Baker last night blamed the so-called Swinging Sixties for the "ambiguous" moral climate of the 1980s.

Backing criticism of the "do your own thing" decade, he said that "so-called liberalisation" culminated in "killings by radical left-wing terrorist groups."

Meanwhile, the Church had become absorbed with social policies, and teachers were too reluctant to impart "traditional moral values" to pupils.

Speaking near Bolton, Mr Baker also declared: "I sometimes think that only four-letter word which trendy parents shrank from using, was the word 'don't'.

"The greatest offence of Sixties liberalism and permissiveness was its arrogance — the way it sought to sweep aside the accumulated wisdom and practices which had served society for centuries."

Charles the Silent

PRINCE Charles, a highly vocal critic of architecture at home, decided yesterday that the blame course during his visit to France was to say nothing.

Yesterday, Charles was shown round a housing development by the Mayor of Paris, Jacques Chirac, and was asked by a reporter what he thought of it.

The Prince, who has recently been the scourge of architects and planners in Britain, diplomatically replied "I am trying to keep my opinions private."

He kept his word by remaining silent about other developments that have attracted heavy local criticism.

Earlier, in a speech at a reception, Charles said he "wouldn't dream" of commenting on French architecture, although "one or two French people have already said they would be interested to hear my views".

Charles

81 Combining traditional type style with a modular approach in no way detracts from busy news pages. Note the use of graphics. The *Manchester Evening News*

New directions

The Independent, launched on October 7, 1986, is a classic example of a computer-designed creation. Editor Andreas Whittam Smith, uninhibited by existing print demarcations or any reader tradition, opted to utilize the full capability of the Atex mainframe system and moved straight into direct input by reporters and writers, with electronic editing and full page composition. Although at the time of writing pages are still having to be printed out as bromides to take adverts and pictures by paste-up, make-up with inputted materials, including graphics, is being done with 'mouse' controls on screen straight from the page design.

The result is a model of modular design based upon computer inputs and so is a useful guide to editors in the field of quality broadsheets – which is *The Independent*'s market – of what can be done. The design technique nevertheless reflects *The Independent*'s careful approach to its targeted readership and is as content-based as any good design should be. The pages **(82)** show that modules do not inhibit the use of variable column measures, five different measures being daringly used on page one, despite a standard sized advert, in a paper basically of eight-column format. The result, as it has to be with mixed measures, is a page more horizontal than *The Times*, though type sizes are much the same and picture size, if anything, bigger.

82 A bold and unusual main picture, variable column setting and elegant rulery characterize *The Independent*'s style, as in these page one and foreign news page examples

The foreign news page, with its centred, beautifully cropped picture of the Archbishop of Canterbury receiving President Ortega of Nicaragua, has both elegance and variety. Contributing to this is the bastard measure story tying in the top of the page and the closely juxtaposed lowercase light and bold Century headlines down page; while the end column panel of briefs, as with the news summary on page one, gives an air of busyness. Page one carries fifteen items and page ten has no fewer than twenty-one.

The Independent does more with print rules than *The Times* and, though at first it was much greyer, it is now happy to set a story in bold as a focal point if part of a page is in danger of looking grey. A reason for the greyness of text is that all the body type is down a size on that of *The Times*, which enables it to run its stories longer. Line and paragraph spacing is not generous, and for these reasons it relies for dominant colour on its headlines. Byline style, enhancing the writer's name, is splendidly uniform and less wearing than the brash approach of the tabloids.

The horizontal effect created by the use of rules and variable measures is perhaps the most distinctive thing about an *Independent* page, plus an insistence upon good composition and impeccable cropping in its photographs. The space happily given to good pictures, irrespective of their use as back-up to the stories, makes it a photographers' paper, and it comes as no surprise to find that within two years of existence it had won a handful of design and photographic awards.

More revolutionary in modular design than *The Independent* was the drastic re-styling of *The Guardian* in 1987 from a format which successfully exploited text and pictures at the expense of headlines **(83)** to one dominated by eccentrically spaced headlines and wholly single-column body setting.

The Guardian, partly in the search for stylistic purity and partly to prepare for the economies of on-screen page composition, imposed upon itself a rigid headline format of lowercase Geneva/Helvetica type alternating in modules in black and light across and down the page, with an occasional light italic.

Everything was changed from masthead to the television programmes. With rare exceptions, no headline exceeded four columns in width, and never more than three lines in depth, remaining mostly in two. The unusual visual innovation **(84)** has been to give each headline an eccentric amount of white space below it varying, for reasons which are hard to fathom, from 2 to 5 picas. Bylines have been standardized to one or two lines of 10-point Helvetica black within fine rules, and subject labels to same size single-column WOBs, likewise standard through the paper. Features pages are differentiated by the use of an occasional small strapline or standfirst.

The effect of this rather austere type treatment is to give the paper a great deal of visual continuity and a distinct typographical character. Good sized and well-cropped pictures help to break up most pages,

THE GUARDIAN

BELL'S SCOTCH WHISKY BELL'S

BELL'S SCOTCH WHISKY BELL'S

Printed in London and Manchester   Saturday June 8 1985   25p

Today

Open-air epic
PAGE 13

Lord of the censors
PAGE 17

Monday
FREEDOM FIGHTER
The new ideological guerrilla: Guardian Women meets a terrorist from the Animal Liberation Front.

Tuesday
PLACE SEEKERS
Where will 10,000 children end up? Education Guardian on the battle for parental choice of school.

Thursday
BOND AND BIRD
Derek Malcolm reviews the new Bond and Alan Parker's Cannes prizewinner, Birdy. Movie Guardian.

News in Brief

Bank aids Sinclair
THE Bank of England is becoming the efforts to salvage Sinclair Research, Britain's embryo home computer company. Page 18.

Threat to unions

Bitter switch

Bank charges

League gag

Whose gold?

Market moves

The weather
COOL, with sunny intervals. Details, back page.

Inside

Supporters want legislation brought forward

Powell bill fails but embryo battle hots up

By Colin Brown, Political Reporter

Tory backbenchers last night mounted a campaign to force the Government to bring forward legislation banning embryo research, after a private member's bill by Mr Enoch Powell had been "talked out" in the Commons.

END OF QUEST: John Bowker, Isle of Wight chief fire officer, and Tantryalos Gironas telling journalists that Tantryalos's brother Ramanus had been found dead

Rescue workers find body in well

By Seumas Milne

Axe falls on pit that led strike

By Peter Hetherington

US fails to sway Europe

By Hella Pick

The United States has failed in its attempt to secure formal Nato endorsement of President Reagan's Strategic Defence Initiative, but this weekend will not alter US determination to press ahead with the project.

'Inside man' behind £6 m security haul

By Paul Keel

A highly placed "inside man" at the time of a raid on the Security Express headquarters provided crucial information enabling an armed gang to steal £6 million in Britain's biggest cash robbery, according to senior sources at Scotland Yard.

Militia takes Unifil troops hostage

From AP and Reuter
in Sidon

Soldiers of the Israeli-backed South Lebanon Army last night threatened to kill 24 Finnish members of Unifil, who they took hostage earlier in the day, unless Shi'ite Muslim guerrillas free three comrades, a US spokesman, Mr Timor Goksel, said. Late last night, the militia released two prisoners.

Thatcher talks, page 6

Falklands war ferry holed

The North Sea Ferry Norland, which spent five months serving in the Falklands war and was narrowly missed by bombs, was towed back to port last night after being holed by a German ship off the Dutch coast.

Ramanus Gironas — trying to escape

Honest Ed's Old Vic bit part

By Aileen Ballantyne

Honest Ed Mirvish, the Canadian son of an unsuccessful encyclopedia salesman who became a multi-millionaire and bought the Old Vic in London, will today take a bit part — as himself — in the biggest television advertising campaign so far for British theatre.

Gerard Vaughan — Government should act

They've both got heart disease.
We want to know why.

We've already identified smoking and obesity as major causes of heart disease.

What the British Heart Foundation is trying to discover is why, even fit, non-smokers can be affected.

That's just one of the many areas where we need your help to fund heart research.

To find out how you can give it, simply return the coupon to us today.

The more you help us, the more we'll find out.

Name
Address
Postcode

British Heart Foundation
The heart research charity.

---

83 *The Guardian*, June 8, 1985 – a low-key type style shortly to be discarded

Records, page 32
Johnny Cash:
southern comfort of
the man in black

Review, page 29
Marcel Proust:
new light on
things past

Analysis, page 27
Ed Koch:
fighting off the
Big Apple's G-man

Zimbabwe, page 14-17
Robert Mugabe:
Potholes on the
road to socialism

* *
30p
Friday
May 12
1989
Published in London
and Manchester

The Guardian

Bush works hard to win Latin American support

US sends in new troops to Panama

Martin Walker in Washington
and Scott Wallace in Panama

PRESIDENT Bush sent over 2,000 fresh American combat troops to Panama yesterday, and ordered all dependants of US personnel to be moved to protected quarters.

But there was no immediate US military threat to the Noriega regime, and the White House was still clearly relying on building a united front of diplomatic pressure from Latin American nations to force General Noriega from office.

Assuming for the first time the mantle of Commander-in-Chief "with a profound obligation to protect American life," Mr Bush told a White House press conference: "We will not be intimidated by the bullying tactics, brutal though they may be, of this dictator Noriega."

The reinforcements brought the number of US troops in Panama to over 13,000.

"I am worried about the lives of Americans citizens and I'll do what is necessary to protect them," the president said, adding that the US ambassador was being recalled, and the embassy cut back to essential staff only.

"The US will not recognise nor accommodate with a regime that wields power through force and violence, at the expense of the Panamanian people's right to be free." Mr Bush added, "If we fail to send a clear signal, the enemies of democracy will become more dangerous."

Outraged by the beating of the Panamanian opposition leaders, Mr Bush was said to be gripped by the threat to US civilians in Panama from Gen Noriega's supporters.

White House aides said they had never seen the president so angry, as he pounded the Oval Office table yesterday and insisted: "I will not have another Iran hostage crisis."

Mr Bush was yesterday rallying the US's friends in Latin America to join in a united front of pressure on Gen Noriega to stand down before more blood was shed.

In a series of phone conversations with other heads of government yesterday, including Mrs Thatcher, the president sought and apparently won the backing of Colombia, Peru, Argentina, El Salvador, Costa Rica, Guatemala, Spain and Canada.

In London, the High Court ruled yesterday that private documents of Gen Noriega, seized during a drugs inquiry, could be released to the US.

But in a report from Moscow which threatened to escalate the diplomatic reach-of the crisis, the Tass news agency suggested that the Panamanian Government had been justified in declaring the election void. Radio Havana yesterday denounced what it said were "transparent US preparations to use force."

"Our objectives are first of all, to protect American citizens. Secondly, to maintain the integrity of the Panama Canal Treaty. Fourthly, to maintain the integrity and our interests in the defence community there and in our defence establishments. Fifthly, to propose and promote our interest in democracy and guaranteeing the rights and wishes of the Panamanian people. And you can mix and match these any way you want to," the official White House spokesman, Mr Martin Fitzwater, said.

With temperatures on the rise, Panamanians and the thousands of Americans living in Panama are bracing themselves for heightened violence.

On Wednesday night the official election tribunal nullified the results of Sunday's balloting. The tribunal, controlled by officials loyal to Gen Noriega, cited a series of irregularities—including the widespread disappearance of ballots and tally sheets — that made it "absolutely impossible" to pronounce a winner.

Some observers interpreted the annulment of the vote as a conciliatory gesture by Gen Noriega that could pave the way for a rapprochement with the opposition.

But the move was widely seen as an acknowledgement that the vote was so overwhelmingly against the general that it was impossible to designate his hand-picked presidential candidate, Mr Carlos Duque, the winner.

Bush opposition leaders — tending their wounds after they were beaten by pro-Noriega mobs on Wednesday — said they would only negotiate with Gen Noriega if he recognised them as the victors of Sunday's elections. In the meantime, they promised to continue their "peaceful struggle" in their efforts to take power.

The second vice-presidential candidate for the US-backed Civic-Democratic Opposition Alliance, or ADOC — Guillermo "Billy" Ford — was dumped in his front yard late on Wednesday after several hours in detention. Mr Ford and ADOC's presidential candidate, Mr Guillermo Endara, suffered injuries in Wednesday's violence as they led an opposition march to claim a moral victory in Panama's election.

Mr Endara is in hospital, and doctors fear he may have suffered some brain injury.

Noriega documents, page 2

Rifkind admits Tory failings

Peter Hetherington

THE Scottish Secretary, Mr Malcolm Rifkind, yesterday acknowledged that the Government was perceived to be insensitive to Scotland's needs, interests and aspirations. His admission surprised some representatives at the Tories' annual Scottish conference at Perth and delighted the Opposition.

In a self-critical examination of the Tories' performance since the General Election, Mr Rifkind moved to establish a new cross-party consensus based on support for the union with England.

He said it was time for the Government to consolidate north of the border, after new radical measures, implying that Thatcherism had to be slowed down.

With many activists increasingly alarmed by the Tories' inability to challenge a resurgent Scottish National Party, the minister said his party had failed to enlist the support of a "substantial majority" of Scots who found socialism and separatism an anathema.

"If we have only been able to attract a modest minority to the Scottish Tory banner that is, in part, our fault either in presentation or in substance or in both," he said. Support for the Scots Tories, with only 10 of the country's 72 MPs, is running well behind the SNP at just over 20 per cent.

Mr Rifkind coupled his plea for greater sensitivity with an appeal to the Labour and Liberal parties to come to the aid of the union. This followed warnings from the Scottish education and health minister, Mr Michael Forsyth, and the former Scottish Tory Party chairman, Mr Michael Ancram, that the 302-year-old union was facing its greatest threat.

Significantly, Mr Rifkind concentrated his fire on the nationalists and avoided strong criticism of Labour, which he regards as a unionist party in the wood during an emerging constitutional crisis.

Labour is one of the organisations that has formed the Scottish Constitutional Convention, now studying home rule options. Other groups include the Democrats, churches and trade unions.

Mr Rifkind attacked the convention as a gathering of "closed minds". Noting that the unionist parties gained 65 per cent of the Scottish vote at the last election, he said: "What is needed now is a genuine dialogue and debate amongst Scottish unionists of all political persuasions and a realisation that we are all seeking what is best for Scotland."

However, he was unclear over how the opposition parties would meet for such a debate. Questioned afterwards about a meeting place for such a dialogue, Mr Rifkind suggested the House of Commons, or "101 platforms around Scotland."

He offered the Scottish Office, which oversees most devolved government in Scotland, as a vehicle for a cross-party campaign.

Politics, pages 6 and 7; Leader comment, page 20

News in brief

'Duped woman' Lockerbie clue

The FBI is investigating the possibility that the unwitting carrier of the Lockerbie bomb may have been an American student who had an Arab boyfriend. Page 10

Mortgage gloom

The Bank of England says there must be better news on inflation before there can be any let-up in interest rates. Pages 18 and 28

Keeler envoy 'did duty'

The Soviet diplomat at the centre of the Christine Keeler scandal has broken silence to say: "I was only fulfilling my diplomatic duties." Page 10

Inside

Agreeable disagreement . . . Mr Mikhail Gorbachev and the US Secretary of State, Mr James Baker, share a joke at yesterday's Kremlin talks

Gorbachev offers nuclear cuts

Jonathan Steele in Moscow
and Helle Ploh

PRESIDENT Gorbachev yesterday offered a unilateral cut in the Soviet Union's short-range nuclear missiles. He is sending his Foreign Minister, Mr Eduard Shevardnadze, to Bonn to explain the proposals for a "comprehensive resolution of this question".

The proposals were put forward during talks in Moscow between the Soviet leader and the US Secretary of State, Mr James Baker.

Last night, Mr Baker said Mr Gorbachev would unilaterally withdraw 500 short-range nuclear weapons from Europe by the end of the year. US officials also told reporters that Mr Gorbachev outlined for the first time the specifics of a Soviet plan to reduce conventional forces in Europe.

Mr Baker made it clear that the United States would not accept a total elimination of tactical nuclear weapons even if talks on the issue ever started.

The Soviet move comes as Nato is embroiled in a bitter dispute over the future of short-range nuclear missiles. It will almost certainly be interpreted in Washington and London as an unwelcome Soviet attempt to help West Germany's attempt to defer a Nato decision on these weapons' modernisation.

"We have agreed to disagree," Mr Baker said in Moscow yesterday, after confirming that there had been no meeting of minds over short-range nuclear weapons.

West Germany, against Anglo-American opposition, is pressing the Western alliance to enter into negotiations with the Soviet Union on reducing arsenals of this last remaining class of land based missiles.

Mr Gorbachev's offer of unilateral cuts in Soviet arsenals, which are more than 16 times the size of Nato's, underlines Soviet eagerness to reduce and eventually eliminate them altogether.

But the Soviet leader's move will also reinforce the suspicions of the Bush Administration that his key foreign policy objective is to divide the Nato allies and secure the denuclearisation of Europe.

Caution towards Moscow will remain the watchword, even though Mr Baker in Moscow was the bearer of a very friendly letter from Mr Bush who has ended his "pause" in US-Soviet relations and re-launched the entire range of superpower arms talks.

Mr Bush has assured Mr Gorbachev that he considers the changes already brought by perestroika to be "significant, even revolutionary." The warmth tone and content of the Bush letter are music to Soviet ears.

The talks in Moscow were the first formal session of superpower negotiations since the Bush Administration started its strategic review. Afterwards, Mr Baker said: "The president emphasised in the strongest terms his support for perestroika".

The Soviet leader kept his politburo colleagues waiting 45 minutes for their regular Thursday meeting as he discussed the contents of Mr Bush's letter.

Mr Baker said his two days of talks here had laid the foundation for "continuity and change" in US-Soviet relations.

"The president wanted me to say that the US is ready to re-engage across the full range of our relations," he added.

But Mr Baker made it clear that there is little chance of a Bush-Gorbachev summit this year.

He said the two sides had agreed to resume the strategic arms talks, adjourned last November, sometime between June 12 and 19. The standing consultative conference which is looking at anti-ballistic missile issues will start in June, as will the talks on nuclear testing.

The bilateral chemical weapons talks would be ex-

tended to cover missile proliferation.

The Soviet side told Mr Baker that it sticks by the joint draft of a treaty cutting strategic arms by 50 per cent which was worked out under the Reagan Administration. It made it clear there has been no softening on its position that the Star Wars programme is incompatible with the 1972 anti-ballistic missile treaty.

Gorbachev-News talks, page 10;
Leader comment, page 20

Power staff reject 7.5pc as Bank warns on pay

Simon Beavis and Larry Elliott

THE wave of threatened industrial action over pay grew last night as leaders of Britain's 76,000 power workers rejected an increased 7.5 per cent pay offer and warned of a possible overtime ban within a fortnight.

The move came as the Bank of England says it would stand a stiff warning that pay settlements were too high and as nearly 19,000 London bus workers voted to begin strike action from Monday to coincide with a third unofficial stoppage by Tube drivers. The bus vote followed an overwhelming rejection of a 7.1 per cent pay offer.

The decision to begin industrial action in the power industry came after union leaders rejected a 0.5 per cent increase on a previous offer from the Electricity Council of 7 per cent.

Union leaders said they had ordered a freeze on an open-ended agreement with employers on changing working practices to force a further increase in the pay offer.

After meeting leaders of the four unions representing power workers yesterday, the Electricity Council said it was disappointed by the decision, but stressed that it was ready to re-enter negotiations to avert industrial action.

It is thought likely that talks could be reconvened before action begins or that the conciliation service, Acas, could be brought into negotiations.

Union leaders believe that the overtime ban, which begins at midnight on May 24, will have an immediate effect on the industry. In particular it would disrupt annual overhauls of equipment in power stations and could lead to losses of supply and blackouts by the autumn.

They also suggest that five-day agreement on changes to work practices could pose a serious threat to privatisation plans for the industry at a time when employers were demanding greater flexibility in the run up to the planned sell-off.

Mr Fred Franks, national officer for the EETPU electricians union and chairman of the union negotiating team, said last night that the action had been "purposefully set at a modest level to force the employers back to the negotiating table".

He made it clear that, although precise demands for a settlement had not been set out at meetings with employers yesterday, workers were looking for a pay increase well in excess of the current 7.5 per cent inflation level.

"It was noticeable that they did not say it was 'their' final offer. They said they were not in the position to improve the offer," he added.

The offer would mean increases of up to £11.70 a week for the lowest grade, £14.58 for craftsmen, and up to £18.91 for top grade foremen.

The Bank's warning on pay, which came in its quarterly bulletin, reflected government concern over wage deals. Officials want to see settlements lower than they were this time last year, rather than running 1 to 2 per cent higher.

Frontiers, page 23; Bank ruling, page 28

Why are British butchers' shops like abattoirs? Here's your guide to better service, and the 10 tell-tale signs that'll get you better meat

Unkind cuts come close to the bone

Food and Drink

Prue Leith

WATCHING Albert Roux knowledgeably fondling slices of beef and whole lamb carcases on The Roux Brothers one evening, my perennial wrath with British butchers was rekindled. Why do they persist in displaying their ware with all the charm of a knacker's yard?

The only butchers I know to ensure their premises do not smell of blood and warm offal, to display their meat neatly and cleanly and, most important of all, who can cut in a straight line, are French — like the chaps at Lamartine and Baileys, owned, you will not be surprised to hear, by Albert Roux.

There is nothing more maddening than paying large sums of good money for a beautiful best-end of English lamb, only to watch the butcher's lad saw straight through the chine and into the eye of the meat — ruining eight cutlets at a stroke.

Or to watch in helpless fury as the chap cheerfully scores you pork crackling, failing to mark the sides and edges at all, and cutting so deep into the middle with half-a-

dozen vandal's slashes that there's no hope of the skin ever turning into crackling. The juices bubble through and turn it to leather.

I was at a shop in Stow-on-the-Wold the other day and I bought — for £17-odd — 10 large lamb steaks cut through the leg. The butcher cut them with his back to me, which is fair enough, but he failed to show them to me before he bundled them, in an untidy heap, on to the scales.

Wanting to see what I was getting, I lifted the top one by a corner to peer underneath, which provoked the manageress to say, "You haven't paid for those yet, madam. They are not yours and you may not touch them." I'm sure the Health Inspector would approve, but the attitude of those two people, who want me presumably to go on spending large sums with them, is staggering.

In France, even in a street market, the pride and pleasure of the meat salesman in his wares is obvious. The joints of larger cuts are barded, larded, neatly tied. They all on clean trays, with perhaps a sprig of fresh — not plastic — parsley.

The cutlets or chops are trimmed of fat, the bones scraped clean and shortened. The escalopes lying in gleaming rows are all the same size, same shape, same thickness.

The kidneys are arranged with

loving pride in concentric circles, or smart rows. No battered tin bucket here. The chickens and poussins are marshalled like soldiers in descending order of size. No heap of birds upside-down in the window or flung to the back of the chopping block.

And why can't an Englishman joint a chicken? Your average butcher's method is to hack it up with a cleaver, leaving splintered backbone attached to thigh and wing. A French butcher will joint a chicken into four or eight, removing the scraggy bits of skin and the pinions from the wing, and separating the leg from the body to include the oyster but to exclude the backbone.

British butchers think nothing of giving you chops two inches thick on the bone or fatty side tapering to nothing on the meat side, or chickens mysteriously missing half their giblets, or kidneys shrivelled or slashed in skinning, or stewing beef that takes you an hour to trim because it's all in bits. He could have trimmed it in two minutes when it was still in one piece.

I suppose it is the British public's fault, notoriously uncomplaining and quite prepared to queue for half-an-hour if the meat is good quality and the butcher is friendly And never mind if the duck we go home with has legs hairier than an Afghan rug.

Take a butchers

Out to Lunch

Matthew Fort

SO WHERE do we go for a decent piece of lamb or beef? Prue Leith has told us what not to look for in characteristic measured and tempered tones. I thought that it would be a good idea to compile a list of 10 Tell Tale Signs, as one newspaper might put it, that may lead us to better meat. Most of it is common sense. Some of it may be the counsel of perfection. It rather depends where you are.

1. Don't buy your meat in a supermarket (with the possible exception of corn fed or "free range" chickens). It's not that your supermarket won't have decent meat. It may do, but once it is armoured in plastic it's impossible to tell. Supermarkets don't have the facility to hang meat and meat aged in Cryovac packages is not the same as meat aged by hanging it in a chill room.

2. By the same token, don't buy meat that is already wrapped, particularly when it is wrapped in plasticised stretchy stuff which makes it look all smooth and plump and palatable, and which can disguise enough disappointments to make you a vegetarian.

3. Avoid meat that seeps blood or other liquid. At the very best it will mean that it has not been hung for long enough. At it's worst it will mean that it has an unacceptably high water content. You will see plenty of liquid in a lot of supermarket meat, which is why they put in that stuff like happy lining in the bottom of the containers.

4. Choose a butcher who hangs his own meat. I know that fewer and fewer butchers do this. It's largely a matter of economics. Beef can hang for up to three weeks before it is ready. Even lamb, particularly older lamb, benefits from a little judicious ageing. This ties up considerable sums of capital. Then the meat can lose up to 15 per cent of its bulk in the process. The effects of this on profit margins can easily be imagined, so be prepared to pay more. Have you ever noticed the phenomenon of the incredible shrinking roast? That is because the liquid -- blood, water — that you have paid for is leached out in the cooking process and not in the hanging process.

5. Talk to your butcher, even if it's a Saturday morning and the queue stretches through the shop, round the corner and down the street. Ask him where this nice looking brisket came from, or what part of the country is currently producing that splendid leg of lamb. Ask him to trim, to chine, to bone or not to bone. Get him to show you the meat before he wraps it up. Inspect it thoroughly.

6. Don't be afraid of your butcher. He may stand 6ft 4ins in his stockinged feet, have fearsome moustaches, blood all over his striped apron and carry a knife the size of a broad sword, but he is human like the rest of us and craves love and appreciation.

If what he has given you is rubbish, tell him so. If it was tough or had shards of bone in it, or ended up half the size it was before it started, have a quiet word with him. If it happens a second time, have a go at him, particularly in front of other customers. And if that doesn't work, I don't know what to do. If you don't complain at

all, he will serve you rubbish from time to time because he knows that he can get away with it.

7. Appearance is important, although I am not sure that it tells you that much about the quality of the meat. A good display probably means that the butcher is a shrewd marketing man. It's much easier to sell stuff that looks nice and well laid out. It makes for a more cheerful shopping experience. But it also probably means that the butcher cares enough for his produce, and that is definitely a Good Thing.

Frequently, continental or continental style butchers look more enticing, partly because they have a tradition of displaying their meat well, but also because they trim and treat their meat to a much greater extent that your traditional English butcher, where the minimum of preparation is actually done to the meat. It isn't really a matter of sloppiness, but of style. The consequence, however, is that the continental style meat looks much neater, more stylish, and there's less waste on it - and you pay more for it.

8. Don't be duped by fresh looking, scarlet meat, and don't be afraid of brown, dull looking meat. The one was probably on the hoof a day or two before, while the other was ageing gracefully in the hanging room.

9. Lamb and beef should have a tracery of fat running through the meat. This will disappear in the cooking, but helps to keep the meat moist during the cooking process and helps to give it flavour at the end. The hue and cry for lean meat is a modern fad, and is not really consistent with food that is supposed to taste of something.

10. While fat on a joint of beef will almost certainly mean it's hardly seen a blade of grass in its life, being fed on barley. This produces an inferior flavour. Grass fed cattle tend to have creamy fat foaming around the outside.

Eating Out

Tips, ties and tots

Tom Jaine, the new editor of The Good Food Guide, welcomes a small reform which takes us nearer to the tip-free restaurant but asks why we still have to conform to social anachronisms

THERE CAN'T be many businesses that manage to impose their wills on the customer so successfully as restaurants.

Time of attendance, method of payment, mode of dress, age of guests, even the language used on menus and notices — all these may be dictated by the proprietor with never a thought for the convenience of a thousand potential customers.

They may even have to go through a complex initiation ceremony, called booking a table, to be admitted to the shrine: telephone the first time, give home and office telephone numbers, give credit card numbers for insurance against non-appearance, then phone a second time on the day of the assumption itself. And Lord help you if you are late. In a seller's market, the customer can get away with quite a lot.

For all the strides that have been taken towards a consumer's nirvana of straight dealing, up-front admissions of origin and ingredients, and consideration for minority groups, the customer still gets a number of raw deals.

How about good old tipping? A chestnut if ever there was one. In the early Sixties, faced with public uncertainty, Trust House (before Forte) instituted the ser-

85   Justifying the unjustified – a daring approach to body setting in the *Weekend Guardian*

but the prevailing effect of the type use is to lessen the influence of the designer in the helping the scanning eye through the pages. The stories, although some are set in bold type as a variant, lie curiously flat and unaccented in the pages and one is more conscious than one should be of the obtrusiveness of the type style. A novelty is that drop letters, which appear on all stories apart from the smallest fillers, are chosen not to a house style but are of a size and type to match the headline above. There is a recognisable logic in this, but unfortunately the result is that two facing pages can have on them as many as ten different sorts of drop letters, some bold, some light, some roman, some italic, some big, some quite titchy.

On the credit side, the various parts of the paper – home, international, financial and sports news, comment and analysis, and the various features sections and listings are well tabbed across the top of the pages, and the paper is made easy to handle both from the editing and editioning point of view, and from the point of view of the reader, provided its presentation is found acceptable.

The design theme is continued inside the paper's weekend supplement, the *Weekend Guardian* **(85)**. The same 18 point rules made up of eight fine rules are used to cut one feature away from the other. The headlines, though set to the same style, having slipped into Garamond look much softened and the longer texts make the type style less obtrusive. The doctrinaire design approach, however, has resulted in the entire reading text being set unjustified ragged right.

Good and bad design

The variability of newspaper design, each within its market, nevertheless demands some sort of standards by which success or otherwise can be judged, and it is here that we return to general principles and common factors applicable to all styles. To give some examples of the sort of faults that count against newspapers in design contests, we can say that a page fails if it is:

Too fussy. Excessively busy leading to poor visual balance.
Too jazzy. Too many display devices crammed into one page resulting in a failure to establish effective highlights.
Overcrowded. Trying to get too much into the page.
Dull. Failure to exploit the page ingredients so as to attract the eye, that is, without clearly defined highlights and creative type and picture balance.
Has clashes. With headline type or picture clashing with the adverts or the adjoining page.
Muddled. Failure to properly sort out and order the page ingredients into a meaningful and attractive pattern, resulting in confusion to the eye.
Has poor type balance. Stories fighting each other, or all demanding the same attention. Headlines badly fitting.
Has poor page furniture. Unskilful use of typographical devices such as panels and special setting, bylines and standfirsts in wrong type; failure to utilize artwork; captions badly placed; poor use of crossheads and other breakers.
Has poor picture use. Badly sited pictures; poor cropping and sizing; failure to utilize picture potential.

The examples in the following two pages illustrate the effect of some of these faults.

Faulty meter leads to shocking electric bill

A MOTHER-OF-FIVE was hit with an electricity bill of more than £2,400 — for having a faulty meter.

Mrs. Katherine Bartlett, of Dulwich, was told her meter had been "under-registering" for two years.

The London Electricity Board (LEB) then demanded she pay £2,451.39 for power she was estimated to have used within that time.

But the determined mum refused and last month won a court declaration stating she was NOT liable to pay.

Her lawyer Nik Nicol said after the case, "My experience suggests that Mrs. Bartlett is not the only one who has suffered from such behaviour.

"I hope that other people will take heart from this case and not just give in if they disagree with their electricity bill.

Council rapped over plight of mum

● *A HOMELESS mother-of-two had to wait THREE years to be re-housed after her marriage broke up.*

● *The desperate mum bedded down with family and her children shared cramped conditions while Southwark Council showed "a high degree of inefficiency," according to the local government*

Ombudsman.

● *He has ruled the council should improve links with tenants and apologise for unnecessarily delaying her application for a new home.*

● *Southwark housing officers incorrectly graded her application TWICE and allowed months to go by.*

"If you think your bill is wrong, seek advice to have it checked out," he added.

Mrs. Bartlett said LEB's estimate was totally unfair, especially since she had been paying regular quarterly bills of about £100.

LEB spokeswoman Anne Hewitt said the bill was totalled judging the types of appliances in Mrs. Bartlett's home, using past experience and advice from other electricity groups.

She added, "We try to follow up where we think there has been a history of electricity not being recorded correctly to make it fair on our other customers."

WEST NORWOOD: A man armed with a revolver escaped with £600 after raiding the Woolwich Building Society in Norwood Road on Monday afternoon.

CLAPHAM: Firefighters battled for an hour to bring a blaze in a warehouse in Bromells Road, under control on Monday. Most of the roof was destroyed. Rubbish being burnt next to the building is believed to have started the fire.

SOUTHWARK: A hospital chief has agreed to attend a meeting of health watchdogs to answer their questions on opting out. Dr. Hugh Saxton, chairman of Guy's Hospital Unit Management Board, will attend a special meeting of Lewisham and North Southwark Community Health Council on Tuesday. The meeting, which is open to the public, will be held in the Court Room, Guy's Hospital, St. Thomas Street, Southwark, at 7 p.m.

WATERLOO: Members of the London Cycling Campaign demonstrated by Waterloo Bridge on Wednesday, against the pollution caused by cars.

WANDSWORTH: Two secondhand dealers who sold dangerous electric fires have been prosecuted by the council. The move follows a crackdown by Wandsworth trading standards officers which found a string of faults in fires being sold in local shops, including bare live ports, unsafe switches and cables with old colour coding. The two traders were fined a total of £240 and ordered to pay more than £900 in costs.

(a)

● PLEA — Paul Daniel

Setback for Aids helpers

A CASH lifeline for a voluntary group which helps support AIDS sufferers has been withheld.

London Lighthouse asked Wandsworth Council for a £7,120 grant to pay for this year's running costs in providing three teams of workers. The group has been in the borough for the last 18 months and has already given aid to 10 sufferers.

But Wandsworth has deferred a decision on the grant because of a lack of information about the group.

Labour councillor Paul Daniel, who is pushing for a quick result, said, "None of the councillors on the grants and IAP sub-committee had been given the proper information. No-one was aware that the scheme was up and running.

"London Lighthouse should be given the money now and not be made to wait for months."

The 24 Wandsworth volunteers come from all walks of life to comfort people with AIDS and help with everyday things like shopping, walking the dog and washing.

Communication manager Mary Pipes said without council funding the group may be forced to cut back on service.

"We would find it difficult to operate the groups in that area and we would have to consider whether we could afford to run the service," she said.

100% OR 110% HAPPY BACK

100's OF DISCOUNTED **EXHAUSTS**

2 YEAR GUARANTEE ON ALL COMPLETE EXHAUST SYSTEMS.

(b)

UNBEATABLE PRICES ON **TYR**

DUNLOP HIGH P...

LOCAL BUSINESSES ASK ABOUT OPENING AN ACCOUNT TODAY.

● BRITAIN'S 44 million voters go to the polls tomorrow to express THEIR views on Europe's future.

● THE BATTLE for the 81 seats in the European Parliament — 78 in England, Scotland and Wales and three in Northern Ireland — also gives them a chance to send Mrs Thatcher a message on her policies at home.

● THE SCORE at the moment is: 45 Tories, 32 Labour and 1 SNP. But polls predict Labour will return more MEPs than the Tories.

● MRS THATCHER'S hard-line anti-European stance has led to fears that the nation will not be prepared to meet the challenge of 1992 when the European Community becomes a single market.

● SWEEPING changes to be introduced this year by Education Secretary Kenneth Baker have raised fears over future standards in Britain's state schools.

● CAN Britain's education measure up to Europe? The Mirror investigates . . .

'I may have to go abroad'

THE 16-year-olds at Holden Lane High School are sweating over their GCSE exams in long hot halls right now.

Each will take an

ELECTION '89 USE YOUR **EURO VOTE** TOMORROW

'We get on well with our teachers'

LIKE most French parents Mme Vitel Crepin, a 42-year-old laboratory analyst, keeps a close watch on her son's education.

And she was delighted when teachers at Lille's Franklin Comprehensive school spotted 14-year-old Xavier's computing skills.

Classes in technical training and two rooms filled with modern computer terminals at the school have helped him build up an advanced knowledge of complex programmes.

Mme Crepin hopes the knowledge will enhance her son's job prospects.

Extras

But if he loses interest, he still has TEN...

86 *Design faults*: (a) The rules here have tied the Aids story firmly in with the advert instead of offsetting it. (b) Blobs, stars, big quotes, drop letters, wobs, halftone, underscore . . . the eye hardly knows where to turn. (c) A halftone picture instead of the WOB lead headline would have got the designer out of trouble. (d) A good picture that has turned its head firmly away from the story

(c)

Special survey

SERVICE

closest to a woman's heart

ESTEE LAUDER'S Re nutriv: Frosted Apricot: £7.50.
☐ Definitely kissproof and stayed put for
☐ Neither too greasy or too dry

MARKS AND SPENCER'S im-
ages Range: Golden Glow: 89p
☐ Perfumed and greasy. Stayed on for
1hr 15 mins. Not kissproof.

Detective died after freak car plunge

A DETECTIVE sergeant died when his unmarked police car inexplicably plunged off the road, demolishing a hedge and 85 feet of wooden fencing.

Neil Gibson, 32, was impaled on a fence post which smashed through the windscreen of his Vauxhall Astra car.

A police vehicle exam-
iner told an inquest that Sergeant Gibson did not appear to have been

By Echo reporter

The inquest was told DS Gibson, a member of the Serious Crimes Squad, was back to colleagues from Runcorn police station

FREE CAMERA
WHEN YOU BUY ANY ITEM £10 OR OVER!

TOMORROW ONLY (THURSDAY 9 MARCH)

ACTUAL SIZE!!

(d)

Eleven for for Imperial

THE William Hill Imperial Cup, Saturday's feature race, has attracted the smallest field for years.

Just eleven horses have stood their ground at the five-day stage with the weights set to rise at least a stone for the Sandown contest.

Toby Balding's Beech Road will carry top weight of 11st 13lb, which includes a 6lb penalty for his recent defeat of Vagador at Fontwell.

But the trainer, who also has Little Toro among the entries, was playing his cards close to his chest yesterday.

Asked whether his pair were likely runners he responded: "Maybe both, maybe neither."

Special Vintage, winner of the Tote Jackpot Handicap Hurdle at the Esher course last month, is set to carry 11st 10lb, but his participation depends on the going.

Trainer Jimmy Fitzgerald said: "As long as it's not heavy, he will run but we will leave a decision as late as possible. He wouldn't be happy carrying a big weight, but he's used to it.

"Despite the poor turn-out the sponsors are not disappointed. Hills spokesman Don Payne said: "Considering that we have had such a mild winter, it is not all that surprising.

"There is such a glut of races for trainers to choose from with the Cheltenham Festival and the County Hurdle in particular offering valuable alternatives."

GOING: Heavy.

Warwick

JANUS
2 00—Matchingham   2 30—Strike-A-Point
TATTERSALL
2 00—Somber

Tresidder can go one better

By MATT SEYMOUR

TRESIDDER, runner up at the last meeting, is fancied to go one better in the Robin and John Simpson Memorial Handicap Chase at Sedgefield this afternoon.

He looked a much improved performer landing the Hope Inn Handicap Chase over today's course in December and confirmed that impression when he followed up at Ayr, despite a last fence blunder.

Course specialist Jody's Boy, a prolific winner this season, having scored seven times in 18 outings, is closely handicapped with Tresidder on their running behind Castlevennon in the George Mulcaster Memorial Cup over today's course in January.

On that occasion, second placed Jody's Boy held a neck advantage over my selection at the line, but I am confident Tresidder will come out on top today.

Trailing Rose, prone to the odd jumping error, finally got her head in front at Edinburgh last time, and given a clear round

could be concerned in the finish.

Tsar tackles today's trip for the first time and may prove best of the rest. Tresidder however looks a safe bet to outpace them all.

Extended

Arthur Stephenson, leading trainer at the course, saddles Polar Nomad in the McEwans Best Scotch Durham National. He has progressed quickly since tackling extended distances and has outstayed the opposition, taking the Pintail Handicap Chase at Newcastle and the Tote Eider Chase over the same course on his last two completed starts.

Sure to be well supported to win the race for the Leasingthorne handler, who was successful in the corresponding race last year with Sir Jest, I am, however, inclined toward the chance of Prince Metternich.

He showed a good turn of speed to defeat Cross Master at Southwell in December and divided Rausal and Little Polveir over today's trip at Bangor last month.

The Journal Racing Extra Handicap Hurdle has a very tricky look about it.

Peter Easterby's Sword Beach, caught on one of his better day's, came to head Lottie's Fury at the final flight of the Harry Lane Memorial Handicap Hurdle at the last meeting.

The latter may have held on with a more enterprising ride

and is expected to come out on top in a very competitive race.

John Parkes, enjoying his best season since his move from Richmond to Malton, may have found a winning opportunity for his Beau Guest in the Crook

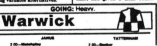

ARTHUR STEPHENSON — leading trainer at Sedgefield

BEST BETS

JANUS
DURBO
(nap, 4.00 Warwick)

Phil's nine-dart game

DARTS player Phil Nixon of Middlestone Moor played the perfect nine-dart game at a competition to choose the Durham rep-
resentative for the British gold cup singles. He hit two 180s, treble 17, treble 18 and double 18 but later lost to Laurence Pratt, his Spennymoor North Eastern Hotel team mate.

Pre-season friendly

ESSEX will play Middlesex in a 50-over-a side match at Chelmsford on April 17 as part of their preparations for the new season.

Tonight's football

EUROPEAN UNDER-21 CHAMPIONSHIP
Albania v England (2.00 Shkodra); Scotland v France (Dundee)

BARCLAYS LEAGUE — Division III
Huddersfield v Reading

Division IV
Rotherham v Grimsby, Wrexham v Hartlepool
B & Q SCOTTISH LEAGUE — Division One
Falkirk v Dunfermline.

Division Two
Albion v Montrose, Brechin v Alloa, Dumbarton v Berwick
SKOL NORTHERN LEAGUE
Easington v Spennymoor Synthonia; North Shields v Gretna; Stockton v Shildon.

Division Two
Cleveland Empas v Prudhoe, Esh Winning v West Auckland, HFS LOANS LEAGUE — Division One Cup
Droylsden v Whitley Bay.

Greyhound results

MIDDLESBROUGH — 7.30. 1 Whitton Farmer (2) 2m 7-2; 2 Cavan Harp (5) 12m 2-11. 5¼l, 28.84. £1.45, £4.76 2.5.1, £9.10. 7.44; 1 Portsrode Tramp (3) 9-4f; 2 Molly Park (1) 11-4. nk, 29.13. £1, £1.82. 3.1.6. £3.82 8.05; Juthal (4) 4m 11-8f; 2 Sandy Park (3) scr 9-4. 6¼l, 26.77. £2.35. £1.72. £3.3 £3.10. 8.22; 1 Glengar Jewel (5) 5-2f; 2 Oaxvali Breeze (1) 7-2. nk, 29.71. £1.60. £2.96. 5.1.2. £11.42. 8.39; Brave Fox (3) 8m 5-2; 2 Cranley Dawn (2) 5m 7-4f. 2l, 28.96. £2.30. £1.16. 3.2.4. £2.62 8.55; 1 Eileen's Empress (4) 7-4f; 2 Highway Five (2) 5-2. 1vl. 29.57. £1.95. £2.12 4.2.5. £13.88. 9.12; 1 Gerry Park (3) 5m 5-2; 2 Gemma s Darling (1) scr 3-11. 1¾l. 29.04. £1.75. £2.56. 3.1.2. £10.26. 9.30; 1 Foxy Fowler (1) 6-4f; 2 Glenbrook Sand (6) 5-1. 1¾l, 29.16. £1.90. £4.08. 1.6.5. £9.18. Jackpot pool ses winning tickets each receiving £91.35.

SUNDERLAND — 7.30. 1 Miss Bruno (5) scr 2-1; 2 Windy Miller (2) 1m 5-2. 2l. 16.34. £4.72. 7.48; 1 Milk Float (3) 5-4f; 2 Sock Thief (5) 6-4. ¾vl. 16.06. £16. 8.02; 1 Supsa (3) 5-4f; 2 Sam (2) 6-4. 5l, 25.46 (record) £19.10. 8.18; 1 Patricia's Hope (4) 3m 5-2; 2 Streamline (1) scr 6-4f. nk, 27.12. £22.30. 8.34; 1 Finish (2) 2m 3-1; 2 Peddler (3) 6wl. 3l, 15.44. £28.85. 8.50; 1 Perseverance (4) 6m 2-1; 2 Wee Mick (3) 5m 7-4. ¾vl, 26.30. £13.85. 9.08; 1 Inchy (4) 9m 4-6f; 2 Fallon Angel (5) 14m 9-4. 4¾vl, 37.91. £7. 9.22; 1 Razor (3) 1m 5-4f; 2 Smasher (5) scr 5-2. 2l. 15.90. £9.75. 9.38; 1 Andrea's Girl (5) scr 9-4; 2 Rasher's Delight (3) 4m sf. 2¾vl. 38.79. £25.45. 9.54; 1 City Lass (5) scr 6-4f. 2l, 1 No Lady (5) 12m 8-4f. nd, 26.19. £11.65. Jackpot two winners each received £22.52.

PELAW GRANGE — 7.15. 1 Picture Book (1) scr sf. 2 Brave Ben (3) scr 2-1. 4vl. 25.27. £7.52. 1.2.4. £43.31. 7.30. 1 Olivier (5) scr 4-1; 2 Michette (3) scr 3-1. 4l, 25.32. £17.07. 4.2.1. £26.58. 7.45. 1 Kevin's Girl (3) scr 6-4; 2 Bely Whizz (4) scr 2-1. ½l. 25.88. £34.65. 3.4.5. £146.44. 8.00. 1 Fawn Tod (2) scr sf; 2 Big Ed (1) scr 3-1. 7l, 24.94. £6.94. 2.1.3. £23.99. 8.17.

BEST BETS

TRESIDDER

12
Creative use of typesetting

It will be clear from the last few chapters and the pages illustrated that each newspaper has a type style based upon a number of chosen faces and the use of a regular range of sizes, either in caps and lowercase, or just in lowercase. Within each style, however, will be found some special uses of type and distinctive sorts of setting that will be resorted to by the designer. Their purpose is to solve particular problems that crop up in the design of the pages. We examine, under the headings that follow, the occasions when these are used and how they contribute to the creative process of design.

Breakers

Long texts, or pages with a number of longish items or that are weak in pictures, can be made easier to read by the use of typographical devices or variations in body setting which we call *eye breakers*.

Panels

Panels, or boxes, can be introduced into the display. A selected story is set, usually in bold body type to differentiate it from the rest of the page, inside a frame made up of type rules or borders, either plain or decorated, as can be seen from example pages in the last few chapters. This can be to create a focal point for the eye, or to give emphasis to the story enclosed in the panel – or to perform both functions at once.

The sort of border used depends on the newspaper's style. The more serious morning papers favour fine or 2-point or thick-and-thin borders, while the popular tabloids, with their bolder style, go for thicker black, tone or milled (Simplex) borders, or even 'shadow' boxes, which are made up of thick black rules on two adjoining sides, opposed to thin rules on the other two. House style should denote which side of the panel the shadow is on, preference for the thicker rule being usually on the right and bottom of the panel. Proportion is important. The thickness of the rules should not be the same on a chunky three-column panel as on a short single-column one. A shadow rule of wider than 6 point (opposed to, say, a 2 point) on a single-column story would leave the body setting at around 6 picas, which is too narrow for most body faces, whereas on a big display panel, a shadow rule on a bold tabloid can reach as much as 18 points in a display-orientated tabloid. There are endless permutations. The shadow can be constructed of multiples of rules; 12 point of screen tinted rule against 2 point on the other sides can give contrast in 'colour' and a real feeling of shadow, compared to total black.

The liking for type panels noted in tabloid papers is said to have started in the hot metal days, when industrial troubles reduced the flow of 'blocks' to the pages and editors could not bear to have their carefully thought-out display patterns destroyed for lack of pictures. Instead, strategically placed panels and heavy white space were used to produce contrast and pull stories away from the surrounding material. These adventures in typography led to the increased use of type panels in tabloid and broadsheet design and proved that, on rare occasions, pictures could be dispensed with.

On features display a large area of a page or spread that requires cohesion can be effectively tied in with a panelled border **(69 and 72)**, while headlines can be enhanced as part of the display by being let into the top rule of a panel, or 'winged in'. This device is useful where a headline is required to be centred for emphasis with white space on either side. In the case of multiple-column panels, care should be taken to balance the white space against the surrounding text and headlines so that it looks like 'creative' white and not a failure on the part of the headline writer to fill the allotted space. The placing of panels should also be checked against the adjoining adverts in case they are using the same device, while another caution is to check the backing page to ensure that show-through from a heavy black rule is not going to damage white areas. Advertisers on the backing page have been known to claim against this fault.

The use of panels, especially big ones, should always be checked in the day's dummy against the opposing page, either editorial or advertising, to see that there is no clash or mismatch.

Panels can be formatted without difficulty in computerized systems in a variety of borders, including shadow box, and delivered complete with text fitted, and are an important part of modular design in papers like *The Independent*. The computer even makes possible what always remained the dream of hot metal compositors – the panel with rounded corners.

Cut-offs

A cut-off performs a similar function in isolating a story from its surroundings but is used more for highlighting an item that relates to a main story with which it is included. The setting, as with a panel, is usually bold to differentiate it from the main text, but instead of having a border all round it is separated from the material above and below by a cut-off rule **(76)** of perhaps 2 point or 4 point, and is often set indented to show white against the main text. It can be run either with or without its own headline.

Break-outs

A long text, especially a feature, can be eased for the eye and emphasis drawn to part of it by taking out a self-contained section and running it with a separate headline, though ruled within the area of the main story. This is often called a *break-out*. Similarly, a related story on a news or features page might be used as a *tie-on* and ruled in with the bigger story under its own headline. The headline type should be chosen to match the main headline, though smaller. Here again the text can be set bold to differentiate it, or in the same type to tie it in visually. Where a tied-on story appears directly under the main intro it is sometimes referred to as a *shoulder*.

Crossheads

Crossheads are the commonest devices used to break up a long text. On a news page they are usually set to a house style, sometimes in 12-point Metro black or similar, caps for a page lead and lowercase for other tops. A common practice is to place them above a paragraph every 4 or 5 inches of text, or sometimes to use them to break up consecutive runs of short legs. The idea is to select a significant word or pair of words from the text that follows. Some purists choose the words carefully so that the crossheads in a story link together lexically, or in idea. Another school of thought asserts that since a crosshead is an eye break it hardly matters what they say, and that readers would not notice if they were nonsense words. Some papers follow this through by using white spaces placed above a drop letter or a piece of decorative rule or graphic symbol **(69)** in place of crossheads, or simply do without them **(74)** and **(75)**, as in *The Times* and *The Guardian*.

On features pages, with their generally longer texts, crossheads can serve a valuable display purpose, appearing often as two-liners in bigger type which deliberately matches the main headline in order to lend cohesion to the type dress. Sometimes the lines are under-scored, and can be set right, centred or staggered. Here, more significant words are chosen with the purpose of giving a taste of the text to the reader. The placing of display crossheads in a feature projection is carefully chosen to help balance the page, and they are an integral part of the page design.

(a) ★★ ━━━ **RONALD REAGAN YESTERDAY** ━━━ ★★

❛You can't massacre an idea . . . you cannot run tanks over hope . . . you cannot riddle a people's yearning with bullets❜

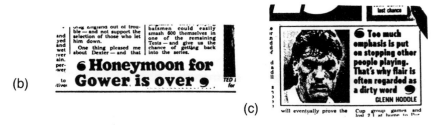

(b) ❛Honeymoon for Gower is over❜

(c) ❛Too much emphasis is put on stopping other people playing. That's why flair is often regarded as a dirty word❜
GLENN HODDLE

87   Quotes used: (a) as the main headline; (b) and (c) as text breakers

Highlight quotes

The projection of long features texts has called into use a number of devices which would rate of little importance on news pages with their busier contents and more numerous headlines. Highlight quotes, in which notable quotations are lifted from the text and set in a special eye-catching type such as 18- or 24-point Ultra Bodoni or Ludlow black, can be found as visual breakers in projections of interview-based features **(87)**. These look well in four lines of single- or double-column placed strategically around a page or spread. Unlike crossheads, these should be located in the middle of paragraphs so that the eye is not tempted, by their extra depth, to stop reading the text at that point. In the case of double-column quotes it is important to ensure that their display purpose does not interfere with the run of the text, and they should ideally be placed at the foot of the display or under an intro or picture where the text can conveniently thread round them. If the layout is heavy on headline, or if the layout style permits it, highlight quotes can give useful 'colour' by being used as WOBs or BOTs.

Bylines and standfirsts

Bylines, which on news pages are often simple lines of 8-point or 10-point Metro or Helvetica set to style above intros, can be harnessed

Applaud the politicians, but don't raise the roof

Charities learn to be City slickers

IN A matter of months complacency has changed to platitude and thence to virtual panic over the destruction of the Earth's ozone layer. The international ozone conference in London closed yesterday amid general feeling that the world is seriously out of joint.

Quite a fright is required for the Earth's major polluters — Britain included — to advocate so strongly elimination of chemicals used in a multitude of household goods, from fridges to floor polish.

The fright over what we now

The international ozone conference has been a step in the right direction, but there is a long way to go, says **Jack O'Sullivan**

escapes, although scientists suggest it is used as an industrial cleaner in Eastern Europe. Each emission survives for up to 70 years.

The conference was a political triumph for Mrs Thatcher, whose "green" conversion was displayed to much congratulation on the world stage. "It makes a real change to see Britain leading from the front rather than following up at the rear," said one of the pioneers in ozone research, Prof Sherwood Rowland from the University of California.

● The long-awaited white paper on control of charities deals with a giving industry that has become big business. NICK FIELDING reports

SEVENTY years old this week, and about to mark the fact by a jamboree for 8,000 people at Alton Towers, Save The Children Fund is the very model of a modern major

88   The standfirst – that is, special setting above the intro – can be used both as a useful explanation and as a design feature

for display purposes on a features spread. They can be panelled in and set in display type, perhaps with the word 'exclusive', and dropped into the middle of a page, or under an intro as a pivot point for the text to turn on. Or they can be incorporated in a *standfirst* run in special type above the intro **(74** and **88)** to explain to the reader why this particular feature is significant, or even – where the name is important – be worked into a 24 point or 30 point strap line above the main heading to introduce the page. Where the writer's name is the most important part of the story, as with a big name columnist or a very special outside contributor, the name can be bigger than the headline, or be worked into a decorative *logo*, around which the display is constructed **(47)**. Such a byline can be the most important offering of the day's edition.

Decoration

Every newspaper has its favourite pieces of type decoration and their use dates back to the flourishes and illuminated capitals of the monastic scribes, which were translated into typographical equivalents by the early printers. Take *drop letters* (which we described in Chapter 2). They have been in and out of favour with the most diverse variety of newspapers and just when they appear to be going out of fashion they reappear in some unexpected quarter, being favoured at the time of writing by such opposed papers as *The Guardian* and *The Times* **(79)** and rejected by *The Independent* and the *Daily Express*.

In many ways the drop letter in its normal position is the most expendable form of adornment since it is the body of the text and the centres of pages that need the benefit of decorative relief rather than the first paragraph of a story. Yet, used carefully, it can give a touch of style and elegance to a page. For instance, in a long feature drop with generous white space above them, spaced out across a long read, can act as attractive eye rests while at the same time marking natural breaks in the text **(14)**.

Blobs and squares

Blobs, either open or closed and ranging from 8 point to 12 point, were once associated with the popular tabloids but have now infiltrated all manner of newspapers. They turn up as text markers on columns of *nibs* (news in brief), summaries, list of things and at the beginnings of *tie-ons* (or *nuggets*) to stories. Black or open *squares* of similar size are an alternative to blobs for the same purposes. The one danger to watch in a permissive layout environment with devices like this is the spotted dog syndrome, which is to be diagnosed in pages in which a rash of blobs and squares has developed into a sinister disease. A side effect of the disease is that the emphasis intended to be given by their use is totally negated by their number **(86)**.

Bold caps

For a less eye-boggling solution in such situations, setting the first word of a (limited) number of items in *bold caps* is effective. The device can also be used to give emphasis to a particular word or quality in a story, although *italic* is perhaps safer since the potential visual damage to the page is less.

Drop figures and quotes

Drop figures, used in the same way as drop letters – set against two or three lines of body type at the beginning of an item – can give a distinctive touch to a bold feature layout in which a numbered list is of great importance and needs highlighting. Drop quotes, another variation of the drop letter and set in a size equal in depth to two or three lines of body type, can enhance and give prominence to a special quoted section in a feature, but not on a number of such sections in the same story. Two drop quotes on a page, one to open the section and one to close it, can be safely accommodated, but half a dozen confuses the eye. When falling badly, such as along the bottoms of column legs of text, or fighting with blobs and squares on the same page, their use can bring on an extreme and terminal form of the spotted dog syndrome, a condition not unknown to some popular tabloid papers on their bad days **(86)**.

Stars

Stars, black or open and from 12 point to 18 point, are used more to jolly up blurbs, horoscopes and competitions than to itemize columns of things and can look right on the right material. There is some justification for them on a column of showbusiness gossip, but little call for them elsewhere in the paper. Use with care.

White space

One of the simplest and most effective forms of decoration to the type area is white space used judiciously and artistically to separate the items and components of a page. It can stop a busy layout looking overcrowded and give great elegance when used in place of dividing rules on a features page **(73)** and **(75)**. Used elsewhere, however, it needs to be planned into the page as an act of artistic judgement rather than fudged in as the spin-off from 'windy' headlines.

Special headline effects

There is little call on news pages for headlines outside the normal type range, but on features pages most papers resort at some time to Letraset transfer type or drawn headlines to achieve a special display effect. Royal features look more seemly in older types such as Baskerville or Bembo lowercase, often blown above normal size, sometimes with instant art crowns woven into headline or strapline. An adventure series can be given great colour with a display heading in 'tea chest' caps from a Letraset sheet, or a period cameo feature in a Victorian cursive. A graceful seriffed lowercase Century light or Garamond (or, if in sans serif, then in the finest and lightest Univers or Futura) gives a feminine look to a women's page display **(14, 73)**.

In addition to the instant stick-on type available, the computerization of printing has made many new type tricks possible. The facility of laser printing of type bromides for paste-up means that no newspaper need go without a wanted type effect.

Some manipulation can be carried out on the art desk on letters to improve display headings. On biggish descending lines in lowercase, knowledge of word shape can be used to enhance the visual effect by tucking the descenders into the ascender space of the line below. Sometimes a design purpose can be achieved by literally entwining the ascenders with the descenders. Kerning of the space between the letters, as we have seen (Chapter 2), can improve the visual effect of lines, especially those with a mixture of straight and rounded strokes.

Ligature

Ligaturing, used knowledgeably, can make an effective line in certain features. This is the method of connecting letters together as used commonly in the diphthongs æ and œ. Originally it was used only with lowercase letters, in particular double *ff*s or in connecting *f* and *t* together on their horizontal strokes, and the aim was to save space in consonents on wooden and metal type bodies. Early font creators were probably influenced by authors' preference for consonants. Dr Johnson Ball, in his biography of the type designer William Caslon, says: 'Charles Dickens will empty the vowel boxes long before those of the consonants, whereas the style of Lord Macaulay's will run heavily on the consonants.'

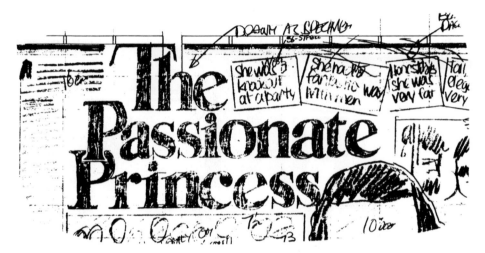

89 Ligaturing – an old device takes on a new design role in these examples from the drawing board

This purpose has long since gone, but, aided by the computer, ligaturing has come back into vogue, especially in book cover, magazine and advertising design, but also in newspaper features page layouts **(89)**. It can draw the eye and in some cases replace the picture content with a stylized titling focal point.

Capital letters now play a greater part than in traditional ligaturing. Curved and otherwise distorted lines of type, in particular, demand that the corners of certain characters should overlap. Ascenders and descenders can be overlapped into the 'beard' spaces of the letters and juxtaposed to create a novel effect. An effective method is to use tints to define or highlight the overlap.

Drawn type

Some papers with predominantly seriffed type formats have tried to improve line counts by mechanically shrinking the width, but this never looks right in lowercase, though it can work in caps. At the *Daily Express*, in the 1970s, a layout artist produced a drawn version of the whole Century bold alphabet to 120 point, with all its furniture, as a mock Century extra condensed. This was used for a time on front page splash headings where it contrasted well with the masthead. It was forbidden, however, inside the paper.

In its search for literate headlines which met with its requirements of heavy sans banner type, the *Daily Mirror*, in the 1950s, adopted a condensed sans face drawn in house by one of its young composing room deputies, Len Kreiner, who had heard that H. G. Bartholomew was having trouble finding the right type. Though the W, N and M were too full by normal sans standards, the type **(90)** struck the right chord for the *Mirror*'s poster style and Kreiner Condensed remained a stock *Mirror* headline face for nearly thirty years until editor Michael Christiansen replaced it with Placard in the 1970s.

90   A famous headline demonstrates the *Daily Mirror*'s distinctive splash type of the 1950s and 1960s: 'Kreiner Condensed'. Its hand-drawn origin is betrayed in the broad 'N' and odd exclamation mark

Special setting

In some areas of the paper visual familiarity is the paramount aim. Nowhere is this more so than on 'listings' features such as the television guide and race programmes. Not only should they appear in the same part of the paper in much the same shape so that they are instantly findable, but they should be set in such a way as to be easily readable for quick reference.

5.10 THE COUNTRY BOY By Bernard Ashley. Six part drama series about a Kent sheep-farming family who are directly affected when a local chemical company dumps pesticide in a river. Ben discovers that Duke is dead and realises that he must have swallowed the same poisoned water. (S)

5.35 NEIGHBOURS (Repeat of this afternoon's).

6.00 NEWS, WEATHER

6.30 WALES TODAY.

7.00 WOGAN Terry talks to Glenn Close and John Malkovich, who star in *Dangerous Liaisons*.

7.35 BEST OF BRITISH Sir John Mills introduces extracts from 50 years of Rank films, focusing on film portrayals of historical figures.

8.00 DALLAS Although Miss Ellie reluctantly agrees to the sale of Southford land and Casey Denault is jubilant, the business does not quite go according to plan. JR is surprised by a visit from his wife. (S)

8.50 POINTS OF VIEW With Anne Robinson.

9.00 NEWS, WELSH NEWS, WEATHER.

9.30 Q.E.D. The Mystery Of Tears. *(See Starchoice)* (S).

7.40 Every Second Counts. Six more spouses fight to win an African safari in Paul Daniels' hurry-up quiz.

8.15 Dynasty: Grimes and Punishment.★

9.0 News; regional news; weather.

9.30 Jumping the Queue.★ In this two-part love story dramatised by Ted Whitehead from Mary Wesley's novel, Sheila Hancock plays a middle-aged woman who has decided to end her life rather than slide into senility. But before she can swim to oblivion off her favourite beach, she meets Hugh (David Threlfall), a young fugitive on the run from the police for killing his mother.

10.50 The Mephisto Waltz. A dying pianist seeks to bequeath a journalist a ghastly legacy in this horror thriller starring Jacqueline Bisset, Alan Alda, Barbara Parkins and Curt Jurgens. Made in 1971.

12.35 The Rockford Files. Love Is the Word. James Garner renews his romance with a blind psychologist (R).

BBC1
8:30 am Roobarb. 8:35 The Raccoons. 9:00 On the Waterfront. 10:55 Cartoon Double Bill. 11:10 Film: "Song of Norway" starring Toralv Maurstad and Florence Henderson with Harry Secombe, Robert Morley and Edward G Robinson. 1:25 pm News. 1:30 Grandstand including FA Cup Final between Everton and Liverpool from Wembley Stadium (kick-off at 3:00). 5:15 The Pink Panther Show.
5:35 News. 5:45 Regional News and Sport. 5:50 MacGyver. 6:40 That's Show Business. 7:10 Bob Says... Opportunity Knocks. 8:00 Columbo. 9:15 News and Sport. 9:30 Midnight Caller. 10:20 Match of the Day: The Road to Wembley. Highlights of today's FA Cup Final between Everton and Liverpool. 11:20 The Odd Couple. 11:45 Film: "The Anniversary" with Bette Davis, Jack Hedley and Sheila Hancock.

BBC2
2:45 pm Network East. 3:25 Film: "Thousands Cheer" starring Gene Kelly with Kathryn Grayson. 5:25 The Week in the Lords. 6:05 Civilisation. 7:00 Ways of Seeing. 7:40 Newsview. 8:25 The Shock of the New. 9:30 Film: "The Go-Between" starring Julie Christie, Alan Bates and Dominic Guard. 11:20 Film: "The Quiller Memorandum" starring George Segal, Max von Sydow and Senta Berger. 1:00-1:35 am Rapido.

LONDON
6:00 am TV-am Breakfast Programme. 11:00 The Chart Show. 12:00 ITN News followed by ITV National Weather. 12:05 Local News and Weather. 12:10 pm The Cup Alternative: "Carry On Again, Doctor" starring Kenneth Williams, Sidney James, Charles Hawtrey and Barbara Windsor. 1:50 The Cup Alterna-

91   Listings setting should combine readability with the successful highlighting of names and times. In these examples the reverse indent of the first two is more helpful to the eye than the run-on style of the third

The formatting facility in photoset systems has taken the hard work out of this sort of typesetting and it is now possible to bring together setting shapes and combinations of body type that will highlight times and names in bold caps for the reader at a keystroke, and identify special information entry by entry **(91)**. Once the editor is satisfied with the body size, width and amount of indent required, and a workable overall page or spread has been devised to allow for pictures in stock positions, the listings subeditor has only to keyboard in the daily or weekly details and call up the appropriate block setting format.

Such a format does not preclude corrections and updates being keyboarded in provided the overall setting depth (and in effect the number of words) of the format is adhered to. The programmes can then either be printed out in blocks for paste-up on page cards, or dropped into position on screen for full page composition.

To achieve speed in page production using this sort of setting it is necessary to stick to a format once adopted and to ensure that the page layout it is designed for is not jeopardized by differences in advert shapes day by day and week by week. A drastic change of setting or page display should be necessary only where a listings feature is felt after long use to have grown stale visually, where it has proved to be faulty in its purpose, or where a radical relaunching of the listings part of the paper is being undertaken to fit in with a new editorial policy.

13
Mastheads

We have said that the aim of the designer is to give a newspaper a recognizable character as well as to make the contents of the pages readable and attractive to the eye. Nowhere is the recognition factor more important than in the title piece or name of the paper which occupies the area at the top of page one usually referred to as the masthead. Strictly the masthead includes the information on date, price and serial number and sometimes the edition marker. It can also include a pictorial motif, or badge, such as the eagle on *The Independent* or the crusader on the *Daily Express*, and so when referring solely to the name of the paper we will call it the *title piece*, although the term *logo* (word) will also be used.

Newspapers traditionally look to continuity in their title piece. Page one has an inevitable shift and flux in contents as the main news of the day is presented to the best advantage; there might, during the course of a few years, be the occasional typographical revamp to coincide with a drive for readership; there might also, though less frequently, be a change in size from broadsheet to tabloid, or vice versa. During all this, great store is placed on the function and typographical appearance of the title piece in assuring the reader that it is the same paper. Consequently, change in the shape and size of the title piece needs to be carefully thought out.

This does not mean that it should never change. An important relaunch of a paper that had gone into decline can be signalled by giving the logo an eye-catching new design. Such a title piece can be an integral part of the publicity surrounding the relaunch, although it will not, of its own, convince readers that things have improved unless the fundamental causes of the paper's decline have been attended to. In the same way a new paper, having carefully thought out its masthead to suit its market, must also ensure that the contents have been properly thought out, too.

The title piece, in short, is the brand name that helps sell the product. Through its use in advertising, street bills, slogans and in other forms of publicity it can push the sales of a paper by planting the notion of its expected character or excellence in the mind of the recipient. It is thus a valuable promotional aid to readership and circulation.

A title piece can also overstay its welcome. Designer and typographer Alan Hutt, writing in 1960, said: 'Papers which redress themselves with agreeable headline and text types, effectively made up, retain hanging over their now smart shop window – the front page – the ancient and grotesque sign which accompanied the spindly news titling heads and the muddy minion text of their founding fathers. It is a position that no ordinary self-interested shopkeeper would tolerate for a moment, and for obvious reasons. That these reasons seem often not to be obvious to newspaper proprietors and managements is a curiosity of trade conservatism quite out of place in the second half of the twentieth century.'

Updates and spot colour

Nowadays one would want to qualify Hutt's general condemnation on the ground that a change of title piece is a serious undertaking akin to changing a brand name of a product. However, in the early 1960s there was some truth in what he said. Worries over the rivalry of television led to newspapers of the period making a close examination of their image and the decade, to some extent, took note of Hutt's strictures by witnessing a revamping, and even the extinction, of some familiar, if dated, mastheads.

The *News of the World*'s famous scroll, showing Britannia presiding over the paper's name in an elaborate Victorian face that would have looked more at home on the side of a canal barge, was jettisoned after more than 100 years in favour of a Rockwell slab serif logo in caps across the top of the then broadsheet. With it went the advertising ear pieces on either side which had earned handsomely but had added to the dated look of the masthead. The new title piece was broken into a two-liner when the paper was relaunched as a tabloid in 1983 **(92)**. It became a white on red colour seal printing off a separate cylinder in the style that had become the practice with the popular tabloids. An interesting postscript to the change occurred during the 'tabloid or not' debate in the 1980s when it was suggested to the proprietor, Rupert Murdoch, that the original logo might be brought out of the cupboard, reduced and used as a nameplate on the new tabloid. 'I'm not in the antique business,' was Murdoch's comment.

The Sun also underwent a traumatic change of masthead in the 1960s. Launched by Mirror Group Newspapers in 1964 as a successor to the ailing *Daily Herald*, which the group had bought from Odhams, it appeared at first as a 7.5 cm wide panel containing a tightly spaced, and blown up, single word SUN in Franklin extra condensed with an orange coloured disc standing alongside it **(93)**. The idea was that the panelled masthead could be moved about the top of the page from

92   *News of the World:* 1910, 1982, 1989

day to day, and even from edition to edition, to suit the size and shape of the splash headline – not a concept that has found many imitators since. One problem was that the orange disc, inked and printed off its separate cylinder under the letterpress system, would wander away from the title piece which printed black and so remained static in its hot metal forme. A more serious defect was that the type of the logo did not differ enough from the surrounding headline type and tended to merge into the page. Thus, in trying to be new and different the masthead gave up the one great advantage of the old black letter or hand-drawn title pieces – their visual differentiation from the type on the page.

Differentiation in appearance from the rest of the page has to be the key to an effective title piece. True, there are successful mastheads designed in the same typeface as the rest of the front page and printed in black as part of the page forme. *The Times* (**78**) is one, and there are others, but they succeed by being placed in a static position clear of the page contents and surrounded by protective white space. Ideally they are in caps against lowercase splash headlines, or lowercase against caps splash headlines.

A total disregard for *The Sun*'s ingenious design was shown by its new proprietor, Rupert Murdoch, and its editor Larry Lamb, in 1969 when they sat down to dinner to discuss relaunching the paper as a tabloid. As the meal drew to a close the new editor doodled the words

93   *The Sun*: 1967, 1968, 1989

THE SUN with a red Biro on a table napkin showing white words on a red background. 'That's it!' said Murdoch.

The Sun's new title piece which has since influenced other tabloids, was successful for two reasons. One, the colour red attracts the eye more than any other, and two, the typography of the carefully hand-drawn sans letters was eye-catching in its own right. Two decades later the only change has been to widen the letters of the word SUN to produce a wider panel of red **(93)**.

One of the reasons for the more decorative mastheads found before the 1960s was the reluctance by editors to choose colour as a means of differentiation due to the unreliability of spot colour as used in the letterpress process. It had long been realized that with the method of printing stop press or edition markers or title motifs in red, blue or green from cylinders separately inked from their own reservoirs it was impossible to place spot colour accurately.

Only by printing the entire title piece in colour, as in *The Sun* example above and as adopted by other popular tabloids, could spot colour be safely used. Even then, in creating a position for it to print on page one, a spare pica of space had to be left vertically and horizontally around it in the page forme to allow the whole panel to 'wander' as the colour cylinder operated independently against the printing plate while the page went through the press.

Old ways and oddities

Up to about 1890 the convention in mastheads had been fairly simple. The Victorians loved the decorative quality of the Old English type as the most effective form of differentiation. Often **(94, 96)**, the title piece consisted of the name of the paper across the top of the page bisected by the Royal coat of arms – to which they were not entitled –in the manner used by *The Times* today. In a modified form, and shorn of some of its embellishments, the Old English has retained its adherents since, as can be seen in the *Daily Telegraph* **(95)** and the *Daily Mail*. Invariably, the type was thickened in stroke so that it would not break up or fill with ink, especially where a brass title plate was exposed to frequent re-use in the hot metal process, while the letters, at first in-lined, were adapted to simpler solid strokes.

With the growth of the popular press, starting with the nineteenth century popular Sundays, of which the *News of the World* is an example, elaborate drawn title pieces came into their own. The 1890s *Daily Graphic* **(97)** displays a highly stylized masthead the full width of the tabloid-sized page and filling nearly a quarter of its depth in which cupids whisper into the ears of goddesses flanking the words *Daily Graphic*. The symbolism of motifs was to endure in masthead design.

94   (a) How *The Times* started life as *The Daily Universal Register* on Saturday, January 1, 1785.
(b) Some nineteenth-century logos – a variety of approaches

95   *Daily Telegraph*: 1872, 1989

96   *Daily Mail*: 1899, 1950, 1962, 1989

Oddities abound in the world of drawn title pieces. The Nazi populist illustrated paper *Illustrierter Beobachter*, published in Munich at the time of Hitler's installation as Chancellor of Germany in 1933, produced an amazing logo which featured its initial letters in an opposed shadow format, making a name plate that covered 20 per cent of the page depth with the initial letters flanked by an enormous scrolled WOB design on which the full name is projected in bold upper and lowercase script. The entire masthead is surrounded by the price and date of the publication, together with the Nazi emblem and eagle. The result **(98)** combines dignity with a feeling of revolutionary fervour. The tints laid against the black of the shadows are daring in view of the crudity of printing presses of the period.

The new printing systems of the 1980s have spurred more ingenuity in mastheads. The American designer Rolfe E. Rehe, in his 1980 revamp of the masthead of the Ecuador daily, *Hoy*, which means 'today', produced a brilliant design **(99)**. He turned the letter O in Hoy into a rising sun with the use of graduated white rules

97   *Daily Graphic:* 1909

98   *Illustrierter Beobachter:* 1933

99   *Hoy:* 1982

across the perfect disc. Small bleach-out motifs alongside the title piece and referring to coverage of the day, and the date lodged around the descender of the 'y', complete the masthead furniture.

Reversals and direct colour

A simple device for differentiation that became popular in the 1950s was the reversal of the title of the paper as white type on black or on tint, or black type on tint, as shown in the example from the *Daily Mail* **(96)**. It was also used by the *Sunday Graphic* and *News Chronicle*. Though few of this genre have survived (the *Daily Mail* quickly went back to a simplified Old English logo) reversal was to become the accepted way with spot colour logos as in the example of *The Sun*, described above.

The movement into web offset printing in the 1970s and 1980s has

South London Press

South London Press

9759   Friday, June 16th, 1989   WEEKEND 20p

100   *South London Press*: 1960, 1989

given further scope for those papers preferring a colour logo since it provides the facility of direct colour printing with its fine accuracy of register. The morning paper *Today*, launched by Eddie Shah in 1986, broke new ground by being the first national daily to have a directly printed colour title piece **(Plate 3)** designed into the page. The initial failure of *Today* under its first management to take the share of the national market it anticipated added fuel, however, to the arguments of the detractors of direct colour. The other web offset launching of 1986, *The Independent*, noticeably rejected colour for its pages, except on special occasions, and opted for a traditional black title piece across the top of the page. In this way it aligned itself in style with *The Daily Telegraph* and *The Times* whose readership market was closest.

A number of provincial papers **(100, 101)** printing on web offset presses have taken the opportunity to use the direct colour facility to bring in new masthead designs, some of them displaying great ingenuity. Such mastheads have become a characteristic feature of the many freesheet papers that have been launched in the last two decades, which have not had to worry about preserving the reader identity of old title pieces.

Designing a title piece

Hand drawing of title pieces, colour and otherwise, has occurred not only in the elaborate cupids-and-scrolls genre but on more recent occasions where a standard titling face has proved inadequate for the effect wanted, or an update has been called for. Northcliffe's title piece for the *Daily Mirror*, the 'women's' paper he launched in 1903, was designed appropriately in a nineteenth century roman Old Face, used at first across the top of the page and, from 1939, broken into two lines in a left-hand corner position. Here it continued unchanged until the 1950s, when it was redrawn in-house slightly bolder. In this form, in an astonishing example of continuity, it carried on into the 1970s, undergoing reversal into white type on a red panel before, under Robert Maxwell's ownership, being given a new hand-drawn

101   *Hastings and St Leonard's Observer:* from black letter to the latest web offset title piece

italic sans title piece, which was later changed again to its current one **(102)**.

The launching of the *Daily Star* on to the national market in 1978 required a logo that would enable it to compete in the popular tabloid field against the *Daily Mirror* and *The Sun*. With the briefing that the design should be something of a 'spoiler' against the other two titles while at the same time having an independent character of its own, Vic Giles designed a drawn logo, using capitals as against the lowercase of *The Sun*. The development of the logo is shown in the illustrated example **(103)**.

The crucial part was the emphasis given to the letter S to match that of *The Sun*. The intention was to make the design roman but the way in which the S developed, with more emphasis across the bottom of the letter against the slope, determined that italic would give a greater legibility at a distance. Compressing the T, A and R, while keeping the boldness of the basically Futura or Antique Olive letter was more difficult until it became obvious that the only way was to ligature the ST and the AR, while pushing the bottom of the A character against the upright of the letter T. The result enabled space to be left for the word DAILY centred on the visual space between the extreme right of the S and the far right of the R, in the same way as with the word THE in *The Sun*. In a subsequent change the style of the logo was preserved but given greater distinctiveness by cutting the red away from around the letters, leaving a thick red outline. Subsequently, the editor changed to a red type title-piece following closely the original white on red.

The revamp and relaunch of the broadsheet *Irish Press* as a tabloid

ALLIES' DRASTIC ARMISTICE TERMS TO HUNS

The Daily Mirror

CERTIFIED CIRCULATION LARGER THAN THAT OF ANY OTHER DAILY PICTURE PAPER

No. 4,696.   Registered at the G.P.O. as a Newspaper.   TUESDAY, NOVEMBER 12, 1918   One Penny.

DAILY MIRROR, Monday, September 4, 1939

Daily Mirror

No. 11,152   +   ONE PENNY
Registered at the O.P.O. as a Newspaper.

Daily Mirror
SAT AUG 29 1959
2¢ FORWARD WITH THE PEOPLE
No. 17,326

BRITAIN'S BIGGEST DAILY SALE
3p   Monday, May 29, 1972   ◆ ◆ ◆   No. 21,268

Friday, June 23, 1989   National Sale: 3,950,664 Incorporating the Daily Record   22p

102   *Daily Mirror: 1918, 1939, 1959, 1972, 1989*

in 1988 presents another example of a logo drawn to suit a particular purpose – in this case the broadening and popularizing of an old-fashioned paper's content aimed at expanding the sales. Again, boldness was called for in a market against existing tabloids. One of the requirements, however, was to incorporate the newspaper's phoenix motif, known as the Gaelic eagle, which had graced its broadsheet masthead and had survived several previous revamps.

Vic Giles, the designer on this occasion too, produced a bold two-line title piece with the lettering in red, and incorporating on the left a silhouette in blue of an alighting eagle overprinted with the paper's motto THE TRUTH IN NEWS – also a wanted part of the design **(104)**. Another requirement was that the whole masthead could be easily reduced or enlarged for use on labels, stationery, posters, vans and television advertising. Due to the paper's imminent replanting, there was more scope for design in that the masthead would be colour printed by web offset as part of the page.

Giles decided, for the sake of continuity, to use the Times bold of the old design in upper and lowercase for the word Press, which would give space in the ascender area for a small version of the word IRISH in extended caps. A difficulty occurred immediately because of the enormous width of the capital P in Times bold when increased in size. This was resolved by using Letraset stick-on type and cutting away the rondel of the P and replacing it with a lowercase O, which worked after retouching.

103   *Daily Star*: 1978, 1986, January 1988, October 1988

A good flow was achieved on the word Press by ligaturing every letter. At 167 mm wide the depth proved to be 67 mm. With the eagle touching the P on the left the whole design stretched to 200 mm, leaving enough space to the right on the tabloid page for blurbs, captions, narrow pictures, etc. to suit the needs of page layout. The word IRISH in Antique Olive Nord 18 mm deep was centred on the visual white above the word PRESS. Finally, the masthead was separated from the page contents below by an 8 mm deep WOB strip containing date and price.

The deliberate contrast between serif and sans serif in the title piece reflected the mix of serif and sans serif in the type dress of the pages, while the caps of the logo meant that splash headlines could be in lowercase, as wanted, with the foil of smaller sans headings in caps.

THE IRISH PRESS

Weather
Cold and windy, with threat of sleet and snow. Details page 2.

Vol. LVII. No. 15   TUESDAY, JANUARY 19, 1988   The Truth in the News   C   PRICE 50p

TUESDAY, APRIL 26, 1988 PRICE 50p (N.I. and Britain 40p)

104   *Irish Press*: January, 1988 to April, 1988 – a dramatic change in market and style

Thus was created a tabloid page of distinctive appearance.

Totally different in its birth was the masthead designed for the new broadsheet *The Independent* for its launch on October 7, 1986, which was the product of a committee working relentlessly at a variety of prototypes by many hands, some handdrawn, some typeset. The final version, an elegant chiselled serif line in black across the top of the page with an alighting (or taking off?) eagle on the left was, in fact, a re-hash of an earlier version produced close to launching day in almost a mood of desperation **(105)**.

THE INDEPENDENT

Published in London   25p   THURSDAY 28 AUGUST 1986

THE INDEPENDENT

FRIDAY 13 JUNE 1986

Published in London, printed in Peterborough, Bradford, Portsmouth and Sittingbourne   25p

 The Independent

PRINTED IN LONDON, MANCHESTER AND PORTSMOUTH

FRIDAY MAY 16 1986 25p

The Independent

FRIDAY 13 JUNE 1986   25p

THE INDEPENDENT

No. 843   FRIDAY 23 JUNE 1989   Published in London   30p

105   Launching of a new daily – four of the many title pieces designed for *The Independent*, and (bottom one) the design that was chosen

Michael Crozier wrote in *The Making of The Independent*: 'The masthead was still giving us problems. We had all seen so many that it was extremely difficult to make an absolute choice. . . . In the end we returned to the beginning and the original idea of Hitchens for a chiselled masthead and an idea subsequently repeated by Thirkell. However, all the previous versions seemed to go wrong in some way and I asked Michael McGuinness if he knew of someone who could hand-draw a new version. He did and the present masthead drawn by Ken Dyster of the Mike Reid Studios in in-line Bodoni is unique.'

More daring and controversial was *The Guardian*'s new masthead **(106)** which appeared with the revamped paper in 1987 displaying a row of cut-out head and shoulder pictures of inside page personalities standing above the title piece. The faces had a distinctive vertical line tint placed across them, making them look rather like bleach-outs, and each carried alongside it a cross-reference to the appropriate page. The title-piece itself broke new ground by having the word GUARDIAN in 120-point lowercase of the Geneva black lowercase splash headline, with the THE lodged closely next to it in a Garamond italic serif face of the same depth, and the whole set right to leave eccentric white space on the left of the page.

106   *The Guardian*: 1951, 1952, 1985, 1989

Giving the pages identity

Not only is a newspaper *The Guardian*, *The Sun* or the *Yorkshire Post* because the title piece tells you it is. It must also, as the pages are turned, feel like what it is supposed to be if the reader is to be satisfied and comfortable with it. This is not just a question of content or attitude, which is what fixes a newspaper in its readership market, but of typographical style. We have considered the relationship between design and market and how this shapes the typographical style of a newspaper. We will now extend this to show how design, while grabbing the eye with the juxtaposition of headlines, text and pictures, also gives the reader this feeling of comfort and continuity by the use of what we call typographical 'signatures'.

The title piece, which we have just discussed, is the first and most important of these – the piece of typography that embodies the brand name of the paper – and its use on stationery, labels and various forms of advertising is vital to the image the paper projects. It can also be usefully deployed inside the paper to stress those areas where the paper's attitude or service to the reader are paramount (**107**). The leader page, on which is found the paper's daily or weekly opinions, is an example of this image projection.

107   Signatures – the title piece as an identity motif

We turn, to illustrate this, to the leader page of the *Daily Mail* (**108**). Boxed in with the word COMMENT on the left, above the regular 10 point setting across 15 picas of the leader, or editorial opinion, is a reduced replica of the *Daily Mail* Old English logo – a logo that, with minor changes derives directly from the very first *Daily Mail* in 1896. The pica black vertical rule alongside the leader, the open spaced-out

PAGE 6

Daily Mail
COMMENT

Building their own future on the Rock

GIBRALTARIANS are braced for today's shock announcement from the Foreign Secretary. When Sir Geoffrey Howe arrives, he will prepare the people of the Rock for a sharp reduction in the 1,800 British military personnel stationed there.

That will, indeed, be tough news for the locals to take. They are heavily reliant on the trade and the employment that the troops bring. But the comfort afforded by the uniformed ceremonial of Empire is psychological as well as economic. Daily on display are the historic ties that Gibraltarians cherish with Britain; a sounding of drums, a blowing of bugles which provide a cocky reminder that there is at least one corner of the Spanish land mass where the inhabitants resolutely refuse to look on themselves as Spaniards.

For all that, most Gibraltarians do not feel themselves British in the same way as, for example, do the Falkland Islanders. The majority on the Rock are not emigrants nor the descendants of emigrants from these shores. Theirs is a cultural mix as distinctive as the most localised of fish stews. To preserve its flavour and prevent it being overwhelmed by Spanish domination, they cleave to the British Crown. That is their right, which the Foreign Secretary is bound to reaffirm.

But they, like other peoples mighty as well as miniscule, are having to learn how to make their home in the fast-developing community of European nations to which Spain as well as Britain now belongs. As allies in NATO and democratic partners in Europe, it becomes increasingly fanciful, not to say paranoid, for Britain to mount so prominent a guard on the Rock to deter hypothetical military attack from Spain.

That is why it makes sense substantially to reduce the number of our troops on Gibraltar. In no way is this a surrender to Spanish pressure. Rather, is it an acceptance of European reality. We would expect Sir Geoffrey to phase the cut-back to give Gibraltar the opportunity to adjust to the loss of jobs and income. Some transitional financial help may also be in order.

But, sooner or later, the Gibraltarians are going to have to build their own commercial future on the Rock; a future which must owe more to the modern challenge of the free European market than to the old-fashioned ethos of colonialism.

Just because there are only 30,000 of them need not mean they have to lose their identity. Even today, Europe has its quaint statelets like Monaco (pop. 27,000) and Andorra (pop. 40,000).

No reason why in time Gibraltar should not become another such independent curiosity: capitalising, under proper inspection, on its off-shore potential for financial business; retaining for as long as is people wish their traditional link with Britain, but one which they would have less occasion — militarily anyway — to parade.

There are bound to be doubts and fears as the British presence is reduced on Gibraltar. But life on the Rock will go on after the regiment pulls out. And we predict that when the Gibraltarians have had their gripe they will begin to discover that they are better placed to enjoy it rewardingly over their very own two square miles of this ever more unified continent.

by PAUL JOHNSON

THE return of John Smith to active politics after his heart attack was a happy event for the House of Commons, where he is liked and respected on all sides.

Indeed it was a happy event for the country, for he is just the kind of politician Britain needs — able, incisive, open-minded and, above all, sensible.

But one man must have had mixed feelings. Smith is exactly the kind of man Neil Kinnock needs on his front bench, and to have him back, fit and eager, is a formidable addition to Labour's fire-power.

But he is also the one man who could topple Kinnock from his shaky perch as its leader.

And shaky is no exaggeration. Last autumn, when Kinnock overwhelmed Tony Benn in the leadership contest, he looked an absolute cert to take Labour into the next election. Four months later, everything is in doubt again.

With Parliament in mid-term, Kinnock has made absolutely no dent at all in the Thatcher monolith.

Even with sky-high mortgage rates, the Tories remain well ahead in the polls. Kinnock's personal ratings have hit rock bottom. His handling of Opposition strategy is dispirited and unintelligent.

It's worth recalling that, in the last parliament, on the one occasion when the Thatcher government really looked vulnerable — the Westland affair — Kinnock missed his chance to go for the jugular by making a lamentable speech.

Last month the government was again in potential trouble over the Currie resignation, exposing the one issue on which it plainly speaks for a nation. Kinnock misjudged the episode completely and allowed the government to slip off the hook.

At this stage of the parliament, Labour ought to be winning by-elections. Instead it is losing them.

Govan was an unqualified disaster in the one area, Scotland, where Labour was supposed to be doing well. Now more trouble for Kinnock looms at Pontypridd, another 'safe' Labour seat.

Blamed

The fact that Kinnock failed, even in his own Welsh back yard, to get the nomination for his preferred candidate, says a lot about the limitations of his power.

If Labour now loses the by-election to a Welsh Nationalist, Kinnock will inevitably be blamed. If it hangs on to the seat, Dr Kim Howells, the lively Leftist whose candidacy Kinnock fought against, will get the credit.

Kinnock's difficulty, all along, has been that the public doesn't take him seriously. The problem may now be beyond remedy.

All the public relations tricks have been tried — the stress on his youth, his happy marriage to the glamorous Glenys, his enthusiasm, compassion and oratorical fireworks.

Now the salesman's patter has run out of breath and faded into embarrassed silence.

The truth is, Neil Kinnock has

Kinnock's danger man

Tired Neil desperately needs John Smith's talents, but he could lose his job to him

been in the shop window too long — a good five years — and it is clear the public doesn't want to buy him.

Kinnock's one hope, in my judgment, is to obtain a clear reversal of his party's defence policy, thereby showing ordinary people that he is a person fit to run the country and that he has the muscle to make his party follow him.

Fudged

Unfortunately, Kinnock is inhibited from making such a demonstration both by his own muddled thinking on the issue and, still more, by the massive

presence of Ron Todd blocking his way. So he will end up with a fudge, and the acrimonious debate, with the disastrous headlines which accompany it, will continue.

Now he faces the prospect of another divisive issue as a head of steam builds up behind the demand for Labour to espouse proportional representation and the so-called Charter 88.

The campaign threatens to split the party down the middle. It has the support of virtually all Labour's few remaining intellectuals, some trades unionists and such Kinnock loyalists as Robin Cook.

But Roy Hattersley has come out strongly against it and Kinnock has not endeared himself to its adherents by denouncing them as whingers.

Hence this internal debate already threatens to degenerate into mud-slinging and has all the makings of a classic Labour Party self-inflicted wound.

Its outcome is pointless anyway since Labour is not, nor likely to be, in a position to impose proportional representation.

Where does all this leave John Smith? If Kinnock loses in 1991 or 1992, which looks increasingly likely, Smith should have little difficulty in ousting him.

Moderate

Other Opposition politicians are already calculating accordingly. David Owen, for instance, feels that if Smith sets about remodelling Labour in the moderate image of its Scottish base, the moment might be ripe to take his Social Democrats back into the party. An electoral pact with the Liberals might also be worth discussing.

The question is, however: can Labour afford to wait that long and risk the agony of a fourth defeat?

Some moderate union leaders fear the disintegration of the TUC and the rapid erosion of the entire Labour movement if they are kept in the wilderness another five years.

They would like to see Smith replace Kinnock before rather than after the election, and so put Labour in with a chance. That is the real threat which must keep Kinnock awake.

He will face no open challenge to his leadership this year. But unless he can decisively reverse the present drift to inevitable defeat, the pressures on Smith to make a challenge next spring will mount steadily.

Meanwhile, two stone lighter and shrewd as ever, Smith is playing himself back into the side. And waiting for Kinnock to score another duck.

Collar your dog by computer

by RAY HEARN

AFTER electronic tags for prisoners, electronic collars for dogs.

Battersea Dogs' Home is to supervise an experiment involving nearly 50 dogs to find out if a nationwide scheme is feasible.

The chairman of the home, Mr Thomas Field-Fisher, has suggested that owners should be required by

law to register their dogs in this way.

'Electronic registration has been tried out in the United States, and does seem to work,' said Tony Hare, director general of the home. 'You inject a small microchip just under the skin using a

syringe. It can last for about 15 years. If the authorities want to identify a stray dog they pass over it an electronic wand, and the result comes up on a computer.'

Trials are expected to start soon. If successful, it could mean

an owner will have to part with around £10 for injection and registration.

The system is about to be introduced in Ireland. Guard dogs will be required by law to have an electronic implant. The Irish Society For The Prevention Of Cruelty To Animals will operate the register.

---

setting and Rockwell bold lowercase headline on the main article, and the use of thick and thin rule breakers, are likewise unchanging stylistic signatures on a page on which high regard is paid to continuity and familiarity.

The byline logos of regular columnists Keith Waterhouse, George Gordon's Letter From America, with its stars-and-stripes breakers, and Nigel Dempster, plus the adaptation of the paper's title to Femail

109   Signatures – inside page logos map out the *Daily Mail*

110   Signatures – a lower key approach in *The Independent*

and TV Mail and Sportsmail are all signatures planted to draw the reader to regular offerings in the paper, and stamp the paper's identity on the pages **(109)**.

The Independent, less chauvinistic in style, deploys its name only once, in replica of its title piece above the leader, but the signatures are still to be found on different pages. The World This Week logo, the stylistic flagging of its home news, foreign news and arts pages, its Economic Outlook and Law Report graphics **(110)** are all recognition motifs deployed in the cause of continuity and identification.

The regular format of the Andy Capp strip in the *Daily Mirror*, the Page Three girl in *The Sun*, the various 'agony aunt' columns of the popular tabloids, even the repetitive typographical shape of the television programmes, plus the fixed position of these items in the paper, perform a similar function. They give easy access to favourite features while providing oases of familiarity amid the flux of the day's news. Such devices are planted discreetly in all manner of newspapers to help give a continuity of image a newspaper cannot do without.

Typographical signatures also perform a useful service for the designer. They enable the visual identity of the paper to be secured in strategic areas, leaving the designer to display the editorial contents without feeling so tied to the pursuit of continuity that design relapses into formula.

14
Special markets

In examining newspaper design we have seen that there are common factors that apply across the board and that there are techniques that apply to particular types of newspaper and styles of design. Differences in market and purpose can influence design style even with general newspapers, whether national or regional; in fact, geography of distribution is of least importance in arriving at an acceptable format.

In this chapter we look at some of the special requirements and special markets outside the main run of newspapers and at how these affect the approach to design, and how the methods we have discussed might need to be adapted.

Sectional newspapers

Some newspapers have discovered that their content and market can be best served by dividing their product into a number of separately folded sections, each with its special logo. The practice originated in the US as a means of coping with the large editions that grew in response to heavy advertising placement in newspapers serving big city conurbations. It enabled publishers to offer advertisers space in particular editorial environments – world news pages, local news, sport, women's, weekend magazine, financial, etc. – and also of offering readers a bulky product in which areas of interest could be found more easily, and which could be split up for reading within family and works groups.

The advertising-conscious retail trades and services and extensive mail order businesses thrived on the penetration achieved by the dailies published in the cities, and by the relatively cheap advertising rates that concentrated circulation made possible. The result was the growth of monster papers with ever increasing numbers of sections, culminating in the celebrated occasion on October 17, 1965, when the *New York Times* brought out fifty-six sections totalling 956 textsize pages.

Sectional newspapers – and the ultimate section, the colour magazine – first appeared in Britain in the 1960s when Sir Roy, later Lord Thomson, bought the *Sunday Times* and other Kemsley titles and set about building up their advertising revenue by high-pressure space-selling techniques. The method suited the wide news coverage and lengthy magazine content of a quality Sunday paper and was eventually taken up by *The Observer*, and to a lesser extent by *The Times* (when it also became a Thomson paper) and the *Financial Times* and some of the bigger provincial papers. It did not, however, become widespread in town and city papers as in America until the pioneering launch of *Plus* magazine 1988, which was inserted into thirty-five regional British evening papers.

Identity is the important thing with sections. In design terms they need to have enough individuality for them to be distinctive one from the other, and to give the pages of each a particular character, while sharing sufficiently in the overall design style to be recognizably part of the same newspaper. This can be done by introducing into each section a distinctive 'signature' type which will blend in with the types used elsewhere in the paper and common to all sections; or a condensed or lighter version of the paper's stock type can be used as a dominant headline type for the section. Another way is to keep the same type range but to introduce design characteristics such as indented setting or pages set within panel rules (using fine or 2-point rules). Creative use of rules and white space will give opportunities of making the pages look special without making them look too different.

111 The sectional newspaper – unmistakeable identity in *The Times*

For easy identification a distinctive logo or title piece is necessary, which should incorporate a miniaturized version of the main masthead **(111)**.

A decision has to be taken about pagination – whether to page the sections through from the carrier paper or to page them separately. A useful ploy, if the pressroom folders allow it, is to fold the odd section into half size as in the books section in the *Sunday Times*.

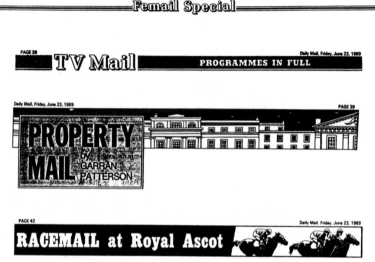

112   Pull-outs and other devices – the *Daily Mail*'s way

Pull-outs

Now common, and especially so in the popular tabloid dailies and many provincial papers, are pull-out sections consisting usually of the four or eight centre (tabloid) pages. They can be devoted to special news or features content, often under a separate logo such as 'four-page supplement on . . . etc.', or to such things as holiday, shopping or property guides with heavy advertising sometimes accompanied by editorial back-up.

Most are paged through with the rest of the paper, a practice used originally to circumvent print union restrictions which insisted that separate supplements to an edition should be charged extra on the wage bill. The notion was that a separately designed but paged through section in the middle fulfilled the purpose of a supplement – though the use of the word 'supplement' was carefully avoided – without incurring extra print charges. It was also less of a problem for the press-room folders than separate sections.

Pull-outs offer two main options to the designer. They can either be designed as an extension in style of the main paper, with perhaps a simple motif (which can be numbered) flagging each page; or they can be given their own special design characteristics within an overall format in the run of the paper or with separately folded sections. The latter way is adopted by papers running regular labelled supplements such as the *Daily Mail* **(112)** the *Financial Times* and the *Evening Standard* **(113)**.

A particular problem arises with pull-outs in the case of popular tabloid papers as a result of the practice of carrying 'under-spreads' across what is in fact the centre spread of the paper proper. What would normally be a spread on pages 24 and 25 of a 48-page paper thus becomes a spread on pages 22 and 27 where there is a 4-page pull-out. The psychology of readership assumed by editors is that people will detach the pull-out and read across the under-spread as if the other pages were not there. This works with readers who expect to have to do it, but can annoy a percentage of readers who start reading the first half of a spread to find their way unexpectedly blocked in mid-headline by an unrelated page, and that they have to turn from page 22 to page 27 to find what happens next.

113   Type and motif signatures – *Evening Standard sections*

One answer is to make the under-spread two separate pages so that the interruption of the pull-out does not upset the sequence. Another is to keep the under-spread but have material on it that can be divided so that neither headlines or pictures cross the gutter. The problem for the page designer who has to accommodate a central pull-out is one of reader psychology as much as design – how, by means of typography and pictures, to make the pull-out seem an additional benefit to the reader rather than an intrusion. If the pull-out embodies the main editorial offering, such as a four-page special feature or series instalment, it becomes the vital part of the paper and to try to maintain an under-spread would seem to be in danger of distracting attention from it.

A solution to the page sequence problem caused by a centre pull-out (though now little used) is to have a *wrapround*, in which a folded sheet forming four pages, separately paged and with a suitable recognition title piece, is attached to the outside of the newspaper. This can be useful for a commemorative edition in which a paper is, say, celebrating a centenary, or wants to display special material with perhaps flashbacks to earlier papers; or for a Royal or similar occasion in which a pre-printed colour souvenir is prepared on special quality paper to be detached for keeping.

Unlike separate sections, neither pull-outs or wraprounds offer any problem in printing and folding, and the pagination adopted – either paged separately or paged in – is a matter for editorial choice.

Desktop design

The use of desktop publishing (DTP) has greatly increased the number of organization, civic and similar tied circulation newspapers which exist in forms as varied as the systems upon which they are produced. It is difficult to lay down design techniques that would apply to all DTP systems; but a good yardstick would be apply the factors common to all newspaper design as described in Chapters 1 and 8 of this book and then to formulate styles that take into account the market of the product and the facilities built into the system.

A system such as the Apple-Mac can offer a wide range of typefaces with a useful graphics facility and laser printer. It would be pointless, however, to try to imitate newspapers produced on a sophisticated mainframe computer system. The result would simply be an inferior looking newspaper. The style would have to relate, for instance, to:

1 The sizes and ranges of types available for body setting and headlines.
2 The sort of pictures available.
3 Required text lengths.
4 The method of page make-up used, that is, paste-up or FPC of whatever limited sort.
5 The paper quality.
6 The size of page and column format adopted.

The last two items are important in DTP publications. A small format of, say, five 7-pica columns would offer scope for some varied layout ideas and headline patterns, and a variety of picture sizes, provided the items were not too long, whereas fewer but wider columns – a three or four column format – would suit longer texts, especially where the emphasis is more on words with just occasional pictures. A few pictures of good size would be the perfect foil here.

If the paper is of reasonable quality and the right pictures are available it would enable the design to utilize magazine techniques with perhaps bleed-offs and the creative use of controlled white space, or special setting round cut-out picture shapes, producing a result which is a hybrid between a newspaper and a magazine. Fine paper means that a finer screen can be used for halftones so that with correct inking subtle picture tones can be rendered and an effect produced which approaches that of gravure.

The best sort of effect is that which arises naturally out of the materials used, both editorial and software. Thus a factory newspaper on fine coated paper might make an attractive feature out of a series of linked pictures of an industrial process accompanied by a descriptive text printed in the knowledge that it would be meaningful to the paper's captive readership. Such pictures would be less effective on ordinary newsprint and less interesting to more general readers.

Pictures of social occasions can give a repetitious feel to a company newspaper writing mainly about its workforce, but variety can be injected and useful layout ploys set in motion by, for instance, inviting readers to submit their best snaps or best holiday pictures or pictures taken of novel or unusual things.

Most DTP products fall down on poor type style, lack of layout ideas or a general failure to make full use of the system and paper available. Thus a product produced on a shoestring, but making full use of what there is can score over an amateurish job turned out on good coated paper with full colour facilities.

Poor type style and lack of layout ideas are the inevitable result of the absence of trained staff. This can be solved in three ways: one, by making a serious study of similar products to learn from other's ideas; two, engaging at least one trained production journalist who can pass on the needed techniques sufficiently for one or two assistants to help bring out the paper; three, farming out the design side of the work to one of the many small companies or one-man outfits who do a design-and-pre-press package. A general briefing of requirements is sufficient for a skilled designer to produce a variety of dummies for selection to establish style, and thereafter to design pages and type up material on a regular basis so that printing costs are kept within the economics of the desktop system.

Chapter 2 contains all the information needed to use type creatively in this field. The essential principles are:

- A type style needs to be based ideally on one or two main typefaces in different sizes and weights, along with one opposed typeface to give emphasis and colour in the right places.
- Indiscriminate mixing of serif and sans serif types should be avoided. Two different but similar serif types will match badly and would be pointless. One sans serif type, provided there are reasonable variations of weight and size, is better than trying to use two. A decision should be taken to give the product either a dominant serif format or a sans serif, and not to vacillate between the two.
- To refine the type format further a decision should be taken whether or not to use a wholly lowercase format, or perhaps to exclude italic type as a matter of style. A small product needs fewer types and variations than a general newspaper or big

magazine. The greater the mixture of faces, sizes and variations the more difficult it is to achieve a consistent design approach.

- Variations in choice and setting of body type should likewise be limited to avoid pages becoming hotch-potches. Panelled items should be used as structural points in the design in the same way as pictures.
- White space should be used creatively as a design element and not to point the failure of type to fill its allotted space. Space within and around headlines should be consistent. If type is indented or set 'ragged' there should be a design reason for it. On good paper with a sharp register white space is a boon to the designer. A study of gravure fashion magazines is a useful source of ideas in the creative use of white.

Chapter 7 will help with picture use. Points to note are:

- Pictures should be cropped for their relevance to the text. What they need to show is enhanced if the image can be made bigger by the exclusion of what they do not need to show.
- Similar pictures, whether of work processes or of people doing similar things, can usually look better if grouped together on a page or pages.
- Good tonal quality is essential to avoid disappointment in reproduction. In choosing a picture any greyness or indistinctness will look worse, not better, when the picture prints, however good the paper.
- Avoid big enlargements of small snaps unless the negative is available. The detail disperses rapidly in proportion to the increase in enlargement made from a print.

Free sheets

Free sheets – not the favourite term of the Association of Free Newspapers – is the name given to newspapers in which advertising income is pitched at a level which enables the proprietor to give them away. To bring in the advertising they usually go for house-to-house distribution in heavily populated areas so they can offer saturation coverage to potential advertisers. Circulation can thus be pegged to a potential target figure, unlike with paid-for papers, although distribution cannot be said to guarantee readership.

To win readership a free sheet has to make itself a viable alternative to a paid-for paper serving the same market, and therefore it has to take seriously the presentation of its editorial content, even if it does occupy a smaller percentage of the paper. In fact, the impact of frees has resulted in paid-for papers in some parts of the country increasing the proportion of advertising to boost falling revenues and the local free sheet increasing the proportion of editorial matter to win readers, to a point where the two have drawn closer together in their overall mix.

In design terms, in order to succeed, frees need to pay at least as much attention to layout as paid-for papers, which means that the editorial content should be used to the paper's advantage. A type style should be evolved as part of an identity. Too many frees fail not through insufficient editorial material but through insufficient care being taken in presenting what there is. Whether they are produced through desktop systems or on contract by printers (the more usual way) the typesetting and graphics facilities should be studied to get the best possible utilization from them and design principles as examined in this book applied.

This does not mean a rash of 'hype' or self-publicity but rather a measured use of type and illustration to create attractive page patterns that are helpful to the eye and right for the sort of readers receiving the paper. Identity and continuity of format allied to properly planned editorial content and services can win over readers who might otherwise equate frees with mail-shot advertising. It is not a market in which readership should be taken for granted.

Contract printing

Many specialist and tied circulation publications, including free, and some bigger papers, are printed by contract printers who specialize in this sort of work. Some regional papers who have invested in big mainframe systems and new web-offset presses have found it profitable to make their facilities available to other newspaper publishers. This should not alter the approach to design. The contractor will print whatever you prepare for the press and if need by, typeset and make up the pages as well. An art desk can operate just as effectively without the composing room being just round the corner, though the separation has to be taken into account in arranging time scales for production.

The geography of such and arrangement, with typesetters and printing presses sometimes situated hundreds of miles away and not necessarily both together, does slow down the production cycle. Layouts with edited text and pictures scaled, and if possible shot to size, have to be sent by messenger or express delivery, and page proofs brought back for cutting and adjustment. The advantage of direct text inputting with its speed and accuracy in screen editing and casting off is, of course, lost where text and headlines are keyed into the typesetters by the contractors from edited copy. A useful hybrid system to get over this problem is where a contract arrangement allows for electronically edited copy from direct input to be entered straight into the contractors' own typesetters. There is no reason why distance from keyboard to typesetter should prevent this. It makes editing and page fitting easier and faster and cuts labour charges by avoiding keyboarding text twice.

Also useful is where the editorial office has its own Autokon laser printer enabling it to shoot pictures to page size and set up camera artwork so that page-ready pictures and artwork can be delivered to the contractors. Otherwise, some useful advantages of the Autokon system are lost to the designer (see Chapter 7). A much better arrangement is when an editorial office can undertake its own typesetting and page make-up up to camera-ready stage, leaving only the plate-making and presswork to the contractor – as is often the case with desktop systems.

The main disadvantage of the contract system in its normal form, in fact, is the loss of fine control by the editorial that exists with in-house printing over the making up of the pages, and the detaching of the art desk from the end product of its efforts. Deadlines and delivery times of page material become of vital importance, especially where proofs of colour pages and covers are needed. The design, editing and production schedules have to be planned very precisely for weekly and monthly publications, with several issues running alongside each other in various states of planning and production. The usual method is to number them in sequence so that work can be correctly delivered and logged.

Even with the most efficient remote control it is useful to arrange for an editorial and art desk presence at the printers on vital page production days as an insurance should late problems arise.

15
The international scene

The development of a strong mass circulation national press, arising out of high population density and short lines of communication, has given Britain a special position in newspaper readership. The fact that national titles aim at a variety of social and income groups means that they exhibit, on the newsstands, a diversity of content as well as of presentation which leaves every taste catered for. At the same time the pervasiveness and high readership of the national press means that most provincial papers, their main topics having been hijacked by their national rivals, are pushed towards a predominantly regional, or even local content in the effort to woo readers. This content colours their presentation both in the pictures that are used and in the topics and words, and even the attitudes, that leap from the pages.

One of the consequences of this is that regional morning papers published in provincial cities have found it hard to be accepted by readers as purveyors of a spectrum of national news and have, during this century, suffered a decline.

Thus, while the design and the quality of the writing of many provincial titles is of a high standard, the feel of these papers is usually markedly different from that of a big national paper. The effect of this – as becomes clear to anyone studying the subject – is to divide the British press into two camps: the national press and the provincial press.

The first noticeable thing about looking at newspapers abroad is that this dichotomy does not seem to apply. There is a vigorous growth of city and region-based papers in most countries that compete successfully with the few mainly political titles that go for national distribution. This situation is justified in big countries such as the USA and Canada by the simple logistics of time and distance and, to a lesser extent, by the rich pickings of conurbation advertising. Out of this can grow a strong regional loyalty to titles. The punchy *New York Post* with its blockbuster sans headlines **(114)** is in a

NEW YORK POST

SPORTS FINAL

THURSDAY, SEPTEMBER 8, 1988 / Mostly sunny, 75-80 today; increasing clouds, 60-65 tonight / Details, Page 2   35¢ in New York City; 50¢ elsewhere

Tortured Tyson is all alone

The champ is alone and barred from seeing the real friends who have rushed to his side but been turned away. This is the sad truth about Tyson revealed in searching stories by PETE HAMILL and MARK Di IONNO on Page 5, MICHAEL MARLEY on the Back Page and JERRY IZENBERG on Page 98.

A CRACK BABY IS BORN

By ANN V. BOLLINGER

Theresa had her baby. He's an 8-pound boy with black curly hair and blue eyes.

But Theresa's baby cries more than most of the other babies in the maternity ward. He's a crack baby.

Theresa is the 16-year-old crack addict The Post wrote about on Tuesday who was 9 months pregnant and still selling her body on the street.

She gave birth on Tuesday night.

Theresa isn't very comfortable. She hasn't

Continued on Page 3

A teen hooker and her pimp, ready for business at the Lincoln Tunnel

FAT CATS IN WALL STREET SCAM BUSTED
Page 4

'BILLIE BOGGS' SEIZED ON DRUG RAP
Page 9

114   *New York Post*

different geographical and cultural as well as typographical world to the sedate *Los Angeles Times*, while both are light years away from the *Detroit Examiner*, in whose city neither titles would find favour. The *Toronto Star* (115) which presents the whole world to Ontario, gives no thought to the *Vancouver Sun*, at the other end of Canada. Likewise Sydney, Brisbane and Perth, Western Australia, happily go it alone.

Yet in old world Europe the same situation is found to apply. There is nothing about *La Gazzetta del Mezzogiorno*, with its bold serif dress and confident use of pictures, spacing and rules, and front page news choice **(130)** to suggest that it is published and printed far away from the centre of the universe down at Bari, at the heel of Italy. The raucus poster layout of Abendpost **(Plate 3)** might encapsulate the world in Frankfurt, but not in Hamburg or Munich where the world and Germany are looked at from a different axis in the pages of their own newspapers. The *Tribune de Geneve*, with its air of final authority **(126)** might trickle into airport bookstalls in Athens and Rome, but it speaks not for Zurich or Berne.

What we are looking at in the old and new worlds, from our vantage point in the home of mega-circulations, is a rich and varied growth of – by our standards – small- and medium-sized titles that combine within their pages the national and regional function of a

115 *Toronto Star*

116 *Atlanta Journal*

newspaper. They are bold and vigorous in opinion and record, while staying alive through sensible regional distribution arrangements and the enjoyment of national advertising income unmolested by mass circulation national predators.

It would be natural, looking at a cross-section of foreign and Commonwealth papers, to expect design styles to be as varied as the geography of the titles, and indeed there is variety. Yet the more we examine the world's newspapers – those printed in the European alphabets at least – the more a number of consistent traits can be identified.

American and Commonwealth

The US has been a leader in print technology and type design for nearly two centuries and American designers claim for it a powerful influence on the world's press. By British standards their wide

columns, generally 9-point body type and heavily spaced headlines and body setting lead to pages that lack impact and waste space. And yet broadsheet papers such as the *Atlanta Journal* **(116)**, and the *San Diego Union* **(117)**, with their open six-column format and simple horizontal layouts typical of American state journals, are easy to read, as is the Mississippi town evening, the *Vicksburg Evening Post* **(118)**. The interminable turns from the front page to inside pages in the *Union* and the *Journal* would annoy European readers, and excessive advertising on many pages makes design as we know it impossible, yet their long expanded lowercase headlines, wide fat paragraphs and well-flagged pages have a dignity and a comfortable feel that grows on you – and with the number of pages there is, in the end, plenty of room for the words.

The American style, if it might be called that, in its simplicity is the product of thick, many-sectioned papers crammed with advertising in which technique has to take second place to the sheer logistics of getting the hundreds of pages of each edition together. It is an

119   *Toronto Globe and Mail*

120   *The Australian*

unlikely model for the very different societies outside North America. It is perhaps natural, therefore, that its nearest clones can be found in Canada, where the *Toronto Globe* and *Mail* (119) and the *Toronto Star* (116), though with less weight of advertising, exemplify the American approach with the same six-column format (seldom found in Europe), long headlines and stories in horizontal segments. It is noteworthy that the *Union*, the *Journal*, the Vicksburg paper and the *Globe and Mail* all have traditional lowercase Old English title pieces.

With the prestigious titles commonly seen in Europe, such as the *International Herald Tribune, Washington Post* and *Wall Street Journal*, following the traditional American pattern it comes as a novelty to find that New York also supports a bold sans type tabloid in the *New York Post* (114). One is tempted to see in it the influence of the British popular tabloids through its long spell under the Rupert Murdoch ownership. Its bold caps headlines BORN A CRACK ADDICT, WIFE-MURDER TRIAL DAD WEDS WITNESS, and TORTURED TYSON IS ALL ALONE have the taut whiplash effect of authentic

121   *Sydney Daily Mirror*

low-count tabloid blockbusters. On the occasion of the Pope's visit to New York, twelve TV stations broadcast football games and only two the Pope's arrival. The *New York Post* splash headline was FOOTBALL 12, POPE 2. Yet after the first dozen eye-catching layouts it settles down to being a staider newspaper than it first appears and gets on with the job of packing text and adverts into its 100-plus pages in a way unlike a British popular tabloid.

With the formative years of the Commonwealth press coinciding with the growth of empire and political institutions in the UK, British newspaper practice was well placed to have global influence. It is not surprising, therefore to find in India, Australia, parts of Africa, and even Hong Kong, British language papers that have a familiar look.

In Australia there is the same division into eight-column broadsheets (occasionally nine) at the serious end of the market, and seven-column city tabloids at the popular end. Rupert Murdoch's *The Australian*, the country's only true national paper **(120)** achieves eye comfort and readibility for its up-market readers with an elegant modular design based on Century bold and light lowercase well broken by bold pictures. There is a feel of the British quality Sundays of a couple of years ago here, though without the preoccupation with artistic rulery, daring picture crops and utilization of white space, or self-conscious artiness.

Down-market, the *Sydney Daily Mirror* **(121)** and the *Brisbane Truth*

and its city clones proclaim, though again with a slightly dated feel, their kinship with *The Sun* and Fleet Street's *Daily Mirror* through their use of heavy sans headlines, page leads mainly in capitals, comic strips, glamour pictures and liberal use of WOBs and BOTs. Only the fatter size – 72 pages and more – betray the influence of American-scale advertising. The 78-page broadsheet *Sydney Morning Herald* pictured here **(122)**, while sharing the modular design approach of *The Australian*, moves further towards the American model with a three-section Wednesday edition crammed with advertising, with strips of news horizontalized above. It also has the Old English title piece much favoured in American papers in comparison with the *Times* style logo of *The Australian.*

The *South China Morning Post*, of Hong Kong **(123)**, and its stable-mate the *Sunday Morning Post*, both many-sectioned and crammed with news and advertising, could have been produced by the same art desk and on the same presses as the Australian broadsheets, though displaying more original and imaginative feature page ideas inside. Both are presented with great style and a newsy feel. Unaccountably, the daily has a nine-column format and the Sunday an eight-column.

European

European newspapers look to a different lineage. Here exist such anomolies as the broadsheet-sized poster layout and the tabloid sized quality sheet, thus contradicting the old notion that design philosophy is somehow related to page size.

Le Monde (50 mm × 34 mm) with its small wordy seriffed headlines and 10½ pica columns of readable 7 point **(124)**, is by no means the exception that proves the rule that a quality newspapers opts for broadsheet. Spain's *El Pais* (41 mm × 29 mm) and the Swiss *Tribune de Geneve* (49 mm × 33 mm), have a similar headline dress and words-orientated design, and appeal to a similar readership market. Having in recent years finally permitted the use of pictures (cartoons were always a feature), *Le Monde* is relaxing sufficiently these days to allow such departures as 3-pica indented stand-up drop letters, the occasional cut-out picture, WOB page flags and the odd bit of bold setting and spot red. It remains, however, a distinctive, well-signposted, comprehensive journal of comment giving emphasis to the words. Its small headlines work through being attractively whited out, while the geography of its items, clearly identified in strap-line or label, persuades the reader by the time page 48 has been reached that the world has been well and truly reviewed. It gives generous listings to 'arts and spectacles', but has no place for sport.

The Madrid daily *El Pais* **(125)**, with similar small size seriffed heads (no more than 42 point) all in lowercase and well whited, adopts the same pattern of flagging its coverage to help the reader. The pages are uniformly of five-column, as opposed to *Le Monde*'s six, and the type a particularly elegant and readable 8 point set to

124 *Le Monde*

125 *El Pais*

advantage on a 9 point body. It uses thick and thin rules effectively across the tops of its pages, often incorporating subject labels. There are rather more pictures, a good business coverage but still no sport. It could be almost a Spanish edition of *Le Monde*.

The *Tribune de Geneve* (126), like *El Pais*, is a five-column tabloid, though slightly bigger, with a 13 pica column width in 8 point, seriffed headings of up to 60 point page lead size, and with capitals used on the page one splash head and on strap lines and identification flags. The typographical treatment of the pages and the feel of the paper is similar to *Le Monde* and *El Pais*, but underscored standfirsts and spot colour are used as eye-breaks and there is slightly more variety in page design. It has an unusual masthead in blue and there are colour pictures on page three and also an adventure strip cartoon in colour. The paper is in three sections, one of which does include sports pages.

The poster broadsheet

At the opposite poll to these sedate tabloids comes the genre of poster-style popular broadsheets in colour, illustrated on **Plates 2** and **3**, which are perhaps the most distinctive aspects of Europe's contribution to newspaper design. It is a trend that has drawn no takers in Britain. Yet it is a style that can be found on bookstalls all

126   *Tribune de Geneve*

over Europe. The fact that the examples shown come from Germany, Greece and two from France is coincidental.

The poster broadsheet is for the newspaper reader who wants everything on page one. It is a contents lists, a taster, a vast, colourful, concentrated distillation of the day's news; it is a grandiose buy-me, read-me-now feast for the eye; it is the ultimate use of display, not in wild or 'circus' fashion but in a controlled assault upon the impulse buyer who is the mainstay of the popular market. It is saying: 'This is it! This you must know! We have the lot – look no further!' It turns upside down the traditional notion that a popular paper should be a small sheet containing, on the front, blockbuster type on the best story of the day with one big eye-catching picture, offering the reader instead a cornucopia of goodies that dazzle the eye.

The *Abendpost*, of Frankfurt **(Plate 3(b))** is an extreme manifestation of this genre. Page one manages to carry three lines of 144-point heavy sans lowercase type on a splash that consists of a one-paragraph summary of a jet crash with cross-reference to page 2; a 29 cm wide picture of a broken bridge with headline in 84 point, one-paragraph taster and cross-reference to page 4; a sports summary with 60-point headline, main results, picture and cross-reference; a self-contained down-page story 15 cm long with an 84-point head-line; a picture with caption of a couple in fancy dress on a tandem;

seven short self-contained stories, competition winners, weather report, TV programme cross-reference and, 12 cm down the page on the left-hand side, the *Abendpost* title piece used as a fulcrum for the stories swirling around it. The main items are clearly flagged with WOB labels, and the stories are kept apart by a mixture of 6 and 10-point red and black rules so that in the vast mosaic of type no one piece can be confused with another.

It is a page for the reader looking for instant easy-to-read news, who knows the rules of the typographical game by which the paper makes its name. Yet note the careful slotting of text in relation to headline and halftone, the strength derived from the long horizontal picture of the bridge, the studied intrusion above the fold of the sports summary and vital big type results – an important item for a large body of a popular paper's readers. The picture of the jets let into the WOB above the splash sends the eye to the centrally sited text. The bridge caption is arrowed, and so is the tandem one. The weather and competition winners are instantly findable in what, on closer inspection, is by no means a jumble of type.

The Athens daily, *To Fos* (The Light), in a similar market **(Plate 2(b))** relies on the same technique with the added facility of highlighting in blue and yellow as well as red. Again, the title piece (in a red and black panel) is lowered from the top of the page for the stories to swirl around it. Many of the twelve items consist only of headlines and cross-references, an important football result taking the entire top of the page in yellow on black. The top half is virtually an extended contents bill for the newsstands, with the main pictures used as focal points round which to assemble the stories below the fold. It is this form of presentation that makes *To Fos* distinctive to its down-market readers. It is bold and instantly recognizable, although the ruling and separation of items is less helpful to the eye of the uninitiated than in the more disciplined German product.

The Paris evening *France-Soir* **(Plate 3(b))** and the *Nice-Matin* a big seller on the Riviera, are less strident examples of the broadsheet poster technique. *France-Soir* follows the German pattern of using sans lowercase in a wide range of sizes, though introducing italic and even a serif variant for some down-page items. The splash story consists only of a headline and cross reference, as do three other items, while the dominant colour picture also funnels down into a caption and cross-reference. The title piece again drops below the top of the page so that it is surrounded by items with once again a football story taking top position although, as a result of the large picture and the longish story on the right, the overall pattern is less complex than the German or Greek examples.

Nice-Matin **(Plate 2(b))**, rich in colour pictures, and with smaller, lighter sans type, carries nine items with the minimum of text, while slotting in half a dozen advertisements at the top and bottom of the page. Every item is cross-referred to inside pages with the exception of one picture with a caption story. The page, with its clearly ruled off

127   *Ultima Hora, Brazil*

128   *Corriere della Sera*

La Gazzetta del Mezzogiorno

La Stampa

items and spread-around pictures, gives the impression of an attractive news menu containing a little something for everyone.

Two new world examples of this genre are to be found in the worldwide circulating USA *Today* **(Plate 4(a))** and the exotic *Ultima Hora* **(127)**, of Brazil. In a front page remarkable by any standards, the title piece of *Ultima Hora* comes 43 picas down the page. It is difficult to identify a columnar format since on all pages there is an eccentricity of measure which, as on page one, manages to convince the eye by the sheer confidence of the presentation. The page illustrated is immaculately put together with the minimum of body matter, giving the reader sixteen headlines in assorted sizes and dwelling in poster form on some of the serious issues arising out of Brazil's mega-inflation. Not sport but the new price of petrol runs across the top of the page.

There is, of course, a wide middle ground between the two extremes discussed above. While there is little influence to be seen of the mass market British tabloids, there is a variety of styles to be

131   *Die Welt*

133   *De Telegraaf*

132   *Le Figaro*

found in the broadsheet newspapers published in the main European cities. Milan's *Corriere della Sera* **(128)** with its unvarying nine-column format and sparse use of pictures is typical of the more serious city-based Italian papers, strong on comment as well as news, and with excellent world news coverage, as is Rome's *La Stampa* **(129)**. Headlines tend to line at the top with stories running across the page in a series of legs resting on similar horizontal segments lining below. Type is a mixture of serif and sans serif, often condensed and invariably in lowercase, with multidecking column and variation provided by light and bold headline versions. Pictures tend to be mainly small and used out of relevance to the text more than for design purposes.

La Gazzetta del Mezzogiorno, of Bari **(130)**, is typical of the middle market, both visually and in readership, using a version of Century bold and italic, all lowercase for headlines, but up to 84 point. Here a more creative use of type, pictures and typographical devices results in pages that allow a good read to the stories while still providing bold focal points to move the eye about.

In the more austere class of product, even by the withdrawn standards of *Le Monde*, comes Axel Springer's broadsheet *Die Welt* **(131)**, published in Bonn which, on page one, offers its celebrated world coverage in seven columns of 8 point unrelieved by a single picture. Meanwhile, *Le Figaro* **(132)**, as national and conservative a paper as can be found in France, is daringly moving away from its stiff format of old, and adopting, though without their boldness, the shop window techniques of the poster broadsheets. All stories in our example, apart from the column one comment piece, are run at short length and then turned to inside pages, or are simply headlines with cross-references, thus enabling fifteen items to be aired on page one.

Another well-stocked page one relying on turns and cross-references is that of the Dutch daily, *De Telegraaf* **(133)**, which manages to combine the elements of a mixed type design, with traditional masthead and splash position with a flavour of the poster broadsheets. The result is a page one which has great vigour above the fold, while degenerating into a hotch-potch below. The Greek version of this halfway house is the prestigious daily *Alethia* (Truth) which injects boldness and business into an old vessel with more dignity, marred only by the discovery and overuse of reverse video straplines **(134)**.

An oddity in any review of Continental styles has to be the slim Russian newspapers. Our examples of *Pravda* **(135)** and *Izvestia* **(136)**, show how daunting can be solid 6-point unleaded type in the Cyrillic reading text to editors who have to pack a lot of words into six pages unrelieved by adverts. In the face of this, the designers of both papers manage to inject some variety into the layouts by the creative use of rules and panels and the disposal of such white space as can be spared.

Both opt for a good sized picture on page one, though in *Pravda* the

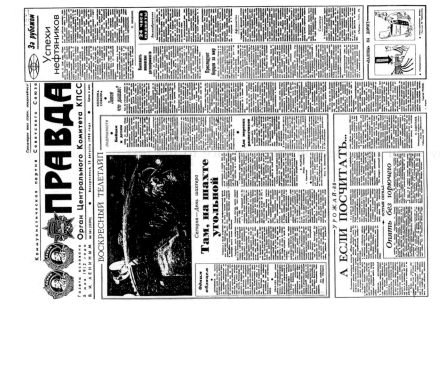

135   *Pravda*

134   *Alethia* (Truth), Athens

136   *Izvestia*

halftone would have looked better moved two columns to the right. *Pravda* is nevertheless the more readable. Its columnar white is effective and its two serif faces include what looks like a Russian version of Ultra Bodoni which, though an oddity on the front page, prints well both in large and small sizes. Also, its columns are mercifully free of the miniscule two-column setting on the two signed opinion pieces in *Izvestia*.

16
Colour

The advances made in colour scanning and the improvements in high-speed heat-set web offset printing have opened up an exciting new world for the journalist/designer. Across the board in newspapers it is now possible to regard colour as one of the normal tools of design. To take advantage of the facilities that are available it is essential for those coming new to page design – and also those who have been familiar only with mono practice – to know something of the process by which a colour photograph or transparency is printed in a newspaper.

As with a monochrome photograph the tones in a colour picture are reproduced by the halftone process. This means that the tones have to be broken down into dots by 'screening' the original in order to reproduce the different colour values. The dots of the screened picture, when transferred to the printing plate, accept ink in various combinations of four basic colours: *yellow, magenta* (red), *cyan* (blue) and *black*. These are printed in that order from four separate plates (that is, the page makes four separate passes through the press) which are prepared from colour negatives made by subjecting the picture or transparency to a process called scanning.

Colour scanning   The scanner **(137)** is an electronic device by which an operator, using a set of balances and filters, given total accuracy by the computer, creates the four negatives from the colours in the photograph. The cyan filter creates a yellow negative; a green filter isolates the magenta; a red filter produces cyan, and a combination yellow-orange filter makes black. These negatives, each containing its own colour, are called separations.

To accomplish this the colour print or transparency is attached to a drum in the machine and the operator keys in the percentage of enlargement or reduction that is needed together with the screen

137   Vital machine in colour-picture editing – this Itek 200-S scanner has a microprocessor-controlled keyboard and a colour monitor

(dot) size. Laser beams then scan the picture as it revolves, isolating and screening every individual image. Within seconds the computer which activates the scanner converts the information into a screened piece of film for each colour. This information is stored digitally in the scanner in case the designer, at a later stage of the page make-up, wishes to use any other pictures or type images to cut into the picture or to overprint on it.

The versatility of the scanner will allow a complete composed page to be produced in the four separations up to its printing size. A single 35 mm transparency can, in fact, be enlarged up to ten times, with the scanner enabling the operator to enhance the sharpness of the image and even the density of individual colours. Modern 'paint box' scanners will allow an art director to change, say, the colour of the sky from night into day, to stretch the image horizontally or vertically, or even take an item out of one picture and transplant it into another. The limiting factor in this sort of operation is the time and expense where page production is on a tight budget.

The operator of the scanner will receive information from time to time from the viewing monitor that the screens are clashing between one colour and another. A crude example of this phenomenon is when an already used picture is used again in a newspaper for a 'flashback' effect. Because the newspaper cutting or old picture has already been screened when originally used, a clash of dots will occur when it is prepared again for the page, giving what is called a 'moiré' effect. The same effect can result inside the scanner from the complexity of the colours of a particular colour print or transparency. It can be cured by the operator simply revolving one or more of the screens on the separations, whereupon reproduction will be seen to return to normal.

Picture quality

Picture editing is more critical in newspapers printing in colour. The more advanced will be calling up photographs in full colour on monitor screens. Sometimes the photographer at the scene of a story will be transmitting, by means of a modem, direct over telephone lines into the picture editor's viewer. With monochrome the dynamics of a picture are traditionally expressed first in its news value and second in its reproductive quality. Faults in focus can, in a curious way, lend a greater sense of urgency to an exclusive hard news picture. More accuracy in focusing is called for with colour since focal 'shake' will confuse the scanner and precious time will be lost manipulating the machine to correct the deficiency.

'Hot' and 'cold' are words that become important in connection with the quality of a picture presented for publication **(Plate 4(b))**. A hot picture is one that shows too large a proportion of red in its colour range. If red is too strong in a transparency it will 'spill over' into the surrounding colours and the blues will take on a purple warmth inappropriate to the subject. Conversely the cold colour blue, if too strong, will dominate and 'corrupt' the warmer colours. Certain types of colour film are notorious for their predilection for cold or hot colour. Good photographers will balance their cameras to the type of film used to correct this problem.

The subject of the picture will influence editorial choice in colour pictures. A disastrous fire, for example, will benefit in reproduction if hot reds are being produced. Conversely the effect of strong red would be wrong in a picture of a snow covered wind-swept mountain. Contrasts, when they occur, can be effective. For instance a picture of a bird like a red cardinal scratching for food in a snow-covered New England garden can deliver a shock to the eye. Achieving colour balance both in the choice of the original and within the scanner is a critical one for the picture editor.

Choosing the picture

The parameters of picture choice, it can be seen, are more complex with colour than with black and white. The editor might want a picture strong on news value and visual impact, whereas production demands are for a range of colour, good tone balance and crisp focus. There are also differences between news and features requirements to be taken into account.

News

News pictures in colour – although this part of the paper remains dominated by black and white – have become commoner since photographers have been encouraged to carry two cameras, one loaded with colour film, the other with monochrome. There are situations where news shots for a colour-reproducing newspaper are a standard requirement. In the case, say, of a major disaster story, the picture editor would deploy several photographers, some carrying colour film, the others black and white. This would guarantee pictures for pages that are not programmed to take colour where a story might spill on to several pages.

If the story is at some distance from the office, modern wiring techniques over telephone lines would be used to meet tight edition deadlines. Mobile transmitters feeding into computerized systems can now be packed into cases the size of a briefcase and both colour and mono can be sent over the same line at the dialing of a telephone and the touch of a small keyboard.

Compared with the old system, computerized methods of picture wiring have become much more economic of time and labour. One consequence, as national papers in Britain have discovered, is that the photographic darkroom's role has had to be realigned since it is not required to such a degree on the news side. With the high-speed turn-round of news pictures handled by the computer, the darkroom function is becoming more to develop and print features material to a higher quality. Computer hardware, as with television, can transmit news pictures from the camera's lens straight to the make-up screen, with copytasting being carried on on the split side of the same screen on which a page is being made up.

Features

The boom area in the supply and use of colour pictures and transparencies is undoubtedly the features, or magazine, pages. The needs of features colour are best expressed in the perfection achieved by the high quality *fashion* photographer. Every aspect is covered by the person behind the lens. Models are chosen for their ability to 'act' the clothes. Their bodies must be appropriate to the type of garment being photographed, eyes and bone structure being paramount, their movements fluid to produce freedom on film. Successful pictures of fashion in colour should give the reader a feeling of excitement, while subtly conveying the fashion editor's view of the features of the clothes that should be brought out.

The disadvantage from the editorial production point of view is the sheer volume of transparencies resulting from a fashion session. The motorized camera enables the operator to demand continuous changes of stance which, in the end, allows the fashion page designer to choose shapes and poses that are unique. The choice can require much discussion between fashion editor and art editor, and it is a good idea to feed the best of the bunch into a display unit for final choice to get a better impression of size. To produce a short list first, the transparencies should be placed side by side on a desktop light box and viewed through a magnifying glass. The chosen ones will be those which, while fulfilling their fashion function, allow the marrying of words and pictures to be made on the page in the most visually attractive way.

Some executives handling fashion pages feel the method of choice with light box and magnifier is simply not good enough, however. Having weeded out the unwanted transparencies, they examine the short list, many times bigger than required for reproduction, through a projector. This can uncover faults not visible to the eye by normal magnification, and give a better reading of the colour. A knowledge of the dominant colour is vital in preparing a colour fashion page.

Agencies

Features colour will in many cases come from the library stock of agencies, and a picture researcher will be sent there to find pictures to fit a given feature. The increased use of colour in newspapers has meant the growth of picture agencies offering colour prints and transparencies, many of them specializing in subjects such as celebrities, gardening, motherhood, country life, money features and so on. A newspaper's researcher will be offered lightbox and viewing facilities, or the agency will research and send round a selection of transparencies to fit a list of requirements, though for an extra fee. The older general agencies still provide news library services in colour film.

Computer retrieval has greatly improved the speed at which a wanted subject can be produced from an agency's files compared to the old mono picture libraries. Another advantage is that trans-parencies take up less space than prints. A less advantageous development is that prices of picture reproduction are increasing with demand. Whenever a new picture fad occurs it is followed by a price explosion. An example is the appetite for celebrities being photographed at night-spots around the world. Immediately this happened the papparazi shifted into gear and began producing immense quantities of mediocre pictures. The agencies responded by setting up specialist departments to sort the good from the bad. Inevitably this was reflected in the price per square centimetre to newspapers for exclusivity.

Special transmission

Pictures for a feature article that have already been published abroad can be airmailed by special delivery and arrive within 24 hours. Some big organizations, however, can send colour 'over the wire' as separations which are instantly usable. The quality, unlike the wire pictures of old, is excellent since satellite transmission is used. The high cost of this method is eased if the pictures can be transmitted via a newspaper's own office in the country of origin. A point to remember is that a picture needs four wiring times for the separations.

A system of instant transmitted display, for which the hardware will soon be available for newspapers in this country, will enable picture editors to simply call an agency which may have a required set of pictures and ask for them to be displayed for viewing on the picture desk VDU. A choice can then be made and a 'receive' command keyed in. The eventual extension of this facility will be the colour scanning by agencies of pictures as ready-to-use separations for transmission to subscribers.

A good picture editor balances these costs of picture procurement against the department's budget. Where a staff photographer can be conveniently sent to do a job it will be invariably the cheapest way.

Colour layout

Despite the fact that colour page make-up can now be done mechanically on some desktop systems, the layout pad has not been abandoned in newspapers that have moved into colour. Nor is it likely to be. The 'same size' drawing of pages still gives the greatest opportunities for creative design.

The semi-opaque layout sheets used for colour are the same as those for mono pages, with a grid identical to the cards used in paste-up. Let us say that the colour picture (or pictures), which usually means a transparency, has been chosen as one of the ingredients of a page along with the type, graphics and other mono components. From the editorial point of view the transparency, because of its colour and shape, is the key element. Copy lengths have been established and perhaps the main headlines written. The designer knows what must be got into the page. It is here that, coming fresh to colour layout, the journalist/designer might be puzzled by the difficulty of establishing on the tiny frame of a 35 mm transparency the specific area required to print. With a monochrome print, of course, all that is needed are the instructions, dimensions and cut-off marks to be marked clearly on the back of the picture, or alternatively by a tracing paper overlay with instructions on it taped to the front.

The transparency

What section of the key transparency is needed? This is the first decision. You place the tiny film on the light box that lives below the lens and bellows of the Grant projector (see Chapter 6). Making sure that the correct long lens is in the lens holder, you locate the transparency in the dead centre of the light box. At this point a movement of as little as 10 mm away from the centre will have you searching for the image that you are trying to project on to a sheet of tracing paper you have placed on the screen at the top of the machine. Is it to be the whole picture, or do you want to crop and blow up part of it? Once you have made this decision you are ready to trace off the image.

You make a final check on which way round the transparency should be. If it is on the light box upside down then you will be tracing off in reverse (left to right). A transparency that has been put in its cardboard frame properly will show the maker's name and other information on the front side and nothing on the reverse. The words on the frame should be facing upwards to you. If the frame is plain on both sides, take the whole thing between finger and thumb, making sure you are not touching the actual film, and allow the available light to strike across the horizontal plane of the film. This should show the correct side as shiny and the reverse side as dull and slightly uneven where the chemicals have created the images of the picture.

Sometimes it can be difficult to read the transparency because of the thinness of its emulsion. In this case be ruthless and take the film out of its frame. Peel the cardboard apart and the film will fall out . . . but not on to the floor! Now the sprocket hole area of the film is revealed. Also showing will be the frame number and producer's name between the sprocket holes. You can be certain the film is the right way round since you can read these words. On the reverse side they read back to front. Now put the transparency back in the Grant machine.

The Grant should be focused up to the size needed for the page and the projected image, whether part of the transparency or the whole, traced off and transferred to the layout sheet.

A snag could occur here. The long lens in the Grant might not be long enough to enlarge the 35 mm piece of film to the full size of the page you are drawing – that is if you are going to make the finished picture that large. The answer in this situation is to trace off the image to the largest size you can, place this tracing below on the light box, and trace up again to the required size. Accuracy in doing this is vital, and so you should be using a very hard pencil or ball-point. Litho houses on publications where page make-up and printing are contracted out will rely on your accuracy since they will be composing colour on screen.

Do not throw away the tracing for your colour picture after it has been transferred to the layout sheet. With a different coloured pen or pencil indicate on it the cropped area of the transparency that you are using. The technique here is the same as when marking up a mono picture (**42**). Having done this on no account allow the transparency to be separated from the tracing. Put identifying marks on both to avoid accidents.

A point to note: in cropping a transparency or colour picture be aware of the usefulness of background colour. Not only can the blue of a sky be pleasing when printed – it can also be a useful vehicle for an overprinted headline, especially on a features page. In a special projection a colour transparency could fill an entire page with the essential illustration at the bottom and the rest of it used to take overprinted headline and body text. Remember, the litho house can match trannie colour so if you need more sky than is in the film it can be extended – at a price!

Page make-up

Having traced your colour picture on to the layout sheet, the other parts of the page can be put together round this focal point. Headlines and text must be made to fit accurately, particularly if they are to overprint, or set as a white-out, on to the picture. If body text is used for a white-on-picture be sure that the type used is bold enough to accept white, bearing in mind that there are four colours meeting on the edge of the tiny characters, each of the colours bearing its own screen. A movement in register of thousandths will confuse these edges and make the words unreadable if the type chosen is too small or is too fine in serif or stroke.

Where a colour element is located on a newspaper page that is otherwise to be printed in mono the mono parts of the page must be accurately made up so that the spaces to accept colour are left precisely located in width and depth for the four passes through the press needed to take ink from the colour plates. A useful practice here in the paste-up room is to apply page-size acetates showing colour location to each page taking colour so that the spaces are seen to be accurate before the page is released to the camera and platemaker. This can avert the serious fault of colour intruding into mono areas of the page through make-up failing to follow the page layout precisely.

To this end instructions on page layouts should be generous in what is required to be done in make-up and colour preparation. For instance every piece of colour tint used must bear its Pantone colour number and the percentage of screen needed to effect the colour required.

Any parts of a transparency that have been removed in order to take in another picture, such as in a montage, must be clearly marked. Shade the edges of your tracing of a colour picture where it is to be to be overlapped in order that the litho operator dealing with the page can see your intentions clearly. The shape and nature of the montage must be made precise **(138)**. Every art director has particular ways of doing this. Whatever the shape, all picture edges that require a measurement should be given one. Remember, there is no way instructions can be put on individual transparencies except for the identity number or letter you have placed on the frame to link it with the number or letter on the page layout.

Typesizes must be marked in detail on the edges of the layout as with mono pages, as also should the thickness and colour of rules. Some contract printing houses prefer type sizes to be in millimetres rather than in the old points system. Differences of this sort should be checked before launching into colour layout and design where

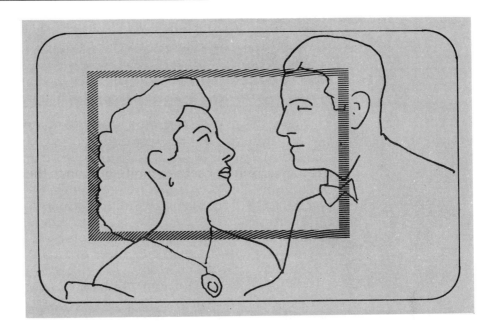

138 To help in design a colour transparency is blown up on a Grant projector and a tracing made. This serves two purposes: it accompanies the trannie to the litho department to show the area of the original that is to be used; it is overdrawn on to the finished layout to ensure accuracy and to provide a means of checking and identification

make-up and printing are by contract. With such arrangements it is a good idea, for safety, to mark any original artwork with its instructions as well as putting instructions on the page. If the colour and the typesetting are at different locations, make sure that the mono part of the layout with its typesetting instructions is made available separately for this purpose. Leave nothing to chance. Your contract printer might be surrounded by pages from all sorts of magazines and newspapers.

Spot colour   The use of a particular colour – spot colour – has been possible for many years under the letterpress system through the provision of a colour duct on the presses, with its own ink reservoir, printing separately via a rubber cylinder. This enabled such basic things as the stop press (fudge) seal, the edition marker and – in more recent years – the title piece to be printed in a chosen colour, though not to a fine accuracy. Usually the colour was one base colour of cyan, magenta or yellow. On some of the older high-speed rotaries this 'fudge box' colour could be used in tabloid newspapers only across a horizontal line at the top of the front and back spread. Two fudge boxes would run simultaneously on the press, one carrying the page one title piece, and the other the back page sports logo, often using red.

Although greater use of spot colour was possible by this method the heavy print runs of national papers, having more press time, did not allow printing time, though some regional papers pioneered the greater use of letterpress spot colour. Advertisers, in particular, were keen to buy such limited colour as could be made available where newspaper companies were happy to offset the slower running of the presses against the extra income.

The switch to web-offset presses, with their easy use for accurate run-of-press colour, has revolutionized the provision of spot colour for editorial and advertising purposes and made possible a more ambitious use of a wider range of mixed colours in the same publication. The production by the Letraset organization of a British Standards Institution colour guide for the industry some years ago, called the *Pantone Guide*, has made things easier both for the ink manufacturers and art editors. The guide lays out the primary colours with a standard series of lighter and darker versions in easily comparable 15 mm squares of colour. Each one is given a Pantone number, and this can be used on a layout to indicate to the printer the exact colour required. The system is now universal, and is used to call up colour on a computer screen.

Each of the swatches in the *Pantone Guide* refers to solid flat colours. Further dilution, however, can be made. Instructions can be given to break down a chosen number by percentage in which the printer or litho house lets 'white' into a colour by screening it.

The technique is effectively used by the newspaper *USA Today*, the undisputed leader in this sort of colour **(Plate 4(a))**. Its four-colour run-of-press reproduction, good though it is, is outshone by the clever editorial and graphic application of a range of spot colour both in rules and panels, and to enhance its characteristic use of charts and graphics. A broadsheet paper, *USA Today* has evolved a type of 'tabloid' journalism in which colour is used instead of big headlines to increase readability and convey information. This quantum leap has been achieved by thinking colour where in the days of hot metal the designer achieved variation through the use of tints and 'shades' of black.

The freedom resulting from the easy resource to spot colour has proved invaluable in the enhancement of information graphics in many British newspapers and in the range of options available to advertisers to highlight parts of an advert.

Duotone colour

A version of spot colour used more in magazines but worthy of greater use in newspapers is duocolour, or duotone, in which a good quality black and white picture is given the benefit of colour tinting. The technique is comparatively simple. A second negative printing the chosen colour is placed under the black and white one with the same screen. Variations of visual depth in the resulting colour are

Plate 1(a) The quill work on the right is from Einhard's *Life of Charlemagne*, written in the early ninth century and demonstrates the style of illuminated letters known as the Caroline, upon which modern Black letter and Old English typefaces are based

(b) This example of early sixteenth-century printing shows how closely the formation of the letters follow the quill work of the monks as in the example at the top

Plate 2(a) The *Daily Mirror* in this front page makes a virtue of the clashing disposition of headlines on a day when there was no prospect of a good colour picture. The night editor has rung the changes by the use of white-on-black and white-on-tone lowercase lines against a dominant splash story

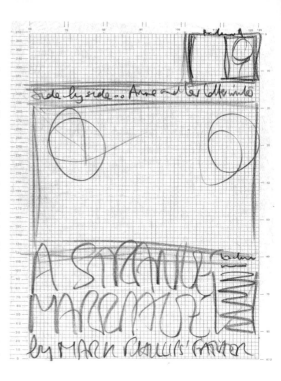

(b) The Athens broadsheet on the left, *To Fos* (The Light), is almost surrealist in its approach with a very European saturation blurb technique. *Nice-Matin* uses a more reserved typography to project similar ideas

Plate 3(a) A superb *Today* page one in its three stages of production – first the editor's rough, which is interpreted by the art desk in the second version, which leads to the finished product in chromaline form

(b) *France-Soir* page ones are noted for the strategic positioning of colour. Here, although there is a mass of headline type, the colour is carefully placed to avoid clash. *Abēndpost*, left, suffers, as German broadsheets do, with 'portmanteau' words which demand plenty of Extra condensed type. However, this page one cries out to be read – a process greatly helped by the effective use of spot colour

Plate 4(a) The combination of a striking blue masthead, a dominant approach to full colour pictures and spot colour create a unique blend of tabloid and broadsheet techniques in *USA Today*. Below: the newspaper's USA Snapshots feature is a good example of a down-page eye-catcher using colours drawn from the halftones in the page

achieved, before printing, by reducing by percentage the dot of the screen on the colour version beneath. The results depend upon the subject and the mood required. It is no use using blue for a second colour if flesh tones are wanted, while blue is reasonable on a holiday scene with masses of sea and sky. Sepia, to give an effect of an old picture or a feeling of mood in an article dealing, say, with antiquities, can be achieved by a reduction of percentage of magenta or red as an under colour. An important point: the black and white picture used must have good definition and contrast. Detail that is too fine can get lost in the applied colour.

The Konica colour copier (referred to on page 96) can cut corners in the duotone process. It carries an at-the-touch colour balance which can be used to rule out one or more of the four colours in a transparency or flat colour picture, or intensify one colour at the expense of the rest. It will also apply a colour directly to a black and white picture. Using this machine the colour wanted can be balanced precisely. When the production of the Konica machine is applied to the page as original artwork the printer then matches the second colour required to print the picture on the page to that indicated on the Konica original.

Colour or not   When to and when not to use colour depends on the type of newspaper and even on the part of a newspaper. While features offer more scope for the mood and atmosphere of a good colour picture and news seems to demand black and white, certain vivid news subjects can produce a shock effect in colour. A general point to note is that research has shown that a colour picture is at its best when surrounded by black and white. There is general agreement that coloured headlines do not improve its effectiveness.

Colour can be effective in columnist or feature logos or motifs, especially those where the typography does not follow house style. Cartoons or sketches drawn by artists should nowadays be submitted with colour. Where the artist has not identified the area where colour should be applied the art editor will usually decide. A common usage is to apply colour in the areas to which mono tints might be applied. Rarely would the main outlines of the drawing be in colour. Care should be taken in artwork with flesh tones since it is easy for such colour to give the impression of crude comic strips.

Using colour on body type is not to be recommended. It is difficult even with modern sophisticated methods to prevent the register from fractionally slipping on printing, thus giving an out-of-focus appearance to the type. To take colour, body type should be set at least above 10 point and be ideally in a sans serif face, that is, Metro or Helvetica. A point to remember is that newsprint is inferior to magazine paper and has an inescapable blotting factor which makes the fine work achieved on magazines impossible.

Spot colour for certain rules and borders can be effective in newspapers, if not used too indiscriminately – and not on the news pages. It can also illuminate charts and graphics, as in the example quoted of *USA Today*.

Where on-the-run colour can go in a newspaper depends, of course, not on the editor's whim but on the arrangements in the press room. *Colour imposition*, as it is called, is based on the concept that priority for colour will be given to the 'title press', that is the press that prints page one and the back page of a publication, together with the middle pages. What additional colour can be made available is a local decision since machine planning in the press room will have established where the colour units stand in the press line. Editorial choice is determined by this fact. Allowing for this there are more single page possibilities in a broadsheet paper than in a tabloid since the tabloid pages print in pairs.

The uses of colour in newspapers is still experimental and, while mistakes are being made, there is an enormous scope for originality and potential for the designer who can adapt it to the paper's market.

Pre-print colour

We have been talking so far about the most commonly used form of colour printing, found in newspapers that have electronic text origination and printing web offset, which is usually referred to as *run of press* colour, that is, the colour parts of the paper are printed on the presses at the same time as the black and white. The other quite different method is *pre-print*, in which high grade newsprint has colour material printed on it in advance on one side of the sheet by the much slower but better quality rota-gravure method and is then re-reeled to be used on the presses when the normal pages are printed.

The advantages of pre-print is that it gives a colour option to publications that do not have an in-house facility for colour printing, and it can be used by papers printing either web offset or by the older letterpress method on rotary presses. There are, of course, publications that use both methods, especially if an advertiser wants to utilize the more expensive pre-print method to give stunning quality to some product promotion as a contrast to black and white editorial and other advertising on adjacent pages.

Pre-print colour, with the advantages of gravure and better quality paper, has become an art form in its own right, so in making editorial use of pre-print, design teams must rise to the occasion and give the same devotion to detail to their colour pages. The first thing to remember is that the pages must be produced well in advance of the on-the-run daily or Sunday paper in which the pre-print will be used. Also, the pages will not be being designed for offset plates but for cylinder-etched production. A meticulous magazine approach is therefore needed.

If there are several of them, or if they are to run consecutively in several issues, a routine must be involved of sending the colour parts of the page for gravure processing several weeks in advance. Time can then be given to the mono words and pictures for printing on to the pages on the night. The editorial layouts must be impeccable since the gravure production could be at the other end of the country or even abroad. Contact will have to be by telephone so it would be useful to have a copy of each transparency blown to size for reference together with its layout in case of queries. Nothing is more frustrating than a printer at the other end of a telephone querying a project that left the editorial department several weeks ago.

Bleed-offs

An important difference between colour pre-print and the adjacent mono pages, is the option of *bleed* on the colour pages. This is the term used when pictures are cut off at the edge of the page **(139)**. Usually 3 mm are needed by the printer to allow for the machines to trim at the printing stage, although the requirement can be up to 5 mm to take account of the possible 'wander' of the paper. Dealing with 35 mm transparencies in terms of bleed can be clumsy when thinking about fine detail on the edge of the page. The new colour machines by Canon and Konica can be of immense value here. They will help to point up any pitfalls across the area to be covered by the picture and, in particular, the bleed edges. The colour copy made should be retained in the editorial dummy for captioning and colour reference and for page and position identity.

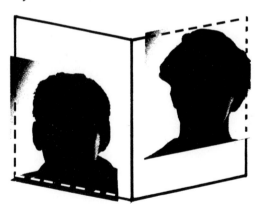

139 Bleed-offs – how a 3 mm cutting allowance is indicated on the layout

Blank make-up sheets used for this sort of work should show the bleed dimensions and also remind the designer of how close type can come to the edge of the page. The page number should be noted carefully since where a picture bleeds depends on whether it is a left-hand or right-hand page, there being no trimmed edge on the fold side. Some editors, of course, reject the bleed facility on pre-print in order to make such colour pages conform with the paper's mono pages.

Colour correction

For newspapers printing *run-of-press* colour, colour correction during production is an almost impossible task. That is why it is necessary to be right first time with colour densities of pictures and of any words in colour on the pages. The reliability of machines is now making this more possible.

In the case of *gravure* and, indeed, of *heat-set offset litho* work, where the drama of on-the night production is not a factor, high quality art proofs can now be available or, even better, *chromalines*. These are produced by litho houses to give absolute definitive guidance to the printer, and are reproductions of the actual film colour separations on stiff plastic art board.

Editorial art and picture people should treat these colour sheets as correction proofs. The colours must be compared with the originals by using a light box for the transparencies and a flood-lit examination wall with the necessary clips to hold the chromalines in place. An examination wall is usually concave and is mounted on a horizontal flat plane that is illuminated. With this shape, every part of the chromaline can be lit and, when placed alongside a light box, will create the absolute conditions for comparison.

Instructions to the process house can be relayed in the white margins and should be written confidently in ball-point. Wax pencils were used in the past and the instructions written on the offending part of the chromaline or colour proof, but problems arose when the marks became smudged during transit or, worse, when they disappeared under heat or light.

It is best for a journalist to tell the experts they think a flesh colour too lurid or red, or to darken the grass rather than to add more cyan. Too knowledgeable an approach can upset people you have to rely upon.

Appendix:
Some problems occurring in the designing of a newspaper

by Vic Giles

New and unusual tasks come to light for the designer engaged in launching or revamping a newspaper. Laying down a format for a new newspaper, as was the case of my work for the *Daily Star* in 1978 involves, for instance, not only the creation of a masthead and a type style to suit the size and market of a newspaper but to decide such things as the printed area of the pages, and with it the column width. Here, a false judgement can land a paper with an obstacle for the rest of its life.

In the case of the *Daily Star* the figures provided by the production director for the size of the new paper, that is, based on newsprint width – were 600 mm wide by 380 mm deep for a double-page spread. From this the column measures could be established together with the width of the column gutters and the gutter space of the fold.

To work this out I needed to establish the accuracy of paper tension through the presses, which were at this time rather old rotary presses. On older presses there will always be a tendency for the printed area to 'wander' on the paper surface, and therefore an awareness of the extent of the wander is necessary.

If the presses are already printing a newspaper, as was the case with the *Daily Star* presses, then the evidence of the eye should reveal the movement from page to page in the existing publication. Some new newspapers 'take fright' at this stage and create type areas at the outset that are wasteful of space and produce oversized margins. Looking at the *Daily Star*'s existing sister paper, the *Daily Express* it was obvious that the press executives had little confidence in their machines since the leading edges of the paper were excessively wide. The aim was to achieve 2 cm each side of the page. There were, in fact, variations of up to 3 and sometimes 4 mm divided between each outer edge.

My decision was to take the pages very close to the centre fold in order to achieve the maximum type area overall. The added advantage of the narrower fold gutter – a gain across the spread of 2 picas – was that when splitting a picture across the fold there was a visual improvement. With the metal chases in use at the time this meant that a narrower tabloid 'bar' had to be put into the chase to separate the pair of pages. More accurate and modern rotary presses such as those used for *The Times* allow a much greater saving on the leading edges, while the problem is eased even more with modern web-offset presses. The effect from the design point of view is that a well-filled page gives a more compact look to the design. It also puts expensive newsprint to better use.

The resulting setting for the *Daily Star* worked out at 8.3 picas to give a pica of gutter between the columns. This made a type page width of 64 picas (380 mm), and with a double-page spread taking 132 picas. To give a margin top and bottom that balanced with the leading edge I made the depth of the type area 81 picas with the folio space standing clear on top.

The change in the *Irish Press* from broadsheet to tabloid in 1988, which I was commissioned to undertake, was intended to broaden the readership of an old established paper by moving moderately down-market. The journalists producing the paper found this something of a shock. They had become used to the grey columns of their paper and subediting attitudes were relaxed towards the wordy writing styles of reporters and feature writers. Pictures were not being used to advantage even on the huge broadsheet canvas and my first job in reforming the design was to talk to the staff and reveal, against examples of rival papers, how their product had become unwieldy to all but its most devoted readers. The breakthrough needed was to wrap up the facts in fewer words and it was going to take some practice if the wanted change in design format was to work.

The change would also have to be sold to readers unused to the tabloid format. There was a need to label pages with 'puff' strap lines to help the eye accept the contents and at the same time emphasize the confidence that can emanate from good tabloid style layout. I used the repeat title piece of the paper (as redesigned) whenever it was appropriate thus, in an almost subliminal way, involving the readers with the paper's name. The word PRESS of the title piece was used in Press Briefing on columns of news briefs, and appeared again in the sports logo on the back page . . . I placed the detailed weather information on page three where it could be suitably anchored on a page where spot colour was expected to become available for the maps and weather graphics.

When it came to the Gossip page, as in the style of all classic gossip columnists, I used the writer's name as the headline in a font different from those used throughout the paper. I put it in Antique Olive capitals, very bold, with the *Irish Press* eagle motif, which had always been part of the paper's masthead, as an integral part of the graphics, thus giving a useful touch of continuity. At the time the name was Michael Sheridan and since the surname was longer it made a very good perch for the eagle to alight upon when the two words were set left. I allowed small stories to run above the byline logo to combat any visual interruption from the full page advertisement on the left. This also had the effect of pushing the main focal point down the page and thus got away from the news page style with the main headlines at the top.

A problem with the revamping of the Newcastle-based *Sunday Sun* (1989) was with the masthead, which suffered from show-through and from poor printing quality. The Pantone colour chosen for the title was an indifferent orange. Even a full cardinal red would have lost something to show-through due to the way the masthead was printing. The washed-out appearance was aggravated by the poor ink impression, which gave more ground for show-through from page two.

A cause was in the styling. The word 'Sunday' was slipped into the space left by an upper and lowercase 'Sun' and in both cases the characters were kerned with too much space. This visually reduced the impact of the words because the orange was not packed tightly enough across the area. The weak colour could have been improved by using a reversal (white on orange) in a squared-up shape. Even more apposite, instead of using the old method of the fudge box to print the masthead, the paper should have printed it using its run-of-press facility, which would have produced a denser result to combat show-through.

There was a problem with the adverts. The holiday feature were unconnected with the holiday adverts which should have been part of the attraction to both readers and advertisers. There seemed to have been no attempt to proportion the weight of advertising against editorial requirements on most pages. The use of page seven, a premier right-hand page, to a full page advert robbed the paper of valuable space for editorial projection and would not have been allowed by the paper's competitors, especially the national Sundays.

The use of reverse, or hanging, indent for the columns of small adverts on a seven-column page was wasteful. The area taken up by the indent could have provided an eighth column of adverts in the same type area, thus increasing the revenue while at the same time economizing on the space available.

We have said in this book that familiarity is an important factor in reader loyalty. Yet there are times in a newspaper's life when changes have to be made. A dramatic example occurred in 1953 when, as one of my early tasks, I was despatched by the Kemsley Organisations's Editorial Director, Dennis Hamilton, to oversee the removal of the Classified adverts that filled the front page of the *Western Mail* at Cardiff. The Kemsley directors in London, who had made the decision against the wishes of the morning paper's then editor, had instructed me to change the appearance of the *Western Mail* into one 'worthy of the second half of the twentieth century.'

My first move was to increase the size of the paper's Times Roman masthead by fifty percent. I then had to plan a virgin broadsheet news page beneath it. I chose Century Bold, Italic and Roman at the unheard size of 72 points for the splash typography. The real breakthrough, however, was to up all the other headings in size; including those used on the inside pages and to give boldness to one page by using a big picture. In fact, apart from briefs with two lines of 18 point, there wasn't a news heading of less than 48 point.

The editor was horrified that I had acted against the traditions of this great and ancient Welsh national newspaper, and showed it. Angry memos were exchanged between Cardiff and London during the run-up to the re-launch, but Dennis Hamilton was insistent that the enterprise should go ahead.

So it did – with the result that on the morning of its debut in its new clothes the circulation of the *Western Mail* fell by more than 30,000 copies.

A man of few words, Dennis Hamilton's reply to Giles's timid telephone call on the dreadful day was, 'Stick with it man! The readers will come back.'

The opposite occurred. As day followed day, the readers, not recognizing the new version of their own newspaper, fell away by the thousand.

If Giles had lost his nerve, Brigadier Hamilton was not going to lose his. 'Stick with it, Giles, damn it!' he repeated.

Three weeks later, the circulation manager began to smile again, and the smile grew broader day by day as he was able to report the return of the faithful readers to the fold. Two months later the figures had recovered to their pre-launch level and had begun climbing above it. The battle was won!

Thirteen years later, in 1966, Sir William Haley, in his last year of editorship, followed suit and did the same for *The Times* – the last daily paper in Britain to lose its front page adverts and replace them with news.

Glossary of journalistic and printing terms

AA Author's alterations. The abbreviation is used by proofreaders alongside the correction on the clean proof. Editorial mark as an instruction.

Accents Stress and acute marks used above the appropriate letters. Their names are:- acute, breve, cedilla, circumflex, grave, macron, tilde and umlaut.

Airbrush Ink and water colour spray machine powered by compressor for use on artwork and photographs. Combined with the range of water colours for tonal effect.

Alphabet length Type when aligned horizontally in alphabets of the same size will give a comparison of lengths.

Amberlith Orange acetate sheeting with a coat that peels away that is used on artwork to mask unwanted areas from light exposure. Amberlith is a trade name.

Ampersand A one character version of the word and (&).

Antihalation backing Coating on the back of photographic film that prevents halation, the effect of a diffusion of light across the developed negative film.

Aperture The measure of openness of a camera lens that is expressed in f-numbers.

Apochromatic A type of lens that will focus red, blue and green in the same plane.

Archive Off-line storage of data in the computer memory.

Artwork   Original copy and/or pictures made ready for camera.

Ascender   Part of the type character in lowercase that rises above the x-height, as in b, f, h, k, l and t.

Asterisk   Reference mark alongside, shaped like a star that takes the reader's eye to the foot of the page for explanation or bibliography.

Assymetric setting   Type line set with no attempt at pattern.

ATFX   Trade name for a comprehensive computer setting and laser printing output system.

Autokon   A monochrome scanner producing line and halftone reproductions in screen rulings up to 175 lines per inch in either negative or positive form. Autokon is a trade name.

Automatic heading   On screen, page make-up systems are able to position headings on consecutive pages by means of a general instruction at the beginning of the designing process.

Azerty   European keyboard able to incorporate accents as opposed to the English qwerty keyboard.

B-series paper size   International ISO range of sizes falling between the A-sizes for use in poster, wallcharts and other larger printed areas.

Background   A piece of computer language indicating that a hyphenation and justification mode is operating at the same time as other copy is being input.

Back number   An older copy of a publication than the current issue.

Backslant   The opposite to italic achieved by photographic distortion.

Bad break   Undesirable end to the line of body type caused by clumsy hyphenation. Editorially a bad turn from the grammatical viewpoint of a headline can be described in the same way.

Bar code   Unique symbolized code in vertical bar form that is readable by machine or light pen and used for stock purposes on the outside of goods, book jackets and other sold printed materials.

Basic   Beginners all-purpose symbolic instruction code. A high-level computer programming language.

Bastard setting A width of setting not regular to the system adopted by the newspaper or magazine.

Beard The area between the x-height of a lowercase letter and the boundary of the metal base in the hot metal system.

Bed The flat metal area of the proofing press that holds the galley with the set type ready for an impression achieved by the roller above.

Bell Gothic The exceptionally economic typeface used extensively for stock market prices and racing cards developed by the Bell Corporation of the USA for telephone books.

Biblical P A reversed in-line P (back to front) used as a focal point symbol at the beginning of a paragraph, or on a well displayed introduction.

Binary Computer numbering system using the base of two as opposed to the decimal which operates out of the base figure ten. The only figures used are 0 and 1. *See* Bit.

Bit The basic unit of information in a computer system. It is referred to as a binary digit. Each bit is either 0 or 1 and eight bits is called a byte.

Bit blaster High-speed laser printer that produces finished computer-set material at a great rate.

Black letter The form of Gothic or Old English mediaeval letter type form based on the script lettering of the monasteries of the mediaeval period.

Blanket Clamped around the offset litho cylinder, the rubber surfaced blanket transfers the printed image from printing plate to paper.

Blanket to blanket Blanket cylinders here can act as opposing impression cylinders printing both sides of the web simultaneously.

Bleach out An illustrative method where an existing picture is exposed in negative form on to a hard surface bromide paper where the tone values are eliminated. This gives a stark and artist-drawn appearance to the original photograph. An Autokon produces the effect automatically.

Bleed When producing pre-print colour in gravure or full page colour reproduction in magazines the facility exists to take the colour to the edge of the cut paper. The make-up is produced with the colour areas running over the page limits by 3 mm. When the publication is in the final stages of production it is trimmed to the pre-ordained printed size. This will enable colour to run to the extreme limits of the page area.

Block   Letterpress printing surface image etched after screening and mounted on a lead block to achieve type high in order to print from. Also a computer term for a group of bytes (information).

Blow up   Enlargement of pictures or type and artwork.

Board   Fashion board and hard tooth board or Bristol board are forms of surface boards for producing artwork upon. Mounting board can be of various weights and is used for giving backing to artwork produced on a thinner surface. These are glued to the board. Also the frame upon which pages are made up under the paste-up system.

Body   Solid metal, either in type form of 12 point and below in the letterpress system. In phototypesetting the actual line of type, including the line space white.

Bold face   The designation of a typeface the weight of which lies between Roman and extra bold.

Borders   Decorative rules that surround pieces of type or entire pages of many thicknesses and weights.

Brad   An essential book that lists all UK publications and their advertising specifications. The full title is *British Rate and Data*.

Broadsheet   The large version of newspapers as opposed to tabloid. Also text-size.

Bromide   A light sensitive paper used for printing photographic images.

Burn or burnt out   Term for exposure or over exposure.

Byline   The authorship of a story or feature, well displayed at the beginning or the end of the story. At the end also a sign off.

Byte   The amount of space needed to store a character in the computer memory. It represents eight binary digits (bits).

C and LC   Abbreviation for capital and lowercase letters.

C series   Range of sizes for envelopes that will fit the A series international size paper.

Camera ready   Artwork, pictures and type ready for the camera and pasted down in position.

Caps   Capitals. Uppercase letters, e.g. ABCDEFGH.

Caption   Body type description of a picture alongside or below.

Carry forward   To read the text forward into the next column.

Cartridge paper   Drawing paper, sometimes used for high quality printed work. Has a good weight and high opacity.

Cassette   Light-proof container for unexposed film, or in the larger form for laser printers.

Casting off   Assessment of manuscript length in terms of type taken to fill space.

Catch line   An identifying heading set at the top of a story to be eliminated before it gets to the publication.

Centred type   Multiple lines of headline of uneven length centred upon each other.

Centre spread   The two facing pages in the middle of a newspaper or magazine. In tabloid terms there would not be a gutter down the centre of the combined pages.

Character   Letters, figures, symbols and punctuation marks of a type range.

Character count   The number of letters and spaces in a line of type.

Character generation   The formation of type images on a visual display unit in association with a high-speed photo composition system, computer driven.

Chip   A small silicon electrical component that contains extensive circuits of logic.

Chromaline   A finished high-quality acetate laminated proof of a finalized page of colour on which small corrections in the colour balance can still be indicated from printing, editorial and advertising viewpoints.

Cicero   European type measure that approximates a pica. Equal to 4.511 mm.

Circular screen   Rotating halftone screen that will set to the proper screen angles for colour printing.

Classified   Small adverts, usually of a column width for jobs, personal, births and deaths, etc.

Clean proof   A finalized proof of copy requiring no further correction.

Close up   A correction mark that indicates a reduction in the width of spacing between characters or space.

Coarse screen   A coarse screen, up to 72 dots to the square inch used particularly on newspapers.

Coated paper   A fine clay coating on the surface of paper to give a smooth finish to halftone pictures.

Cold colour   The blue-coloured tone values of the spectrum.

Cold composition   Typesetting that does not use hot metal.

Cold set   Web printing where ink is allowed to dry with no heat applied. *See* Hot-set.

Collate   Sections of books or magazines gathered together in the correct order for binding.

Colour bars   Strips of colour alongside finished colour proofs, in the margins for comparison of colour values across the images.

Colour correction   Dot-etching, retouching or masking to improve the colour rendition either on a transparency, photo print or plate.

Colour filters   Coloured masks placed in front of camera lens in order to leave the single colour required for each of the separations in four-colour printing.

Colour match system   A system such as the Pantone matching method that gives the total variation on each of the colours of the spectrum. They are numbered for easy instruction to the platemaker and printer.

Colour separation   The full colour original pictures or artwork separated into the four primary printing colours by the use of filters.

Colour swatch   Specified colour as a sample.

Colour transparency   Often abbreviated to tranny. A photopositive film in full colour.

Command   An instruction to a computer.

Compose   To create lines of type or pages. An operator is called a compositor or a key-stroker.

Computer setting   Setting and storing typesetting by computer that will then display on a VDU. It will also perform the hyphenation and justification required. The mathematical calculations required for this operation are extremely fast thus reducing costs. The laser printer will then accept the command from the computer to produce an accurate output (proof).

Condensed type   A typeface designed with form narrower than its regular brother in the same font.

Console   Mainframe computer keyboard control.

Contact print   A photograph, reproduced same size by exposing a negative to light which passes through to create an image on bromide paper.

Contact screen   A screen that is in contact with a photograph to achieve a screen print by light passing through. This is then processed to make a plate for printing.

Contents page   Page with the index to a magazine or book.

Contrast   A wide range from fine to coarse, or highlight to shadow, of colour or black when printed.

Copy   A manuscript, artwork or photograph considered for publication.

Copyfitting   Typographical specification that will determine if a piece of copy will fit the given space.

Copyright   The proprietorial rights in a creative work as assumed by law. The type symbol that indicates this is a letter c enclosed in a circle, with the appropriate explanation.

Core memory   A computer's main storage capacity.

Cromalin   An alternative spelling of chromaline. *See* Chromaline.

Crop   To mark a picture to bring up the major point that a reader should see, that is, to exclude unwanted parts. To place parameter lines around the area required as an instruction to the printer or platemaker.

Crosshead   The smallest of display headings used to interrupt the flow of body type and set either aligned or centred on the column measure. It rests the reader's eye from the continuous flow of body type.

Cross line screen   The standard halftone screen.

Cross-reference   An indication that a story continues or is resumed on another page.

Cursor   Indicator, usually a moving dash or arrow shape on a visual display screen, telling the operator the position of the next input or correction.

Cut-off   The length of a printed sheet as determined by the pre-set web offset press, and the circumference of the printing cylinder. Also an item cut off from the rest of the text by print rules.

Cut-off rule   The fine black rule used in newspapers to indicate the end of one story and the beginning of the next. Applied both horizontally and vertically.

Cut-out   Illustration with the background masked out or painted out to leave the image cut out on the page background.

Cyan   The colour blue used in colour printing.

Dagger   Second symbol after an asterisk to indicate a cross-reference or footnote.

Daisy wheel   Flat disk with letters attached to the stalks to be used with typewriters or for removable elements of a quality printer.

Deep etch   The process of etching away the non-printing areas of a litho plate or zinc plate with acid, or by mechanical means.

Default   Start up setting identity on VDUs to indicate computer is waiting and ready.

Definition   The detail and sharpness of a reproduction.

Delete   Proofreader's mark on a proof meaning to remove.

Developer   Chemical used to remove unexposed area of a litho plate or to develop a photograph.

Diazo   A photographic chemical coating. Used in plate making. A copying process that uses light sensitive compounds. Facsimile wire prints are produced in this way.

Didot   Typographical measure used in Continental Europe named after Francois Didot. 0.376 mm is the measure.

Dimension marks   Picture parameters marked on the original copy or overlay or on the back to indicate reduction or enlargement.

Direct input   Inputting of text into a computer by an originator of copy (stories) to be retrievable for editing and typesetting.

Disk or disc   Hard or floppy disk to hold computer information.

Dot   The individual segmental dot of which a halftone is constructed.

Dot leaders   Three dots that indicate a suggested word or a pause that leads into another line of thought. An ellipsis.

Download   Command to transfer information from screen to laser printer.

Downtime   The period during which a piece of printing machinery is out of action.

Drop cap   A large capital letter that fills several lines at the beginning of a paragraph. Derived from the ancient monastic art of illuminating scrolls with colourful initial letters.

Drop-out halftones   Highlight areas of the picture are left with no screen dots and just show the white of the paper.

Dummy   Mock up of a projected publication.

Duotone   Two negatives produced with different screen angles used to produce a two-colour reproduction from a single-colour original.

Edit   Checking for grammar, spelling and punctuation before instructing the typesetter: in newspaper terms cutting to length.

Edition   Copies of a publication from the same typeset originals or plates.

Egyptian   Serif typeface noted for the solid slab nature of its serif feet and shoulders.

Electronic scanner A revolving drum on which the original is strapped while being scanned across its full colour areas for colour density readings.

Electrostatic print A process of copying where an electrically charged drum receives the reflected light from the original copy. The charge is lost on the areas affected by the light but the 'toner' retained by the charged areas is fused to the paper and creates the image.

Ellipsis *See* Dot leaders.

Em A lowercase 'm' width in any typeface, also a standard measurement width of 12 points. Six to an inch. One em equals 0.166044 inches.

Em-dash The long dash (or hyphen) a quad wide as opposed to an n dash, half the width.

Em-quad The square of any m font size. Traditionally called a mutton.

Emulsion Photosensitive coating to bromide paper or film that produces an image by light reaction. When there is no indication around the film sprocket holes on a colour transparency as to the correct side up of the picture, look for the emulsion side of the film, it will appear dull. The transparency should be viewed and used through the glossy side.

Engraving Copper, zinc or steel sheet sensitized and acid etched after a picture or illustration has been exposed on the surface by means of a screen. The acid etches away the highlight sections of the dots to a greater degree than the shadowed parts and gives a reproduction when ink is transferred from its surface on to the paper. Can be hand engraving with an engraving tool.

En-quad Half the width of an em-quad.

Exposure The time taken for the light reflected from the photographed subject to impinge on the camera film. *See* F number.

Extended A term applied to a typeface that is designed to be much wider than its regular type alternative, e.g. Geneva black and Geneva black extended. Another description is expanded.

F number The aperture of a lens. The setting is formed by dividing the focal length of the lens by the diameter of the aperture, e.g. F 2.8 and F 16. Sometimes called F stop.

Face The style of a typeface or the printing surface of a piece of type.

Facsimile The precise copy of a document. The exact transmission of a document, e.g. facsimile transmission, or Fax for short.

Family A series of typefaces that are related.

Fillers Small stories on newspaper pages to fill areas of the page where the more important stories have fallen short. They can add to the readability and design of the page.

Filter Coloured glass, gelatin or plastic placed over the lens in order to prevent certain colours reaching the film. This allows the colour separation in the four-colour printing process.

Film processor A machine for processing exposed film, producing negative and positive results. It develops, fixes, washes and dries at high speed.

Financial setting A description of the most economic way to set stock exchange prices and race cards, etc. The most favoured face for this job is Bell Gothic, created by the Bell Telephone Company of America for its telephone directories and now used all over the world. It is very legible at 6 point and 5 point.

Fine screen 120 lines to the inch and over.

Fixing Image on film or paper made permanent after developing by chemical means.

Flash A photoflood or flash that for a split second illuminates a darkened subject and allows more reflected light into the wide-open camera lens. In process work it is a flash exposure that allows the halftone to enhance the areas of shadow.

Flatbed Printing press that prints from a flat surface rather than from a cylinder.

Flat plan The projected plan of a newspaper or magazine drawn up in small two-page rectangles to create an instant recognition of the pagination. The rectangles are used in page production for notes on the contents of each page and marked off as completed.

Floppy disk Plastic flexible disk used for the magnetic storage of information on computers.

Flush right or left Multiple-line headlines where the words are of different lengths and are visually improved by being set with the type flush on the right or left of the column.

Flyer   The launching of an editorial idea or an advertising hand bill.

Focal length   The distance between the film and lens when the image of the subject is in focus through the viewfinder.

Focal plane   When a sharp image is formed by light passing through the lens on to the film, this area is termed the focal plane.

Fog   Extra light impinging on the film surface causing over-exposure in those areas is fogging.

Folder   Newspaper slang term for a printing press.

Folio   The area at the top or bottom of a page reserved for the page number, date and name of publication. This is usually 18 points deep, to contain a 12-point line of type.

Font   *See* Fount.

Footnote   Explanatory pointer to the main text, usually carried in smaller bodytype at the foot of the page.

Format   The computer typesetter's most used set of commands such as type names, sizes and alphabets and stored as codes. Also, specifications for a page, magazine, newspaper or book.

Fotosetter   Trade name for the first generation of photographic display headline setters.

Fount   A complete set of type of the same face together with the furniture of the fount.

Four-colour process   Printing in colour with the three subtractive primary colours, yellow, magenta and cyan plus black. These colours are separated out photographically.

Free sheet   Slang term for publications given away free. American phrase for paper that is wood free.

Front end   Another term for direct input. Editorial method of inputting original copy into the main frame of the computer for later retrieval for editing by the subeditor, applying setting commands and then setting from these original keystrokes.

Full colour   Four-colour printing.

Full out   Setting square with no indentations of any kind.

Full point   The full stop at the end of a sentence.

Furniture   A hot-metal term describing the pieces of wood and metal used for wedging and locking together the metal slugs of type for proofing on the galley. Also used to describe the extras in a type font such as symbols, arrows, hands and fists.

Galley   A three-sided tray used in hot-metal letterpress. The sides are under type-high in order that columns of type laid on the tray can be proofed on a specially designed proofing press. The proof that results is often also called a galley, short for galley proof. Name for laser printer output.

Gate fold   A magazine page that folds out of the body of the magazine to double its size.

Generation   The production of typesetting from computer. Stages in reproducing from an original.

Gigo   Slang term for bad results from a computer caused by faulty input. Garbage *in*, garbage *out*!

Gloss print   A finished photograph that has been 'glazed' to give a shiny effect. Often the best form of original for reproduction, as opposed to a matt finish.

Grain of paper   Direction of the fibres in paper making.

Grainy   Film speed that creates an artistic grain on the finished photograph.

Gravure   An abbreviation of the term roto-gravure. A high-speed mass production system of presses producing sixteen pages across each cylinder. These are engraved (etched) into the copper surface and finally chromed to give the surface a longer running life.

Grey scale   The ranges of density, progressing from white to black and identifying each shade of grey.

Grid   The arrangement of fine rules to create columns on a layout sheet, often backed by a graph grid in squares of 6 point or 12 point. The sheet is at its most efficient when semi-opaque with the lines in a non-photographic ink. The same grid is applied to paste-up sheets, but on a heavyweight paper that is non-transparent.

Grid of composing   Used in some typesetting systems; a rectangular carrier of negative type fonts.

Hairline   The finest thickness of column rule. Usually 1 point. Also used to describe white space particularly in kerning between serif faces. At the larger sizes a hairline of white between serifs gives a more pleasing visual appearance. Here, it would be a unit of space.

Halftone   A photograph that has been screened photographically for a printed reproduction. The screen can be of various dimensions to be determined by the quality of the reproduction desired. On newsprint the screen would be between 65 and 100 dots to the inch. Better quality paper would demand upwards of 120 dots to the inch. *See* Deep etched.

Hanging indent   The first line of a paragraph left hanging over a pica indent from the rest of the paragraph and so on, throughout the story. Newspaper parlance abbreviates this to 0 and 1, or nothing and one.

Hanging punctuation   If the typesetter has hyphenated and justified but still leaves a full point over the measure then the computer can be commanded to leave the point hanging.

Hanging quote   For decorative reasons a quote or quote marks of a much larger size than the body type is allowed to hang at the front and back of the paragraph. However, the measure must then include these larger quotes and the entire story indented to allow for the hanging punctuation.

Hard copy   News editor's terminology for reporter's copy going forward to the copytaster or chief subeditor with all the facts in place. Also typewritten copy produced at the front end simultaneously with punched or magnetic tape for setting. The original copy can be used as a first proof since it will be justified and hyphenated as shown on screen.

Hard disk   Opposite to floppy disk . . . a disk permanently inside the computer on which information is electronically inscribed from a floppy or from keyboard commands.

Hardware   The generic name for typesetting and word processing equipment as opposed to software – programmes, disks, etc.

Head   The top of the page.

Headline or heading   Display lines from 14 point up to 144 point and even larger that will summarize the story beneath. An editor's decision about the importance of the story to the reader is illustrated by the headline sizes and where it appears on the page.

Hold lines   Designer's lines on the layout (or mechanical) that define areas of picture, type or colour. They will have instructions with regard to these lines in the layout's margin.

Hot type   An expression that refers to the melting and re-casting into typographical shapes of the lead or metal (lead, antimony and tin) for the letterpress process.

Hyphenation   A pre-programmed command in the computer that will ensure the word at the end of a set measure breaks at the correct grammatical point and still allows space for the hyphen. Application of the command is in four sections: exception dictionary, true dictionary, logic and discretionary hyphen. The commands are usually coupled with the line justification and abbreviated to H&J (hyphenate and justify).

Illustration   Any kind of drawing, photograph or line and tone artwork that will enhance the page.

Imposition   The arrangement of pages for the presses that will ensure them appearing in the correct order.

Imprint   The name, address and details of the printer, designer and perhaps proprietor of the publication. Usually placed in a discreet position in the newspaper or magazine in small body type. Originally the imprint was imposed at a separate printing which accounts for the word 'imprint'.

Indent   Setting a paragraph, on the first line, at less than the full column measure. Also indent to allow for a drop letter to be inserted.

Initial or illumination   The first letter of a printed piece that the designer feels should be decorative. It could be simply a large capital letter or one reversed white on black or in colour. The term derives from the ancient monastic art of colour-illuminated letters that enhanced written texts. Initial cap can also mean a line of capital letters where a larger cap is set at the beginning of each word.

Input   The copy to be processed by the computer typesetter as opposed to *output* which is the finished sheet of paper covered in type that leaves the laser printer at the command of the computer.

Insert   A piece of printed material that is inserted into a host publication by hand or with the aid of a machine blower attached to the printing press. Also the term used for the addition of a piece of written copy inside the main flow of the author's work.

Italic   All fonts of type that slope to the right and follow the ancient skill of writing script in this way. The computer will slope the type in either direction at the touch of a key.

Jobbing   The work of a commercial printer running a jobbing shop. One that does not publish.

Justify   To set lines of body type correctly spaced by the computer to create a straight edge on both sides of the column. Unjustification will give the opposite effect of a poetic or ragged edge.

K   A computer storage measure. The main frame can store 1024 words to every K. An abbreviaton of kilobyte.

Kern   Deleting or inserting units of space between letters and words in order to achieve visual balance. Letters that will always require this balance are the badly shaped ones A, W, V and Y together with all the rounded letters. The hot-metal process was restricted by the physical fact that this could only be performed on individual characters by cutting into the beard or body of a letter with a saw to create a joint with the next letter in line. Computers allow a house style to be achieved with a once-only command inserted into the memory. Entire alphabets of every font in the house can be kerned to the taste of the editor or house designer. American producers of the hardware and software leave this to each individual customer. A newspaper or magazine will not bear resemblance to the same publication that was processed with hot metal until a copied kerning programme is installed.

Key   The copy code that distinguishes typeface, size and column width at the top of the copy set by computer. It will appear at the top of the screen before the copy begins to run.

Keyboard   Set of keys on a linecasting machine, computer type-setter or word processor to allow text to be enlined and commands given.

Keyline   Outline laid down by the artist or designer to contain an area of tint, colour, photograph or type, usually as a guide and not to be reproduced.

Kicker   Different definition in Britain and the USA. Here it means a scene-setting intro to a story with independent display in the front of the main story or a specially displayed story on a page. In the USA it would be a strap line, a small display line as a lead in to the main headline.

Kill   To delete a story or illustration. To erase type already set in the computer.

KPH The number of keystrokes per hour achieved by a key stroker (compositor, typesetter).

Layout A hand drawn page, on a semi-seethrough surface, which the rays of a light box can penetrate. It has the format of the page already printed on it in a light colour that does not interfere with the design. The columns are in vertical rectangles with the appropriate gutters indicating white space between, usually a pica. The designer draws the page, indicating type and written instructions in the margins. On each outside edge of the paper is a centimetre scale that gives instant access to advert sizes without need to use a ruler; sometimes called a scheme. Also the process of designing or laying out a page.

LC An instruction for lowercase setting only.

Leader A row of dots, dashes or squares or any other set pieces to guide the reader's eye to the next word or point.

Lead-in The first few words of a story that achieve emphasis by being set in capitals.

Leading (pronounced ledding) A hot-metal term for spacing the lead lines of type with metal. These were produced by a casting machine called an Elrod which could be set to turn out any length at a given thickness from 1 to 18 points.

Legibility Quality of the readability of the printed word and the definition of the halftone pictures.

Letraset Corporate name for a waxed-back, rub-down, transferred typeface.

Letter spacing For lengthening or reducing the length of a given line of type. Used creatively a spaced line can accentuate the purpose of the words. Letter spacing should be a house style achieved by kerning the original type systems installed by the system designers. Any subsequent change should be for the enhancement of individual lines of a story or feature.

Ligature Metal setting containing particular letters that are joined for the sake of ancient grammar as in two lowercase ffs. Free-thinking designers have extended the use of ligaturing. Many characters marry naturally together and doing so can enhance a masthead or a corporate logo. The technique has become easier with computer setting since the removal of units can be made with a minus command.

Lightface   A thinner version of any regular typeface.

Light pen   Light sensitive stylus used to edit on a VDU screen, or to read bar codes.

Linecaster   Any hot-metal line caster setting machine that will set in lines such as the Linotype and Intertype; also the single letter casting machines such as Monotype and Ludlow.

Line drawing   Any piece of artwork made up of lines and solid masses and no tone area, usually in ink.

Line engraving   A printing illustrative plate that prints only lines and tints with no tone areas.

Line gauge   A ruler calibrated in printing measures for calculating types and size. Type gauge.

Line negative   A high-contrast negative giving open spaces for the lines and black masses with solid areas that do not allow light through. The reversal on exposure will create white areas from a black negative.

Line spacing   Computer setting's word for leading (ledding).

Linotron   Linotype Corporation's trade name for the CRT high-speed photosetter.

Linotronic   The range of computer setting systems using the laser technique.

Linotype   Mergenthaler's trade name for his line casting machine. A typesetting machine that sets slugs of type in hot metal (lead, antimony and tin).

Lithography   A planographic printing process. The image areas are separated from the non-image parts by the repulsion of oil and water, oil being the etch.

Live matter   Type already set, original copy to be used in the publication as opposed to dead matter.

Lock-up   A letterpress term for the page of type being locked up with a key. The metal type is then immovable inside its metal frame (forme) and can be transported from department to department.

Logo   Or logotype; a trade mark or masthead.

Loop   A series of computer instructions that will be repeated until a condition is reached which will divert from the loop.

Lowercase   Shortened to lc, small typeset letters, not capitals.

Ludlow   Trade name for a hot-metal casting machine where brass matrices are assembled by hand in a metal 'stick' one letter at a time and then cast as one type line. Used for display headings of above 18 point.

Mainframe   The computer core. The memory.

Magazine   Metal container, angled on the top of a linecasting machine. It contains matrices of body type that freely flow into the casting area of the machine at a touch of the keyboard. Also area containing sensitized paper inside a laser printer.

Magenta   Process red. One of the colours used in four-colour printing.

Magnetic tape   Narrow tape, magnetically coated for the storage in serial form of computer data.

Make-up   Elements for the printed page gathered together and arranged into an attractive and readable whole in accordance with the page design. The process of making up a page on paste-up or on screen. Sometimes used as a name for the layout, or page design.

Manuscript   MS for short. Handwritten copy ready for setting.

Margins   Space around the printed page that will allow the proper cut-off on three sides plus the consideration for the fold area gutter.

Mark-up   Instructions for setting on a make-up.

Mask   Opaque overlay that masks out the area of a picture not required.

Masthead   Design or logo of the newspaper's title with a distinctive identity.

Matrix   Or matrice. The mould or digits from which type is cast, photographically or laser produced.

Matte finish   A non-glossy surface to a photograph.

Mean line   More commonly called the x-line or x-height. It is the imaginary line that runs along the top of the lowercase characters.

Measure   The em or pica width of a line of type. The measured and set width of a column of type body.

Mechanical   A camera-ready paste up.

Mechanical tints   Patterned sheets, usually of a rub-down transfer variety that give tonal value to artwork.

Memory   A computer's temporary and data storage area. *See* RAM and ROM.

Metric system   Decimal measurement now applied to the printing industry. Metre: 39.37 in; centimetre: 00.3937 in; millimetre: 00.0394 in.

Merge   A technique in photocomposition (typesetting) to combine sequences of tape into one, using a computer to incorporate new copy and produce a clean tape for typesetting.

Misprint   Typographical error.

Misregister   One or more of the four colours printed out of register and causing distortion of the image.

Mixing   Refers to the mixing of typefaces in one line of setting of a display face. The effect is to produce a common baseline.

Modem   Device that transforms and translates telephone transmission into digital form and vice versa.

Modern   Describes typefaces developed in the late eighteenth century.

Modern figures   Numerals the same size as the capital letters in any given typeface, unlike Old Style where the figures drop below the baseline of the type.

Moiré   A wavy screen pattern that appears on colour reproduction when the four screens are wrongly angled.

Mono   Reproduction only in black and white. Also an abbreviation for the Monotype Corporation's typesetting equipment.

Montage   Several pieces of artwork, pictures or both assembled in an artistic format as one.

Morgue   Newspaper reference library.

Monotype   Trade name for typecasting machines that cast individual letters in hot metal.

Mutton   Old name for an em measure. See Em-quad.

Negative   The reverse of the photographic positive image. First film development in the process of the finished bromide photographic print.

NLM   Newspaper lines per minute. Standard measure of photosetter speed. Output measured to an 8-point line at an 11-em width.

Newsprint   Paper made specifically for the production of newspapers usually between 45 and 58 grams with the ability to stand high-speed production.

Nut   Old name for an en quad.

Oblique   A roman character sloping to the right, italic.

OCR   Optical character reading or recognition. Interpretation of typewritten material by machine which scans the text and stores it for subsequent typesetting.

Offset   (lithography) Planographic printing method. Image and non-image areas on the same plane and separated by chemical means, by the principle of the replusion of oil and water. The ink (grease/oil) is transferred from the printing plate on to a rubber blanket and thence to the paper, offset.

Old style   Type designs developed in the seventeenth century.

On-line   Connected to a centralized computer processing unit and communicating with it.

Opaque   Painted out areas on film that will not be required in the reproduction. The chemical paint is often referred to as a tin of opaque; impervious to light.

Open matter   Well-spaced lines of type with many short or widowed lines that will produce large white areas.

Optical centre   The visual middle of the page from bottom to top considered to be 10 per cent above the centre line. The main focal point.

Original   Original photograph or drawing presented for reproduction.

Ornamented Embellished character based on monastic capital illuminated letters.

Overmatter Set copy that is too long for the space designed for it and therefore left over.

Overprinting An extra printing on top of existing printed form. Black or coloured type that overprints art work or a photograph.

Over-run Copies printed in excess to requirements.

Ozalid Method of copying used for proofing film. Blueprint.

Page proofs A hot-metal page or galley was 'pulled'. Ancient proof pulling presses had a static roller that pressed down on the metal or wooden type and the paper covered type was pulled manually through beneath the roller, by hand. Pressure from the heavy roller impressed the image on the paper. Development of the proofing press allowed the bed of the press on which a galley stood to be drawn to and fro mechanically. The system was eventually reversed in order that the roller moved over the static type mechanically. In computerized systems the proofs are called outputs, perfect reproductions in their own right produced by a laser printer at the computer command. The output appears as a continuous sheet of bromide paper. Also a copy of a pasted-up page produced by a photocopier.

Page view terminal VDU screen that will allow the viewing of a complete page.

Pagination The consecutive planning and numbering of pages.

Pantone Reference book of a colour-tone system. Patches of colour that are numbered and accepted by printers. Variations through the spectrum are recorded and will match the printer's numbered references.

Paragraph mark A symbol used to draw attention to the beginning of a paragraph of type. It could be a solid square, a blob or a biblical P. In each case it would be indented or set hanging as desired. Paragraph marker in written copy indicates that a para starts here. The abbreviated indication is a three-sided bracket drawn around the first letter of the word.

Paste-up Output bromides of set type and headlines waxed on a stout card printed with a non-photographic grid of the format of the publication. The process of making up a page by the paste-up method from a page design, or layout. The paste-up person works to a layout. Screened pictures are likewise waxed and laid down in position.

Parenthesis   Rounded brackets at each end of a grammatical aside.

Pasted dummy   A blank completely paginated dummy giving advertisement positions in which drawn pages are pasted as they are editorially produced. It is used to avoid clashes in typefaces and headlines across pairs of pages, and should be available at all times during the preparation of a newspaper or magazine to people who have a part in the planning.

PE   Printer's error. Normally a literal in typesetting.

Perfect binding   Adhesive back binding. Used extensively in magazine production. Provides an up-market square backed look.

Perfecting   Printing on both sides of a sheet of paper at the same time.

Photocomposition   Setting achieved mechanically by exposing individual letters to photographic film.

Photostat   Instant image reproduction created electrostatically. The attraction of metallic ink dust to statically charged paper. Used in instant copying machines.

Piece fraction   A fraction made from two or three parts. A half-size three, a dash beneath with a half-size four below to make ¾.

Pied-to pie   Accidently mixed type. Sometimes caused in hot-metal days by a compositor dropping a galley of type.

Pi font   A stored computer font containing characters that have no place among alphabets of type. Rules, corners, ligatured letters, arrows, logos, trade marks, column headings etc.

Point   The smallest measure in printing. There are 72 of them to the inch and each one measures 0.013837 in or 0.351 mm.

Positive   Opposite to negative. The finished photographic image, reproducable as such. The stage preceding is the negative where the whites are black and the blacks white.

Primary letters   Lowercase letters with no descenders.

Proof   A rough reproduction in order to test for corrections. *See* Page proofs.

Proofreading   Checking proofs for errors and literals.

Quad   Left, right or centre. The headline style. The squaring of a character of type.

Quire   One-twentieth of a ream.

Quoins   Expandable metal wedges for holding type in place on a metal galley (tray).

Quotes   Double or single commas set around something said by somebody. The style is the shape of the figures 6 and 9 with a quote looking like 6 at the front.

Qwerty   Name for the standard typewriter keyboard. The title comes from the first six characters of the keyboard. Computer type setting uses the qwerty method.

Ragged right   Text type set as poetry. Lines of varying lengths. Computer is commanded not to justify the lines to a conforming column width. Unjustified setting.

Raised cap   Initial letter of the introductory paragraph of a type-set story. It should line up with the bottom of the first line of body type in order to stand above the setting in its own white space.

RAM   Random access memory of a computer main frame. RAM is usually erased when power is turned off.

Range   To range a headline right or left is to square it with the right or left of the column setting.

Rate card   The price stated on a card by the advertising department for the various advertisement positions available in a publication.

Reading head   A device that is capable of reading or sensing information punched on a tape or signals from a computer.

Real time   Method by which computing operations are carried out simultaneously.

Recto   Page on the right side of a publication spread carrying an odd number. The even side is the verso. The back and front of a two-sided printed sheet.

Reference mark   Any symbol that will direct the reader's eye from the paragraph being read to information embellishing the facts at the bottom of the page, e.g. asterisks, daggers, etc.

Register   Colour positioning to create a good readable picture reproduction and text. When register is out of position the effect is of an out-of-focus picture.

Register marks Cross wire motif drawn by the processing departments to maintain absolute register. Each of the colour originals will key into the other three and maintain this when placed over each other.

Reel A roll of newsprint.

Repro Work for the camera before it goes to press.

Retouching Correcting a photograph or transparency with fine painting or scratching before making for repro.

Reverse Copy that will appear white on black or on colour or on a photograph to appear white on the finished product. To print a photograph from a wrong-way-round negative.

Revise A revised proof for subsequent reading by the reader.

River Unsightly stream of white space running through the body type of the page and distracting the reader.

ROM Read only memory. Information the computer uses to run system. Does not erase when power is turned off.

Roman type A regular typeface coming, in density, half way between bold and light.

Rop Abbreviation for the term run of paper or run of press. Material printed as part of the main text.

Rotary Printing from revolving plates on the cylinder. In gravure, printing from the actual cylinder.

Rotogravure Rotary press gravure printing. *See* Gravure.

Rough A sketch or page layout at its first conception.

Routing Cutting away the areas of the metal plate not required for printing.

Rules Printed lines measured in points of thickness and used to divide stories and add decoration to the page. Panels of different thicknesses will give the page variety.

Run around Type of bastard measure that sets around a shape usually at body sizes. A picture of non-standard width, will require bastard setting alongside to fill the width of the column.

Run on　The continuation of a line of body type on the same line. The removal of a paragraph to create a run of sentences; the instruction will be to run on. Also the cost of an additional run of copies beyond the original requirements.

Running head　or headline. A line that repeats itself or is a continuation of the same phrase on continuing pages, such as blurbs.

Running text　The body text of an article or news story as opposed to display headlines.

Saddle stitching　Binding with wire stitches through the centre pages of a publication in order to hold the publication together.

Safelight　Coloured lamp used in a dark room that will not 'fog' film as it is being developed.

Sans serif　Typeface designed without a serif.

Scaling　Calculation of the enlargement or reduction in proportion of a picture or piece of artwork that will be required at the printing stage. Achieved with the use of a pocket calculator, scale, logarithms or disk calculator. A simple and accurate system can be achieved by establishing an overlay the area of the picture required and then drawing a diagonal line from the corner and extending it, if need be, to the finished required dimensions. By joining the area as a rectangle the area to be printed is established.

Scanner　Equipment that scans original copy electronically or that scans colour transparencies or flat colour photographic material, to establish densities and colour values that will determine the separations.

Screen　See Halftone.

Screen angles　The correct positioning of the four screens in colour reproduction to avoid the moiré effect. See Moiré.

Separation　The process of scanning colour originals to achieve separately the four subtractive primary printing colours of yellow, magenta (red), cyan (blue) and black. The colours are separately scanned with the use of colour filters.

Sequential access　Items in the computer memory that are read in sequence rather than by random access.

Serial interface   Interface from which information is transmitted one bit at a time.

Series   The complete range of sizes from the same typeface.

Serif   Face designed with horizontal cross strokes that create 'feet' on the bottom of the letter and 'shoulders' at the top, together with curlicues, and sometimes blobs, at the extremities of the capital letters. The use derives from the script style of the quill pen.

Set width   To set a given measure of type at its em width. The width of an individual character with the appropriate space in front and behind it.

Shadow   The dark part of a photograph, colour or tint. Also: an adjective that follows that name of a typeface that is embellished with a shadow, e.g. Granby shadow.

Sheet fed   Printing on separate sheets as opposed to a roll.

Shift   The key that when depressed on a keyboard changes all the characters into capital letters.

Shoot   To take a photograph or expose a process camera.

Shoulder   When widely set body type runs into a single column and then turns into a second column under the original wide setting a shoulder is created in the second leg. To prevent the reader's eye from being diverted into the wrong reading area, by-lines or pieces of half rule can be used to create the division required. A shoulder in hot-metal production is strictly the part of the brass matrice that supports the ascenders and descenders on appropriate letters.

Show through   When the printed word and picture shows through on to the next page and distorts or interferes with the image on the backing page. Usually caused by too heavy an impression on the top side.

Sidehead   A small cross heading to relieve the greyness of the body type. Either set flush left or right of the column.

Sign-off   The writer's name at the end of a story.

Small caps   Caps that will line up top and bottom with the x-height lowercase line alongside.

Software   Computer programmes on a soft disk or diskette.

Solid   Type set with no line spacing.

Sort   A single character of type.

Spacebands   Linecasting machine's brass spaces used to justify the length of a line of type.

Spaces   In metal type, spaces are created with pieces of metal of varying thicknesses that are less than type high and will therefore not print.

Spec   An abbreviation for specification. It is type and space specified on the layout for the printer.

Specimen   Sample of page set to specify the display method advocated and the mood of the editorial words.

Spectrometer   An electronic device to measure paper colour from its reflected light.

Spot colour   An additional colour available to the basic black on selected pages of a publication.

Spread   A pair of facing pages with a gutter in between. Middle pages, without a gutter are referred to as the centre spread.

Sprocket holes   Feed holes in paper tape. Feed holes in film.

Square back   Flat back to a book or magazine often called perfect binding and achieved by glueing sections together.

Square serif   Common to the Egyptian faces such as Karnak, Beton or Rockwell – sometimes thicker than the verticals of the character.

SS   Abbreviation for same size.

Stabilization paper   Dry processed paper used in phototypesetting. In some ways a misnomer since it has an output life of only six weeks and can change 'colour' even in less.

Standing type   After proofing and correcting the type stands and awaits its subsequent use. A hot-metal term.

Stat   Photostat. An electrostatically produced copy print for high-speed production.

Step and repeat   A machine that will repeatedly produce reproductions of an original picture or printed product to instructions.

Stet A proofreader's mark to indicate that copy already deleted should be reinstated.

Stipple A dot effect, often used in artwork to give an effect of light and shade. A type of screen.

Storage Magnetic computer memory on a hard disk.

Straight matter Uncomplicated setting in a single measure.

Strapline A small display line that will set the scene above the headline, and sometimes alongside it.

Stripping-in Piecing separate segments of film or bromide together to create one complete printable element.

Sub An abbreviation of sub-editor. A person who will edit, re-write, trim or grammatically improve text from the original source, and prepare instructions for setting.

Subhead A more discursive line of type to follow the main headline but in a smaller size.

Subtractive primaries Process colours in four-colour printing. Yellow, magenta and cyan.

Swash letters Italic capital letters with long descenders and flourishes that follow the principals of illuminated drop letters.

Swatch A colour specimen. Often describes the entire colour specimen chart.

Swelled rules Rules that are thicker in the centre than at the ends. Used in a decorative sense.

Tabular material Typeset columns of tables or figures such as stock market prices, race cards etc. To be set in the most readable, smallest and economic face available.

Tails Bottom margin of the page.

Take Part of the copy allocated to one typesetting operator. Parts of the copy subeditors have split up and sent for high-speed setting.

Terminal Keyboard and visual display screen for the generation of copy in type form.

Text Body typesetting as opposed to display headings. From ancient monastic quill writing called textus.

Text type   Body type of any face below 12 point.

Thumbnails   Small drawings, sometimes pocket cartoons.

Tint   A solid colour reduced by screening on a percentage basis.

Tint laying   The laying over drawings or type of a filmed tint cut to the area dictated by artist or designer. This is often produced as a waxed-back sheet for easy adhesion.

Titling   Alphabets of foundry type only in capital letters. They are square at the top and bottom with no beards and this allows them to be set with a minimum of line spacing.

Tone   Variation of a colour or a shade of grey.

Tooth   Surface of paper rough in texture. It is best to define the quality of surface required when ordering layout paper since the harder the tooth of the paper the faster it wears out pencils and felt-tip pens.

Tracker   In hot-metal composing rooms, this was the description of the person who kept track of the prices of setting, monitoring piece work and collective rates of pay per operator for each item set.

Transducer   Electronic device for converting signals into readable material.

Transfer type   Produced on a transparent plastic sheet with a waxed back in order that type can be dry transferred on to the surface of art work or pictures. The method can also be used by paste-up operatives on the finished paste-up. The best known of producers are Letraset and Mecanorma.

Transitional   Typefaces designed with the characteristics of Old and Modern styles, such as Baskerville.

Transparency   Photographic film as a finished picture from 16 mm upwards produced by the developer in a card frame. It is viewed by passing light through on a light box or inside a light viewer. Also trannie.

Transpose   Is abbreviated to /trs. It means one element of a word page or design has interchanged with another.

Trichromatic   Using three colours.

Trim size   Final size of the publication after trimming.

TSR Terminate and stay resident. A computer command for do not erase when ended.

Type Alphabets, digitally, photographically or metal produced.

Type family Variations of one basic type style of alphabet. The components of a family are Roman (regular type weight) bold (a heavier, thicker version) and italic (sloping to the right). Each can vary further, e.g. Helvetica extended, Helvetica extra bold, Helvetica compact, Helvetica condensed, Helvetica extra condensed, Helvetica light. Eccentric faces also have descriptive titles: Granby shadow, Compacta outline, Balloon drop shadow and Broadway in-line, etc.

TS Abbreviation for typescript.

Turn A story, usually in a newspaper, that turns from one page and continues on another. It has a small line of cross-reference at the end of the first part and the beginning of the next.

Type area The area of a page. The parameters to set to.

Type gauge A steel, sometimes plastic ruler calibrated in points and ems. The more sophisticated will have metric and inches as well.

Type high Height of a standard piece of metal type, 0.918 of an inch. Any material for printing and cast in metal is required to be specifically and accurately type high and is mechanically planed to assure it.

Type metal Metal for melting down and casting into type by pouring it into a mould. The metal is an alloy comprising lead, antimony and tin.

Typesetter Person or company that sets type.

Typographer A designer of type material.

U/c Often expressed as C, upper case, or caps.

Unit Parts of an em squared. Used primarily by computer type designers in the original high digital formation of each letter before being produced as masters. The more sophisticated productions are created in 100 units wide format to each letter. When kerning (spacing) computer set type for visual impact the measures of space between the letters and words are defined as units.

Unit value The number of units in a character of type.

Unjustified type   A column of type set with a ragged edge on one side or the other. It is created by using even spacing throughout with no attempt by the computer to hyphenate and justify. Unjustified right is the version most popular to achieve an eccentricity in page lay-out.

Untrimmed size   Outside dimensions of a printed page before the trim to the finished size.

UPC   Unique product code. The computer bars of identity and price attached to goods and printed matter. Also known as the bar code.

Update   Incorporating into a file or computer the newest material or programme. To include new information in a story running through the edition throughout the day or night.

Uppercase   Capital letters.

Vacuum frame   Framed glass covering camera-originating table into which is placed the artwork or pictures for reproduction. The frame is then pumped free of air and the resulting vacuum forces the artwork completely flat. This prevents any uneven light reflections from interfering with the final camera image.

Value   Refers to the darkness or lightness of photographic tones across the picture.

Van dyke   American term for a dye-line proof produced in brown.

Variable space   Technique used in computer setting to create a justified line of type.

Verso   A left-hand page with an even number. Opposite to recto.

Vignette   Halftone picture or illustration fading through the tone values to white.

Visual   See Layout.

Visual display unit   A computer terminal consisting of a cathode ray tube screen and keyboard for the input and correction of copy. The input is displayed on the screen together with instructions keyed in by the operator. A VDU can be used to edit copy with the aid of a cursor which indicates on screen where words are being changed. The text can then be 'downloaded' to a typesetter.

Volume   A book. The thickness of paper indicated as a volume number equal in thickness to 100 sheets of paper at 100 grams.

Weight   An expression used, particularly by designers to describe the visual impact of a piece of type or picture on a page layout. Type weight is described as Roman, light and bold.

Warm colour   Spectrum shades of the red and yellow range.

Wash drawing   An illustration using tone values created with the use of water colours or inks, usually in shades of black or grey.

Wash up   The cleaning of the ink ducts and rollers of a printing press prior to the change of ink colours. It can also mean the shutting down of the presses.

Web   A continuous length of paper, a roll as opposed to a sheet of paper.

Web offset   Offset litho, reel fed and could be heat-set or cold-set. In heat-set the dry finish is hastened by heat blown on to the paper. This will give a more glossy, luxurious finish to the product. It will also ensure the ink stays on the paper.

WF   Abbreviation for wrong font. Used by proofreaders to indicate that a mix of typefaces has occurred in a word or line.

Widow   One word left on the last line of a paragraph. Ugly rivers of white space can be caused in text by excessive widows.

Window   A clear panel left in a litho film page for halftone pictures to be stripped in.

Word   A computer term that means a set of bits which can be recognized by the machine as the smallest logical units of information for processing.

Word break   The natural or logical dividing point of a word break at the end of a set line of type. The hyphenation point.

Word processor   A machine like a typewriter that, by using computer logic, will accept, store and retrieve words for editing and reproduction in typewriter style for future reference.

Wordspace   The set space between the words as opposed to letterspace. This will determine justification for a line of set body type.

Workings   The number of passes through the same printing press that will create the finished product, e.g. four impressions on a single-colour machine to achieve a four-colour reproduction.

Wysiwyg   What you see is what you get! Acronym appearing on a visual display screen indicating it is showing an exact replica of the final output.

Xenon flash   A flash of an intense light source used in photosetting.

Xerography   A copying process in which a 'toner' is electrostatically applied to the image areas of the charged copying paper.

X-height   Body height of the lowercase letters exclusive of the ascenders and descenders, e.g. The height of the lowercase letter x.

X-line   Imaginary line along the tops of the lowercase letters on a line of set type.

Yankee dryer   Steam-heated cylinder for drying photographic paper to a glazed finish.

Zip-a-tone   A trade name for a rub down film of tint, tone or colour that has a pre-waxed back for adhesion to artwork or pictures.

Index

5_0y!11?

Design:
  balance, 133
  colour in, 231–43
  creative basis, 144
  desk-top, 208–11
  dynamic approach, 145, 146–59
  emphasis, 135
  faults, 175–7
  features, 50
  freestyle, 145, 146–59
  historical influences, 38–62
  influences, 9, 70
  ingredients, 5
  modular, 160–77
  modular patterns, 161–2
  new directions, 169
  principles, 1–5, 139
  static approach, 144–5, 160–77
  success of, 1
  techniques, 53
  terminology, 34–5
  traditional, 162
  variety, 134
De Telegraaf, 227–8
Detroit Examiner, 214
Dickens, Charles, 184
Die Welt, 226, 228
Digital type, 33, 36–7
Direct colour, 194
Doric, 16–7
Drawing pages, 129–30
Drawings, 102–3
Drawn type, 186
Drop figures, 183
Drop letters, 126–8, 174–5, 182
Drop quotes, 183
Dummy, 125
Duotone colour, 240–1
Dwiggins, W. A., 17

Eastern Daily Press, 139
Edition traps, 135
Editor's influence, 10
Editorial:
  packaging 138
  targetting 138–9
Education Act, 1870

Eggington, George, 59
Egyptian:
  Bold condensed, 13
  type, 15
Ekland, Britt, 86
Electronic origination, 69–70
El Pais, 220–1
European press, 220–30
Evans, Harold, 60, 137
Evening Standard, 139–40, 206–7
Eye breakers, 178
Excelsior:
  italic, 16
  type, 16

Faithfull Scout, The, 41
Fashion photography, 234–5
Faults, design, 175–7
Features:
  pages, 50, 128
  planning, 124
Felt-tips, 98
Femail, 206
Figaro, Le, 227
Figgins and Thorowgood, 15, 17
Fillers, 7
Financial Times, 62, 123, 139–40, 205–6
Flat plans, 120
Fleet Street, 55, 68, 118
Forme, 191
Fowler, H. W., 29
Fox Talbot, Henry, 51
Fractur, 12, 18
France-Soir, 224
Franklin, Benjamin, 13
Franklin Gothic Bold, 15, 19, 189
Freelances, 81
Free sheets, 210–11
Freestyle design, 145, 147–59
Frutiger, Adrian, 16
Full page composition, 62, 71, 161
Futura, 15, 19, 149, 153, 184, 196

Garamond, Claud, 12, 33
Garamond, (type), 12, 19, 175, 184